Humanity at a Crossroads:
Which Way Home?

Other Books by the Author

Envisioning a New World:
Awakening to Life's Oneness

Liberating Masculine and Feminine –
Breaking the Spell of Exclusion

One Light, One Spirit –
A Guide to Transformed Living

The Ultimate Choice:
Armageddon or Awakening

Humanity At A Crossroads: Which Way Home?

Rosemarie Carnarius

PARTNERSHIP PUBLISHING

Copyright © 2013 by Rosemarie Carnarius
Cover design by CreateSpace

ISBN-13: 978-1484981023 Paperback
ISBN-10: 1484981022
eBook

Printed in the United States of America
by CreateSpace – An Amazon Company

Published September 2013

Partnership Publishing
yinyangharmonics@gmail.com

Available on:
Amazon.com
www.CreateSpace.com/4285152
and other retailers

PARTNERSHIP PUBLISHING

CONTENTS

*Dedicated to the spirit of truth and justice
and to men and women of courage
who are maligned for exposing and resisting
the powers of this world.*

~ ~ ~

Dissent is the highest form of patriotism.

Thomas Jefferson

ACKNOWLEDGMENTS

As I prepare for the publication of the fourth volume in a series on the urgency for personal and societal transformation, I look back in amazement at the journey that has brought me thus far.

Early in life, I see a little girl watching through a shuttered window the collapse of a regime and the end of a war that devastated a world; see the ominous shadow of Soviet tanks charging across Eastern Europe, collecting satellite countries and subjugating people to build an empire; see a determined 17-year-old escaping to West Germany and see her, finally, arriving in the land of her dreams, America, like millions before and after.

There were some enormous challenges along the way, but also many unexpected gifts, and always the most vital of them all, love and friendship. I am filled with gratitude for everyone who has been inspiration, enrichment and support. The growth of my being, and deepening of my understanding, are the results of many caring hearts and hands.

Although some passages were dark and dangerous, I learned that we, indeed, never walk alone and that each life, in its own particular way, is blessed and full of opportunities to seize the moment, to become in actuality what potentially we already are. There is nothing missing, except that, as human beings, we have fashioned a strange habit of standing in our own light and then bemoaning the darkness.

At this perilous time in history, thanks be to all who have had the courage to end their exile and return home to their heart and spiritual center – thus generating the light to help illumine the way for others.

FOREWORD

Professor Alfred McCoy, a TomDispatch regular, in a recent article summed up the awful future into which the United States is rushing headlong: "If all or much goes according to plan, sometime in the third decade of this century the Pentagon will complete a comprehensive global surveillance system for Earth, sky and space using robotics to coordinate a veritable flood of data from biometric street-level monitoring, cyber-data mining, a world-wide network of Space Surveillance Telescopes and triple canopy aeronautic patrols."

Rev. Rosemarie Carnarius seeks to awaken the American public's conscience to become actively involved in reversing this trend as well as ending the perpetual war imposed on the world by vested US interests and their military-industrial corporations. In this thoughtful book, she gives a timely prescription for solving the problems generated by those developments.

Carnarius has already written a number of other books on this general theme, works that point especially to the absence of spiritual and moral values regarding domestic and international policies which are being relentlessly pursued by the United States in the wake of 9/11.

She has the prophetic insight to communicate eloquently, appealing to our spirituality and our common moral fiber to tackle the issues America has engendered regarding the fate of the world at this juncture. Our citizens have to begin to see the truth as it is described in this excellent book – not the propaganda constantly fed through the media. And they must work earnestly on enlivening the spirituality within that connects us with the rest of humankind.

Earlier this year I published a hefty 666-page book on *Muslims At The Crossroads* detailing the human and financial costs, violations of international treaties and agreements, along with distorted or inaccurate reporting regarding Muslims that the American public has been subjected to for more than a decade in the post 9/11 developments.

In her writings, Carnarius explores a number of those events, and with her unique incisive ability, gives abundant examples, juxtaposing them with the underlying spiritual and moral ills of which the American public is either not aware or does not seem to care about. It is high time that we all become more educated about the wrongs done in our name and take urgent measures to remedy them. This book is essential reading for all those interested in the future of humankind.

Siraj I. Mufti, Ph.D.
Board of Directors
International Center for Peace and Justice
Tucson, Arizona

PREFACE

What do we fight against? Our fight is against lies, mendacity, deceit,
bullying and everything that belittles, enslaves, or would destroy
a human being.

　　　　　　　　~Norbert Capek

No lie can live forever.

　　　　　　　~Martin Luther King

It is impossible to understand the present state of the
human condition without recognizing the staggering significance of September 11, 2001. For at that time, the value system
which had sustained us for generations (imperfect as it was in
practice) came crashing down like the superstructures that sank
into oblivion in New York City that day.

Many of those values and principles were originally anchored in the teachings of a great master, whose birth in Pales-
tine became an extraordinary turning point in human history.
Even the sequence of the numbering of days was radically refit-
ted due to his impact on the consciousness especially of the
Western world, with his birth becoming the dividing line between BC ("Before Christ") and AD (Anno Domini, "Year of
the Lord").

For the sake of contrast, I shall take the liberty of treating the first year designated to read AD as a symbolic year zero
– despite the fact that at the time the concept of zero had not
even been introduced. This allows me to make the point that a
zero also emerged from another world-transforming event: the
ground zero of 9/11. The difference between the two, however,
could not be more vast or stark.

Year zero was a birthing event, signaled by the luminosity of a star. Occurring at night, it brought a powerful new radiance to our world. Or more precisely, it spiritually turned the
very darkness into light.

Ground zero, by contrast, was a death experience, and though taking place in the early hours of a brilliant autumn day, it culminated in a colossal cloud of debris and toxic dust that turned day into night, a promising morning into a bewildering spiritual nightfall.

Put another way, zero as a time component was an ascent into life and love and freedom; spatial zero was a descent into a mass grave followed by brutal war, countless deaths and a world surveilled, controlled and subjugated.

Ironically, then, *ground* zero too turned into a new beginning: the inauguration of something dark and sinister and cruel, a giant step backwards, as though the reason for the reconfiguring of the old calendar had never occurred. For on 9/11, in a flash, everything changed, and there is nothing comparable to it. This was far more than the collapse of two skyscraping towers pulverizing thousands of human beings. This was about a formidable group seizing control and installing themselves as supreme commanders, while exercising a totally new Totalitarianism.

In the process, the United States became a belligerent, anti-spiritual presence among the nations. Driven by a calculating ideology based on an alien, anachronistic mindset, the Bush/NeoCon administration created the most hazardous and ruinous period in American history – constitutionally, politically, financially, economically, socially and especially morally, – with devastating effects on the world, especially countries with Muslim populations.

Unfortunately, despite the 2009 change of administration in Washington, the most destructive element active in our world today continues to be a three-headed monster: the monster of lies and spin, the monster of greed, and the monster of militarism.

To compare those developments and their consequences with being lost in a spiritual desert would be a pronounced understatement. However, from another perspective, it does describe rather accurately what has happened not only over the last decade, but albeit more gradually, for several generations. America veered away from its aim and calling and followed false prophets from disaster to disaster. 9/11, meanwhile, was the big bang of ultimate distress that will either wake us from our sleep – or pave the way for the biggest catastrophe ever, a nuclear holocaust – if those who flippantly sing: "Bomb, bomb, bomb Iran" get their perverse, juvenile way.

Yet, whether World War III or what in religious circles is known as "Armageddon" remains an idea or explodes into physical reality lies in the hands of humanity collectively. No doubt, we are moving toward its yawning chasm, with sabers being rattled especially by the extreme right in Israel. Before we despair, however, let us remember that humanity is greater by far than warmongers and militarists combined. In a word, we have choices – and the militarists have "only guns". (The latter idea is taken from an engraving in stone in Myanmar, 2010.)

There are presently two options available to the human race. They introduce themselves as follows: In one column are those of iron will, the "willful ones", who believe in power and dominance. In the other are those who have surrendered their will to the Spirit of Life, the "humble ones", whose aim is to serve humanity and the Common Good. In advancing toward the future, with whom will the majority of human beings align?

To choose wisely, we need information – facts that can help us to see through the fog of fabrications, truths that can set us free, no matter how painful or difficult.

This is why this work was written, and why the first part of it focuses so rigorously on exposing lies, treacherous lies, that have made possible the herding of America: from the least to the most educated, the vast majority can be corralled, shorn and, if need be, slaughtered. In short, 9/11 inflicted such a horrific concussion on the psyche of the American people that a decade later, the country still suffers from acute Post Traumatic Stress Disorder.

Throughout the pages that follow, we shall explore the cost of self-alienation and reflect on the moral corruption that inevitably arises when humans are strangers to themselves. We shall confront especially the fact that when the spiritual element is missing, terrible wrongs are casually committed or condoned. For that reason, the second part of this work explores options that can lead us out of the grim labyrinth of disempowerment and fear to safer ground and inner healing.

Robert Kennedy was fond of paraphrasing a line from George Bernard Shaw's *Back to Methuselah.* "Some see things as they are and say *why?* I dream things that never were and say *why not?*"

Using these two divergent reactions to the state of the human condition, we will examine some of the critical issues in our world that constantly elicit a frustrated "why?" and at the same time suggest how such a response might be changed to a more hopeful and encouraging, "why not!"

The human condition does not have to remain the way it is. We don't have to be or act like perpetual adolescents. We can mature. However, to convert a "why?" into a "why not!" requires reeducation, and awareness of how to use the various tools at our disposal for self-reform that we might build a different world, a more people-friendly world.

We start by turning in the direction of home, of coming home to self, the heart, our humanity. This is where our roots are, and where our very essence waits to be utilized for fostering love, self-fulfillment and service to life and others.

Our present age is a propitious confluence of circumstances promising the birth of something fundamentally new. But it will be ours only if we develop skills much like those of great mountaineers, since our challenge is to scale the rugged summit before us without tumbling into the chasm below. In other words, we shall need what the revered Abraham Joshua Heschel once described as the greatest requirements of our time: "moral grandeur and spiritual audacity."

Equipped with those qualities, we can begin the demanding journey towards the heights of authentic living, while using our personal and communal achievements in advancing peace with justice for all the Earth's people.

Because of a unique background which introduced me at a young age to the dark side of human nature with its capacity for ruthlessness and cruelty, I long ago dedicated my life and work to the liberation of the human spirit. This includes an intense interest in how we might mend a world carelessly torn apart by ignorance and willfully wounded by arrogance. To that end, I have never ceased believing that human beings deserve better and that we have within the light, the knowledge and the tools to be liberated and healed on all levels, personal and societal. And, being healed, become healers.

As my previous writings have highlighted, I consider a solid dose of spirituality to be the ultimate prescription for becoming well in ways that are lasting. This is the reason for the strong emphasis on the recommendations of the spiritually awakened of all religions for a life passionately and purposefully lived. (See *One Light, One Spirit – A Guide to Transformed Living*.)

Like the other companion pieces, this work has been written from direct experience, with ideas tested in the laboratory of life. It has been my long-adhered-to principle to share only those recipes about conscious living that I have found personally doable and digestible, so to speak.

I eagerly invite readers to test how these collections of ideas might be made meaningful in the context of their own lives, hoping, of course, that they will both stimulate taste buds *and* be deeply nourishing for the demands of the journey home to self and wholeness.

The writing was completed in spring, at a time when ancient nature astonishes with the miracle of resurrected life, when amid garlands of color, bursts of green and songs of jubilance, hope and joy are reborn, and when the festivals of Passover and Easter mark defining moments in the history of two religions. It seems fitting that a work inviting change and renewal would have its completion coincide with such a promising moment in the seasonal rhythm of the year.

Rosemarie Carnarius

Tucson, Arizona

part one

Lost in a Spiritual Wilderness

Chapter 1

SEPTEMBER 11, 2001 –
A WORLDWIDE SOUND OF SOS

I have set before you life and death…
Choose life that you and your descendants may live.

~ Prophet Jeremiah

Experience is not what happens to you,
it is what you do with what happens to you.

~Aldous Huxley

The world is a dangerous place, not because of those who do evil,
but because of those who look on and do nothing.

~Albert Einstein

I speak as one who experienced in utero the Kristall-
nacht in Leipzig, was born nine months prior to the outbreak
of WWII, and witnessed as a six-year-old the chaos and collapse of Hitler's tyranny, only to see it replaced with the Iron
Curtain and total control of Stalin's paranoid and cruel regime.
And I speak as one who at seventeen escaped that stifling societal prison to follow the yearning of my heart for freedom
and the dream of a new home in America. Finally, I speak as
one full of anguish about the conditions of our world, and the
course embarked upon by the leaders of our country in the
wake of the tragedy of September 11, 2001. Though the event
took place twelve years ago, its devastating effect is ongoing
and should therefore be subject to periodic reevaluation.

When towers fell and volume rose

Who could ever forget that fateful day in September
when the unimaginable turned real right before our disbelieving
eyes, when centers of financial supremacy collapsed in New

York City, burying in their fall the pulverized bodies and lives of thousands? Soon huge clouds of dust, dense and billowing, descended like giant monsters, surging through streets and lunging around corners – ominously turning day into night, blinding everyone caught in their menacing grip.

America, a nation thought to be invincible, was being assailed, wounded – not fatally but shockingly – even as in yet another city, the capital itself, a segment of the Pentagon, center of awesome military might, incomprehensibly, lay burning.

A piercing SOS – Save our Souls! – rose as if from a single throat and its anguished cry reverberated around the globe as television stations channeled the staggering news and apocalyptic scenes to millions of homes in numerous countries. Something immense had happened, something that would forever change the life we had known. And indeed, for days eyes and ears were tuned to the unfolding events in the United States of America, trumping all other news.

Something in the psyche of our citizens died that fateful autumn morning so full of sapphire skies and promises. We became a vulnerable people, a people in need of others around the globe. The leadership in Washington somehow acknowledged that need, albeit via the message that this act of terror was an attack on people everywhere, on civilization itself.

Meanwhile, shock, grief, fear and angry shouts for revenge combined to shape a climate of highly charged emotions, creating a slippery track where the hazard of losing one's moral footing loomed large. For almost immediately, without establishing facts of culpability, the government claimed it knew the perpetrators and promised retribution.

With every commercial station having suspended its programming and shifted into "Breaking News" mode, I knew within the first few hours that if I wanted to escape being inundated by the mesmerizing power of the visual images being broadcast ad infinitum, I had to turn off the television.

I focused on radio, the auditory, instead. It allowed for some distance, made room for independent thought. And those thoughts were fed vitally important information by, for example, Amy Goodman and her distinguished guests on *Democracy*

Now! Here could be found qualified voices to keep alive alternative ways of comprehending what was unfolding.

Despite that welcome lifeline, it took several days to find my equilibrium, to sense beneath the tears and fears and strident patriotic sentiments, a deeper truth and guidance beyond the enraged sounds for retribution.

Soon after the tragedy, a personal response crystallized:

Admonition

Do not speak of war, revenge
with easy tongue
do not lightly invoke
getting even in this time
of weapons that mass destroy.
Pause. Grieve. Bow.
Listen. But do not speak
of war casually, from raw
emotions, injured pride.
Pause again. Grieve more
deeply. And listen, listen!
Let your ears bring truth
to you beyond the shock
of the apparent: the images
of crashing planes
and crumbling buildings —
of twin towers of power
collapsing to ashes and dust.
Let your hearts be torn
by sorrow and grief
by the tragic loss of lives
perishing in horror
as they did in Hiroshima
Dresden and Vietnam.

Let investigators find
the plotting serpent
behind the diabolic attack
but do not speak

of war, revenge
with easy tongue
with unknowing.

RC - Sept. 15, 2001

Pausing, reflecting, introspecting were not to be. Not on that day nor any day to follow.

This is not to say that many Americans did not rise in heroic fashion to answer the desperate sounds of SOS generated by the catastrophe. Those dedicated firemen, for instance, who responded to the call, many losing their very lives in the process, or the tireless rescue workers who combed through the toxic scraps and dust for bodies, body parts, those who donated their blood, and those who made generous financial donations. Even eagerly attentive canines bravely served the needs of the hour.

Expressions of empathy and sorrow were also key responses from around the globe. In Berlin, 200,000 people gathered by candlelight near the Brandenburg Gate, unabashedly shedding tears as they voiced solidarity with the citizens of our country. France's *Le Monde* eloquently proclaimed, "We are all Americans now." And Iran was the first Muslim country to send condolences while offering cooperation in apprehending the terrorists who had committed such a heinous crime.

The desperate cry "Save our Souls" emanating from America in its hour of shock and agony was thus answered with solid responses by the people of the Earth and with full assistance from all the members of NATO. Even today, twelve years later, some still commit soldiers to the war in Afghanistan, with not a few of them – 1,050 is the official number as of 2013 – having made the ultimate sacrifice.

When comparing those acts of exceptional solidarity to the bellicose rhetoric of the US government, a striking difference becomes glaringly apparent. Instead of prudence and goodwill, hostility and intimidating statements issued forth from the highest offices of the administration, while all of Congress seemed to have fallen under a spell. For immediately after 9/11, wily operators began to walk the halls of power, presenting policy papers foreign to the values enshrined in the Constitution or laboriously gained in the struggle for human rights. They apparently found acceptance because soon male and female VIPs, cloaked in a mantle of ultra-patriotism, paraded before the ever-present cameras, condemning the terrorists and urging passage of measures that would ensure America's security, even if it meant placing alarming restrictions on the Bill of Rights.

Simultaneously, those who began to speak out in defense of the Constitution were denounced as "unpatriotic", or worse, as aiding the terrorists. Something surreal was unfolding in the oldest democracy in the world.

Within days of the calamity, George W. Bush arrived at the site of the former World Trade Center to survey the immense pile of debris, and to urge those brave and exhausted rescue workers to carry on with their daunting task. Standing on a platform, he addressed the assembled, at times encouragingly placing a presidential arm on a worker's shoulder.

This is how the staged scene affected me:

Beyond black and white

Escorted by police and politicians
and ringed by rescue workers
he stood astride the rubble and soot
and bull-horned his words
into the cheering crowd:
"We vow to rid the world of evil!"

To rid the world of evil
when one person's weed
is another one's flower
when one people's terrorist
is another people's warrior-hero?
Think European settlers and Native American tribes
think colonialists and indigenous cultures
all over the globe –
think existence sliced into
'us versus them'

since time immemorial.

Then ask, what is good and what is evil?
And who is wrong and who is right?

Once the answer used to be simple
once when the world
came simply
in black and white.

RC - Sept. 19, 2001

Theologian Marty Martin wrote: "The demonizing of the enemy inhibits self-examination." Alas, instead of self-examination, instead of assuming at least some responsibility for this calamity, words like "terrorists… terrorism…evil" and the promise to wipe them off the face of the earth, became our national obsession.

Yet, despite the posturing of politicians and sensational-ized headlines in the media, there were voices of refreshing honesty. Author/activist Susan Sontag, in an essay in *The New Yorker* on Sept. 24, expressed frustration, saying, "Those in public office have let us know that they consider their task to be a manipulative one: confidence building and grief manage-ment. Politics, the politics of democracy – which entails dis-agreement, which promotes candor – has been replaced by psy-chotherapy. Let's by all means grieve together. But let's not be stupid together."

It was advice that remained unheeded by the great ma-jority of citizens, and definitely by the government in Washing-ton. This became a very pricey refusal.

Choices that shape our destiny

What I witnessed post 9/11 answered a question that had haunted me since I began to grapple with it: How had it been possible for Hitler to gain such power over an intelligent and well-educated people? Granted, the German realities of the 1930s were immeasurably worse than what happened in the US in 2001, with the loss of WWI, the Great Depression and the punitive Treaty of Versailles devastating an economy and demoralizing a people. Still, the responses in both cases were so similar it was unsettling.

It appears that when survival is threatened, the herd instinct in humans gets activated almost instantly. Flags and nationalistic songs become omnipresent. Those who see things differently are branded "unpatriotic" and ostracized. Worst of all, citizens relinquish liberties for the sake of safety, and are quite willing to become informers – what George Bush euphemistically called, "the eyes and ears of freedom." In other words, fear and suspicion dictate behavior, and survival and security become consuming concerns.

In addition, under conditions interpreted as being a matter of life and death, people will give up almost anything in order to feel safe. Even citizens of a historically pioneering democracy proved not to be exempt from that instinctive reaction. Instead of relying on the rallying cry of the American Independence movement of 1776, "Give me liberty or give me death!" the choice in 2001 was the death of liberties in order to stay alive, in order to be "safe".

The USA PATRIOT ACT – imposing controls by restricting freedoms for the sake of "protection" – was passed overwhelmingly by Congress, and the few voices of caution and concern were drowned out by the shrill and self-righteous, but especially the super-patriots. Ardent nationalistic rhetoric ruled the podium of every Congressional session, even as loyalty to the Constitution began to sag. Fearfulness and unquestioning support for those at the helm across the country added to the weight. After all, prominent TV personality Dan Rather had set the example when he obediently declared: "George Bush is the president. He makes the decisions…wherever he wants me to line up, just tell me where, and he makes the call."

There are those who would suggest that it was the vast amount of dust created by the exploding and collapsing Twin Towers and building #7, which, symbolically, robbed American citizens of lucidity of thought and transparency of vision. The result of that loss was a lack of moral clarity that became the second resounding SOS of 9/11. And in many ways it was the far more serious. For when an angry giant loses its moral compass and ethical judgment, disaster is sure to follow.

A taste of that was to be experienced by the citizens of the world, and those in Muslim countries in particular, long before the removal of the dust and debris at ground zero.

Of course, not everyone was swept up in a tidal wave of hyper-patriotism and vengefulness; a few remained standing tall. They were sentinels of courage during a time of the highest emergency.

Most prominent among them was Congresswoman Barbara Lee of California. On September 14, 2001, she was the only member of Congress to vote against the *2001 Authorization for Use of Military Force*, warning against a rush to war in Afghanistan and the dangers of conceding Congress's constitutional responsibilities.

Nine years later, in September 2010, she was as true to her principles and as determined as ever when she introduced legislation in Congress to reexamine, and ultimately repeal the authorization, arguing that "a blank check to wage war anywhere, at any time, and for any length does not serve the national security interests of the United States."

She explained, "Over the last nine years, this broad authorization of force has had far-reaching implications which shake the very foundations of our great nation and democracy. It has been used to justify warrantless surveillance and wiretapping activities, indefinite detention practices that fly in the face of our constitutional values, extra-judicial targeted-killing operations, and a policy of borderless and open-ended war."

For being such a brave defender of the Constitution, for being a genuine patriot, Barbara Lee received death threats in 2001. Imagine if others had rallied around her, and agreeing, had rejected fear and political pressure. How differently would have unfolded the course of history!

Because adherence to constitutional principles and democratic values, however, was not the choice of the majority, we've paid a steep price in civil liberties and the loss of nearly 6,700 American lives, with more than 50,000 wounded, 16,000 of them severely. Tens of thousands returned battle scarred by traumatic brain injury and Post Traumatic Stress Disorder.

This count does not include those veterans who committed suicide or expired from war-related causes after their tour of duty. Specifically, according to a report published by the *Bay Citizen* and the *New York Times* in 2010, more than 1,000 California veterans under thirty-five died between 2005 and 2008 in just that way after completing military service.

Beyond the lost lives and limbs, there is, finally, the ruinous financial cost of this so-called war on terror, which Reuters reported in June of 2011 to amount to approximately $3.7 trillion. This figure is consistent with a number of government studies, including the Joint Economic Committee of Congress, which estimated that the war will cost $3.5 trillion.

All this supposedly for the sake of a safety that is neither genuine nor lasting, with constant new "threats" able to disturb the phantom security so dearly paid for. Thus, "Operation Enduring Freedom" in Afghanistan and "Operation Iraqi Freedom" are not only cynical Newspeak, but chilling Orwellian operations. They are a tragic moral setback for our country, and by extension, the whole of humankind, proving John Dryden, one of England's great 17th century poets, correct: "Even victors are by victory undone."

These developments illustrate that our greatest peril did not originate from outside our borders but from within: from the Oval Office, the Pentagon and members of Congress as they conspired to authorize combat in faraway places, impose "Homeland Security" and total surveillance of the globe, while approving obscene sums of money to fund them.

9/11 was a test of immense proportions. Today it is obvious that we failed it on every count: Americans panic more easily, are even less informed, and thus more gullible. (See the effect of fear mongering regarding Iran.) In addition, the economy is sickly, after nearly plunging into depression in 2008; almost eight percent of Americans are still unemployed and hundreds of thousands of homes have been foreclosed. Not only has the war consumed exorbitant amounts of money, thus increasing the debt, but costs for wounded vets are projected to exceed $900 billion (Associated Press, October 1, 2010).

Finally, beyond our own war dead and injured, the US

government is responsible for the destruction of two countries and cultures, having sown chaos, death and devastation on a massive scale in both Afghanistan and Iraq.

George W. Bush was on the right track when he asked, "Why do they hate us?" The problem is, he never paused to hear the answer, raising suspicions that he and his administration were not really interested in knowing. If he had been, we would soon have discovered that if they hated us at all, it was not because they envied our values, but because *we* betrayed them; *we* have not been true to ourselves and our democratic standards of liberty and justice for all. One can only presume that George Bush and his NeoCon handlers had already chosen fighting and killing in response to 9/11 and were not in the least interested in answers or options.

For me, the query was not hard to solve, having for years been deeply pained by the deteriorating situation in the Middle East. Realizing that only a win/win approach offered any hope for that tortured territory, I agonized over the escalating deaths and the fallacy of believing in a military solution, while fearing a calamity due to the tinderbox state of the region, the one which Nobel Prize laureate Harold Pinter had accurately described as "the central factor in world unrest".

For those devoted to human rights, the dire situation of the Palestinian people is deeply distressing, crying out as it does for America's honest, even-handed commitment to a just solution. Since, however, our government chooses another path, Palestinians chafe, not only under Israel's merciless occupation, but from our double standards and unconscionable veto of any resolution presented by the UN. A mockery has been made of international law and the principles of self-determination and justice, and millions of innocent human beings suffer daily because of that infidelity to democratic values.

Besides being a brazen betrayal, such double standards are a ticket to disaster. "Why do they hate us?" It is simple: Because we fervently preached, but dishonestly practiced, the ideals of life, liberty and the pursuit of happiness for all.

Consequently, in the Middle East, among the great masses, where truth always finds a refuge during times of duplicity, a deep wound in the heart of millions continues to fester, while numerous voices, similar to a Greek Chorus, cry out "J'accuse! J'accuse!" against the hypocrisy of the United States.

Reaping bitter fruits

"The culture of fear," wrote former President Carter's National Security advisor Zbigniew Brzezinski, "is like a genie that has been let out of its bottle. It acquires a life of its own – and can become demoralizing."

Indeed, beginning with the first airplane crashing into the World Trade Center on the morning of September 11, 2001, the country that institutionalized the concept of liberty and equality for all, thereby giving the world the promise of a brighter future, went into free fall: it became infected with anxiety and obsessed with retaliation. Soon shrewd operators audaciously turned back the clock and reinstated the old paradigm: the idea of absolutized good and evil, the belief in not only one eye, but ten (or a thousand!) eyes for one; the principle of solving disputes through bullying and bullets.

Subsequently, we witnessed arrogance and machinations without accountability in the highest offices in Washington, as devious minds managed to justify defiance of constitutional principles, international law and universal human rights.

That hubris was fully on display when President George W. Bush spoke in early February 2002 to the students and faculty at the University of Pittsburgh. "I view this as a struggle of tyranny versus freedom, of evil versus good. And there is no in-between, as far as I am concerned. Either you are with us or you are against us. Either you stand for a peaceful world…or you are going to be against the mighty United States of America," he threatened.

Bill Tammeus, columnist for the *Kansas City Star*, wrote in response: "Such talk reinforces the image of an imperialistic America led by Sheriff Bush. It's not intended to persuade but to unnerve, not to engender sympathy and cooperation but capitulation. You don't convince people by silencing them."

The President's tough talk made some allies grow uneasy. Most refused to sign on to the "Axis of Evil" rhetoric, despite the remarkable outpouring of worldwide sympathy for our country after the attacks. Reason and courage had not entirely faded from the Western world's political scene.

Meanwhile, a great number of our citizens bought into the idea that on a dust- and tear-filled September day in 2001, America had become a unified nation. But how truly genuine is unity based on shock and a common enemy? This was not a spontaneous awakening, not a spiritual transformation bringing us into alignment with one another in pursuit of a noble goal; this was fear-based nationalism at its most visceral, most emotional, culminating in a climate of shared outrage and cries for revenge. Such components make not for a triumphant but a troublesome state of union – a banding together based on survival-driven angst. It would surely have been more accurate to call such a union a shotgun marriage.

A closer look at its offspring might provide a clue. For what we experience today is a once vibrant, self-confident nation plagued by polarization and paralysis, by a turning of people against one another as though engaged in a "cold war".

America is in peril, not because of terrorist threats, but because of its collective state of psychological health and well-being. Yes, we are outwardly still powerful, but we are far from strong, much less united, either politically or spiritually. We are today an embittered and bitterly divided nation, where dialogue and cooperation are at their lowest ebb, relishing vilification of others at home and abroad, looking for scapegoats. We need to ask ourselves what diabolical seeds we sowed on 9/11 to reap such self-injurious results.

The question, in fact, must be even more basic. Who, we need to inquire, gained control in this country after 9/11, if not before? Who, through skillful subterfuge, inserted alien ways and values into the moral and political fiber of a people, similar to the DNA of a debilitating virus invading the genetic code of an individual and replicating itself?

In subsequent chapters, we will explore answers to this baffling state of affairs. Suffice it to say for now that 9/11 is a tragedy that fits the metaphor of replication, perpetuating itself over and over as a manipulative force in the life of our nation.

Having said that, it must also be acknowledged that not everyone considers 9/11 a tragedy. According to *Haaretz Service* and *Reuters* (April 16, 2008), for instance, Benjamin Netanyahu told an audience at Bar Ilan University that the September 11, 2001, terror attacks had been beneficial for Israel.

"We are benefiting from one thing, and that is the attack on the Twin Towers and Pentagon, and the American struggle in Iraq," the Israeli newspaper *Ma'ariv* quoted Mr. Netanyahu as saying. Further elaborating, he stated that these events "swung American public opinion in our favor."

As will be shown in more detail in the following chapters, on 9/11 neoconservatives became the dominant players in US foreign policy, while simultaneously stifling domestic voices protesting their stratagem, be that in the media, at universities, or at public forums. Democracy in America was sliding precariously into autocracy and censorship.

The appearance of such an oppressive force in, of all places, the United States, was a stunning development, especially alarming because Congress itself succumbed as though hexed, blindly stumbling into collaboration. Now George Bush was calling himself "a war president" with an obliging media faithfully repeating the self-styled, encompassing, designation.

War president, wars fought simultaneously in several countries for years – yet, what have we gained? Do our citizens feel more protected? Is our country more secure? Are our soldiers less vulnerable? The answers are obvious, especially concerning the latter, for how can occupiers ever expect to be kept safe by those and from those they contemptuously occupy?

I believe Americans are in general a decent, tolerant, generous, and yes, forgiving people. If our government, in the wake of 9/11, had built upon those endearing qualities, what a different world we'd live in today!

Instead, showing little appreciation for the worldwide expressions of empathy after 9/11, the Bush/Cheney/NeoCon administration soon poisoned the international atmosphere with belligerent us/them talk, which reached its zenith with preemptive war against Iraq, and fell to its lowest point with photos of the degrading treatment of detainees at Abu Ghraib

– proving to all the world how easy it is to slide from the path of justice into the quagmire of vengeance when a nation reverts to being ruled by emotions rather than laws.

Historian Howard Zinn spoke of the course our government had chosen, saying: "People in other countries deserve to live as much as people in those Twin Towers deserved to live." And Cornel West, then professor of African-American studies at Harvard, outlined in an impassioned speech the crucial shift in consciousness needed to allow for that equation: "We must say not only to this nation but to the world that a baby in Iraq and a baby in Guatemala, and a baby in Tel Aviv, and a baby on the West Bank, and a baby in Oakland, and a baby in Chicago, all have exactly the same value. If we cannot say that…we are only playing games!"

These are the voices that need to be heard and heeded, for without them there will be no future for the human race, since only the recognition of the worth and dignity of every person will ensure that we survive the age of nuclear weapons. We can begin to initiate that process by enlarging our hearts to include not only the victims of 9/11, but suffering humanity everywhere – all the oppressed, exploited, violated members of the human race. This means curtailing our self-absorption and hubris, and accepting the challenge of becoming fully engaged and responsible members of the global community.

A concern for security?

As underlined, when survival is at stake, or believed to be, there arises a willingness to toss aside freedoms and civil liberties for anything that promises security. This is how Senator Joe Lieberman managed to convince everyone in Washington that the country needed a Homeland Security Department "to ensure the safety of the American people" at a cost of $50 billion annually. To that must be added another $80 billion yearly for US intelligence agencies, a figure disclosed by the Obama administration in 2010 for the first time in ten years.

While this may strike a detached observer as paranoid, it illustrates how, in the wake of 9/11, the one thing sold to the American people as absolutely essential was security – a vast and hugely expensive security system, as explained above.

At the same time, and quite paradoxically, there remained the reality of hundreds of thousands of individuals continuing to cross America's southern border with Mexico. Regardless of how one feels about undocumented migrants, this fact should give us pause. How can we be protected from "terrorists" while such large, unchecked masses of people regularly enter the country? How can the government be sure that all of them come merely to find work and better living conditions? Remember, it supposedly took only nineteen hijackers with box cutters to trigger a catastrophe that changed our way of life, and the course of the world, forever!

If it is security the government is focused on providing, then the present border arrangements will not do. And one should think that "Homeland Security" is quite aware of that. So what does "security" really mean for those in charge in Washington? As for critics who have learned to connect the dots, it is not hard to figure out. It means (a) subjecting American citizens to excessive measures of control and the curtailment of civil rights. Think, for example, of the inconveniences of traveling via airplane since 9/11! And (b) fighting wars in far-off places where countless, mostly innocent, people have lost their lives, their property and livelihoods, not only in direct attacks, but through divide and conquer methods.

Domestically, security has furthermore meant a people surveilled – not in the modus operandi of the former Soviet regime, but more shrewdly, subtly. Most citizens living under the communist regime knew that they had no freedom; Americans exist under the illusion that they do. That phone conversations and emails, financial transactions and membership in social justice and peace organizations are subject to surveillance seems to concern a number of individuals, but certainly not the majority. This does not bode well for our nation.

These are only some of the ways in which we are being controlled. Add to that the aspect of a controlled media, and one can only weep for what has been lost. In fact, for the sake of honoring words, we should no longer speak of "security" when it comes to the intentions of our government; the more appropriate word is *control*. And this kind of control would never have been advocated or tolerated without 9/11.

After that defining date in history, America began to serve neither American nor universal humanitarian values. Arrogance and ruthlessness led, among other things, to "shock and awe" carnage amid blatant violations of international law.

Those violations include the inhumane treatment of detainees at Bagram, Abu Ghraib, Guantanamo, and other, secret dungeons of despair, crimes so dark one can only recoil in abhorrence. Committing them has been properly subjected to strong criticism from human rights groups and outraged people around the globe. At home, such dehumanizing behavior has left its mark on our body politic by creating a leak of toxicity oozing like sewage into the stream of shared life, contaminating all. What we do unto others, we do unto ourselves, and it now confronts us in multiple ways.

There are those who will protest that much of what happened under the Bush administration no longer applies to Barack Obama's White House. I am not convinced that genuine change has been permitted. Surveillance, both global and domestic, is still in place, the war in Afghanistan was escalated, drones commit extrajudicial killings, which include the lives of hundreds of innocent civilians on a regular basis in a number of Muslim countries. US soldiers have supposedly pulled out of Iraq only to leave behind an embassy the size of Vatican City. The complex consists of 21 buildings on a 104-acre site, employs 15,000 people and has a security detail of 4,000. It is the largest and most expensive US "embassy" in the world. No other country has anything like it anywhere.

Having been designed and begun under the Bush administration, it is clearly the NeoCons' control center of the Middle East and beyond – a heavily fortified enclave within the larger territory of Iraq.

Finally, as the *Tucson Citizen*, now only available online, made clear, "The war was the most shameful escapade in American history," while concluding that "We must all wear the cloak of shame [because] we let his happen." Moreover, none of "the crass and craven" individuals who authorized the wars or legalized torture has been charged and tried, and many of their behind-the-scenes dealings go on as before.

"I tremble for my country when I recall that God is just," are fitting words by Thomas Jefferson to describe the terrible fate that has befallen our nation. And thus the horrific SOS that pierced hearts on September 11 continues, now for an entirely new set of reasons.

Ignorance is not bliss

Unless they served as soldiers in previous combat, citizens of this country have no personal experiences or recollections of the horrors of war. There have been no carpet bombings of US cities, no advancing tanks and drawn bayonets from invading foreign troops. It has been 150 years since the last great conflict, the Civil War, was fought on American soil.

When the butchery that is war is something one only reads about in a book or watches in a movie crammed with heroes and villains, it is much easier to acquiesce to a unilateral, preemptive strike against another people. What is much more difficult is to preserve one's moral integrity. For as such self-righteous attacks have shown, they have a circular nature, and in the end lead back to the perpetrator, toward self-wounding, resulting in continual moral decline: We cannot dehumanize and kill others without diminishing what is human in us.

It is quite astonishing to realize that, of all the countries in the world, none has been involved in more major wars, one after the other, in the 20th century and now the 21st, than the oldest democracy in the world. What does that say about democracy and people in general? The answers are many, but in the end, they all come down to this: in a democracy, the politicians who get elected reflect the maturity level of the average voter; otherwise their message will not be heard. Representative Dennis Kucinich is a perfect case in point. When he ran for president in 2008 on an anti-war platform, he garnered the support of barely 1% of those voting in the primaries.

As to the wars we have fought: How much of those developments could have been prevented or at least minimized, if we had listened and incorporated into our philosophy of life the teachings of a long line of homegrown prophets who advocated almost from the beginning of our nation for a more spiritual way of life? Emerson, Thoreau, Channing, Parker, Fuller, Whitman, Muir, to mention a few, and in the 20th century, Martin Luther King, all held in their hearts an image of America conflicting with the direction in which it was moving.

One might have thought that by the beginning of the 3rd millennium, we would have recognized the error of not paying attention to those great visionaries, and not be sucked into yet another war, this one lasting longer than any other.

Instead, unable or unwilling to embrace a more spiritual way of life, we made money, technology, economic expansion and military prowess our primary foci. Granted, a fleeting satisfaction may be extracted from such cherished elements of the material world, but one cannot grow a purposeful life on synthetic soil. For that, humans need humus, compost, need seeds of love and inner fertilizer – introspection, reflection, stillness, solitude – to make them grow into a fertile garden offering genuine nourishment for growing souls.

If we could add at least some of those qualities to our busy extroverted lives, we would be able to diminish some of the *real* threats to our survival. We could begin to curb our ferocious appetite for goods, for profit, for energy, not to mention our appalling wastefulness, inhumane treatment of animals, exploitation and degradation of the environment – our whole anthropocentric, unsustainable way of life. In fact, recall how, after the horrors of 9/11, not a single sacrifice was asked of us. Rather, going shopping was extolled as everybody's basic right – and duty!

I would argue that all these components have, in various ways, contributed to 9/11. And since we are all guilty of such shortcomings, none of us can feel exempt from bearing responsibility and hence from the need to change.

Conversely, with Americans having been encouraged to blithely continue the good life, do we know, do we even care, how many tens of thousands, hundreds of thousands, members of the human family were killed or maimed in foreign lands, when war, our country's aggression against them, commenced?

Do we know, do we even care, how many were made refugees, how many forced to subsist on food found in dumpsters, how many compelled to become prostitutes so that their children could survive? Or how many of those children were made orphans? Do we know, do we even care, how many were swept via dragnets into detention centers and subjected to terror and torture – all in our name?

Building on a passage from William Butler Yeats' enigmatic poem *The Second Coming*, one of America's premier columnists, the late Molly Ivins, wrote in 2002: "Before the blood-dimmed tide is loosed, before we become a shape with a lion's body and the head of a man, with a gaze as blank and pitiless as the sun, before we become that rough beast, its hour come round at last, slouching toward Bethlehem to be born ... let's stop. And think."

The great truth-teller's voice was prematurely silenced by cancer, but her warning about the US having morphed into a monster under George W. Bush and his neo-conservative co-conspirators, remains as prophetic as Yeats' chilling preview of coming events, written in the wake of World War I.

In that same column she wants to make absolutely certain that America hears her, hears about what lies ahead, but hears also that people have choices. She does so with a quote from Tom Stoppard's play *Rosencrantz and Guildenstern are Dead*, where at the end of the tragedy the one says to the other, "There must have been a time, somewhere near the beginning, when we could have said no."

Frightened by the sound of horrifying explosions, bewildered by the collapse of two lofty towers, and blinded by massive, churning clouds of dust, we missed our chance. And now, like other nations before, we must, brick by brick, rebuild the edifice of our dreams and earn once again the rights, the respect and the honor we so dismissively squandered.

Until that hour, the SOS of 9/11 will not cease.

Chapter 2

MOURNING TWO LOSSES

*At the end, Saddam was cowering underground with no way to escape.
So why does it feel as if we are the ones who are trapped?*

~*Steven Chapman*

Truth has a way of asserting itself despite all attempts to obscure it.

~*Robert C. Byrd*

Truth is the only safe ground to stand upon.

~*Elizabeth Cady Stanton*

On September 11, 2001, two tragedies occurred: Amer
ica lost 3,000 lives, and America lost its moral footing and direction.

How did it happen?

A clean break

What few could have been aware of in the midst of the
global shock waves that followed 9/11 was that several years
prior to that world-transforming autumn day, two master plans
for a drastically changed US foreign policy had been hatched.
The first, a comprehensive vision for reconfiguring the Middle
East for the benefit of Israel, was outlined in a 1996 policy paper titled *A Clean Break: A New Strategy for Securing the Realm.*
Authors included Richard Perle, Paul Wolfowitz, Douglas
Feith, and David Wurmser – individuals destined to become
prominent members of or advisers to the Bush administration.

A Clean Break was intended for incoming Israeli Prime
Minister Benjamin Netanyahu and was prepared under the aus-
pices of an Israeli think tank, the Institute for Advanced Strategic and Political Studies. It pressed the new Israeli government
to launch preemptive war against its Arab neighbors. "Israel

28

has the opportunity to make a clean break," the paper said, "to engage every possible energy on rebuilding Zionism."

Baghdad was first on the hit list – "Whoever inherits Iraq dominates the entire Levant strategically," they wrote. Thus, according to former insiders, attacking Iraq became the NeoCons' obsession the moment they ascended to power with the Bush/Cheney presidency in 2001.

Along the same lines, a second master plan was spawned and promoted by the ultra conservative think tank Project for the New American Century (PNAC), co-founded in 1997 by William Kristol and Robert Kagan. In it, some of the same ideologues argued for a hard line US foreign policy based on unilateralism, preemptive strikes and "total war" for the purpose of ensuring the absolute supremacy of the United States in world affairs. PNAC's doctrine can be found in a white paper produced in September 2000, bearing the title *Rebuilding America's Defenses: Strategy, Forces and Resources for a New Century*.

From the start, the creators of the document admitted that the ambitious goals would take a long time to accomplish, "absent some catastrophic and catalyzing event – like a new Pearl Harbor."

The full text bears the signatures of a group of ultra-right-wing neoconservatives: Dick Cheney, Donald Rumsfeld, Paul Wolfowitz, Richard Perle, I. Lewis "Scooter" Libby, Elliot Abrams, Jeb Bush, William Kristol, William J. Bennett, Zalmay Khalilzad, Dan Quayle, Norman Podhoretz, Donald Kagan, and others – twenty-five signers in all. Many of those who formulated the audacious plan would one day run the Pentagon and US foreign policy.

Then, a year after the completion of the white paper, the explosion and crumbling to ashes and dust of the World Trade Center became that "new Pearl Harbor" they had calculated needed to happen. In a word, 9/11 proved to be the catastrophic and catalyzing event for the remaking of America in preparation for "total war" in the Middle East. Cunning minds swiftly shifted into high gear to seize the moment.

As it turned out, thanks to their inordinate influence

over Congress and privileged access to the media, as well as the use of ubiquitous think tanks, the group could rather effortlessly persuade the American public to support their audacious objectives.

Michael Lind, in his provocative book, *Made in Texas: George W. Bush and the Southern Takeover of American Politics*, explains from a different perspective the forces at work, even as he provides additional insight into the mind of George W. Bush and his appointees. Succinctly summarizing their defining character and goals, he emphasizes their traditional reactionary Texas conservatism, their belief in minimal government at home and a bellicose foreign policy abroad and their religious fundamentalism.

"With the election of George W. Bush, the frustrated neoconservatives finally had an opportunity to put their ambitious schemes for reordering the world into practice," he maintains. He then goes on to remind us that in his first year, G.W. Bush canceled more international treaties than any president in American history, leaving America's treaty partners insulted and shocked.

Lind's overarching verdict is unequivocal: "The conservative [worldview] of the Bush administration has no precedents in US foreign policy. But it has a striking resemblance to nineteenth-century British imperialism."

Still, it would be erroneous to see these developments as being entirely out of character and disconnected from our national history.

This is because America's belief in its exceptionalism and "Manifest Destiny", fortified by the Monroe Doctrine of 1823, which warned Europe that the Western Hemisphere was no longer open for European colonization, have virtually ensured the nation's long-standing history of conquest by economic, political and/or military means. This was expanded into a political ideology whereby America's mission was seen as promoting and defending democracy throughout the world.

Such attitudes grafted a dangerous shadow early in its history onto the bright ideals of a newborn nation.

From that perspective, the haughty reaction to 9/11 by

Washington's elite did not entirely originate in a vacuum. Tendencies toward it had been gestating for generations.

The consequences, however, have not only been an unmitigated disaster with respect to our country's original purpose, but for the aspirations of the world community. When the strongest nation on Earth callously serves only its own domineering instincts, while lashing out at anyone who dares to disagree, then humanity is deprived of the strong friend it needs to find its way to a more equitable and peaceful future.

How ironic and sad, therefore, that a decade after the demise of Soviet communism and the end of the Cold War, when hundreds of millions were engaged in rebuilding their lives, and international relations were being renewed, unbridled nationalism and a military mindset should have determined the direction of the most ethnically heterogeneous country in the world. By the very standards of its demographic diversity, the US ought to be *the* most progressive nation on Earth instead of being a regressive intimidator.

Post 9/11 with its climate of arrogance of power and rule of the gun inaugurated instead the most hazardous and potentially ruinous period in American history. Individuals acquainted with similar intervals in the life of other nations were alarmed. Though few were willing to listen, those who cared felt, nonetheless, compelled to warn others of how fatal the erosion of liberties would be, especially since fear alone allows for such voluntary surrender of basic rights.

And fear, we know, enfeebles in multiple ways: It robs us of reason, constricts the heart and reduces our humanity. Most alarmingly, fear makes us relinquish our power, leaving us susceptible to manipulation and enticing offers of "security". This becomes particularly acute when fear metastasizes into paranoia. In the highly charged atmosphere of 9/11 and its aftermath, color-coded alerts turned out to be a very handy method for keeping that paranoia alive.

By opting for fear and force, the Bush/Cheney/ Neo-Con administration chose not to participate in the new forward movement that had shown such promise in the early 1990s. Instead, it waged preemptive war, thereby scornfully squandering the oceanic tide of goodwill for our country that had been generated by a grieving world.

It made possible the so-called War on Terrorism with its worldwide invasion of privacy, global tracking of money and information, military campaigns and medieval methods of torture. The rather cynically named "Digital Collection Systems Work" became one of numerous spy systems introduced by the Bush administration to survey and control the citizens of our country and the world.

Meanwhile, as noted in the previous chapter, Benjamin Netanyahu described the events of 9/11 as good for Israel. Beyond what the prime minister had in mind, it turned out that the mass murder was valuable indeed for an emerging sector of the Israeli economy.

In "Laboratory for a Fortressed World" (*The Nation*, June 14, 2007) Canadian author and social activist, Naomi Klein, gives an account of the post-9/11 growth of Israel's homeland security sector. "Before 9/11 homeland security barely existed as an industry," Klein reports. "By the end of this year, Israeli exports in the sector will reach $1.2 billion."

"The key products and services," she explains, "are high-tech fences, unmanned drones, biometric IDs, video and audio surveillance gear, air passenger profiling and prisoner interrogation systems – precisely the tools and technologies Israel has used to lock in the occupied territories."

They become thus what Klein calls, "a living example of how to enjoy relative safety amid constant war." Israel is enjoying "supergrowth" because its high tech companies are exporting that model to the world.

"Israel has struck oil," she concludes. "The oil is the war on terror, the state of constant fear that creates a bottomless global demand for devices that watch, listen, contain and target suspects."

Even though the controlling web was installed during the previous administration, today the forces whose aim is Full Spectrum Dominance keep on monitoring everyone and everything around the world. Its globalized reach and cynical sense of entitlement are making Orwell's *Nineteen Eighty-Four* look positively primitive by comparison. For here is a totalitarianism, the scope and reach of which has never before darkened the planet and human life on it. What is striking is its spectacular ability to disguise itself, and its awesome capacity for complete control. A brilliant, albeit terrifying, coup d'état has been executed.

In addition, the system is also more cunningly lethal because of technological advances such as the 21st century's most deceptive weapon: drones. Drones, invisible and inaudible, can strike the unsuspecting at any time, anywhere, awake or asleep, at the command of a computer operator hundreds, even thousands, of miles away. These truly diabolical weapons should be renounced as being unworthy of humans by every civilized country. For they are as despicable as cluster bombs, another weapon the US insists must remain in its military arsenal, even as most of the world has voted to outlaw them.

This is how we inflict wounds on ourselves, moral wounds at first which then manifest as tangible ones, disturbing ones, in the common life of our own citizens: we despise each other, attack and vilify each other, wish each other ill, and accusingly point fingers at scapegoats. Unbeknownst to most, we are a divided and conquered people – divided by ignorance and conquered by fear.

The people of the Earth want to evolve, grow, outgrow the brutal ways of yesteryear, but, tragically, our country is sabotaging the process. And it is doing it for purely self-serving purposes.

The "Clean Break" envisioned at the beginning of the 3rd millennium by a small group of power-intoxicated individuals is, no doubt, a break. But it is anything but clean. It resembles more of a bloody breakdown, a self-inflicted wound, a soiled bed in which we must now sleep.

The rotten smell of lies

Not a few of us were alarmed when we recognized the course our country had embarked upon after 9/11. We sensed a looming disaster, not only for the people of the Middle East, but as mentioned, the moral fiber of our own country.

Still, one might ask, why did some of us cringe every time we were treated to one of those scripted performances out of Washington? Was it the information gained from alternative news sources that contradicted those calculated assertions? Was it intuition? Or was it, as in my own case, that unique antenna developed while living under dictators, which sensitizes an individual to governmental lies?

Then, an additional possibility unexpectedly presented itself via an article in the *Arizona Daily Star* of June 13, 2003. "Brain knows when deal stinks", proclaimed the headline. Reading on, I learned that based on a study in the journal *Science*, a sense of revulsion that some feel when offered an unfair deal comes from the same part of the brain that detects bad smells. "The concept of a deal smelling fishy is probably not all that far off," the writer mused. "It may be that when you deal with somebody who isn't trustworthy, you have the same emotions as when you smell something bad."

There you have it! Those who opposed the hazardous course of the Bush administration after 9/11, and especially its unprovoked war against Iraq, smelled something fishy, something odious, something very wrong from the start: George W. Bush and his handlers were deliberately misleading the public.

Assaulting truth

Why did the American people so blindly accept all the propaganda presented to them? We have mentioned already the Fourth Estate and its failure to serve the public by repeating and amplifying the lies rather than exposing them. There is, however, one more equally potent factor to consider.

The tactics employed by George W. Bush and his NeoCons were reminiscent of another era and as such reflective of a chilling comment by Hermann Goering, Adolf Hitler's Luftwaffe Commander, made at the Nuremberg trials: "Of course the people don't want war. ... But after all, it is the leaders of the country who determine the policy, and it's always a simple matter to drag the people along. ... All you have to do is tell them they are being attacked, and denounce the pacifists for lack of patriotism and exposing the country to danger. It works the same in any country." (*Nuremberg Diary* by G. M. Gilbert, Signet, New York, 1947.)

Regrettably, history confirms Goering's cynical attitude. On the other hand, one might have thought and hoped that Americans would be the exception. After all, this nation is not a newcomer to self-governance. This is the birthplace of modern democracy. By 2001, generations of citizens had lived under a representative government for 225 years, regardless of how imperfect in practice.

Not all was lost, however, for there was enough opposition to the assault on constitutional rights that the American Civil Liberties Union could report its biggest growth ever in membership. Remaining clear-headed, at least some Americans were ready to take a stand against scare tactics and neo-fascist strategies.

Meanwhile, unfolding events showed that America had, indeed, been co-opted by an alien, anachronistic ideology, and subjected to policies foreign to our basic values. "I want my country back," cried the disenfranchised.

Since the birth of this Republic, nothing quite like it had ever occurred. The crisis of 9/11 and its aftermath were thus of greater significance to our national identity than any other preceding it. Because most of us are ill informed as to what happened behind the scenes in Washington with the arrival of George Bush in the White House, it will not be easy to untangle America from the stranglehold of the NeoCons and their marriage of convenience to fanatical religious fundamentalists. It will in fact be a Herculean task.

Having said that, such a challenge can be more easily faced if we keep our perspective, gather wisdom, and remember the words of the sage: "In the struggle between truth and falsehood, falsehood wins the first round, but truth the last."

No matter how justice will one day come to the perpetrators of those hideous acts, our goal must be to emerge a changed people who realize that what is good for the world is good for us; that is, we must awaken to life's Oneness and the interrelatedness of all beings. Not to achieve this transformation would be ruinous for both our country and the world.

Rubble and revelations

Who could ever have foreseen the vast learning requirements that would rise out of the implosion of two huge towers as they fell into their footprints while spreading dust and debris all over Lower Manhattan and into New Jersey, thicker than a blanket?

For those who had been paying attention and were concerned about the lifestyle of the majority of Americans prior to the event, it was clear from the start that it would take far less time to clean up the rubble of buildings than to rebuild lives that had veered off course, disengaged from their original purpose.

We had forgotten the deeper meaning of our existence, had entrusted it to outer elements, from the power of money to the potency of weapons. We were, subsequently, short on inner, crisis-sustaining strength. When inwardly weak, this is precisely what happens: we become frightened, we succumb to fear, and we can be manipulated.

Although on the whole a decent and generous people, American naiveté and gullibility revealed itself to be our Achilles heel, allowing less than honorable leaders to exploit and use us. And thus, like naive lemmings, we followed false prophets to the cliff at the edge of the sea.

These alarming developments tell us that we have work to do, inner work, by which alone we can connect with the strength and wisdom of our being. For it is not airplanes or tanks that will ultimately protect, much less rescue us, from the emergencies of our lives, but the emergence of a much neglected part: the light within us. That negligence, we can be sure, will always, sooner or later, lead to a moral crisis, and when encountering it, will leave us floundering. Floundering people are easy prey for ruthless predators.

When applying this to 9/11, it is not hard to see why American citizens, caught in the shock of the terror attacks and the ensuing panic and anxiety were so effortlessly duped and manipulated to relinquish civil liberties and in the end support an unlawful, immoral war.

When human beings lose contact with the inner light, they lose their true perception, being blinded by the illusory reality of outer things. This fact continues to make it difficult for many to see why the real loss of 9/11 was not the World Trade Center, a section of the Pentagon, or even something as precious as human lives; the real loss of that day was moral clarity and with it, part of our humanity.

If catastrophes are not only tragedies but opportunities to grow, the staggering impact of that world-shaking, life-changing day could have led to another outcome besides causing so many more deaths and inflicting such devastation on the already war-ravaged land and people of Afghanistan, and later on a country that had nothing whatsoever to do with September 11, 2001.

Why, we must ask, was Osama bin Laden and his al-Qaeda network not hunted down by American intelligence agencies in connection with international organizations, such as Interpol, and brought to justice? Instead, the Bush administration started a merciless war against all of Afghanistan that has by now lasted eleven destructive years. How many innocent lives have been snuffed out, how many mothers, fathers and children buried on Afghan soil because of American hubris and vengefulness? Is this how we want to be remembered by an abused people – *and* the people of this world?

We had, undoubtedly, another choice, one that could have utilized the pain of that day to propel us onto a new level of awareness, to a place of inner strength, empowerment, ultimately letting our country emerge as a pioneering exemplar of a new way of life for the world's people. Except that those who held the reins of power had other plans; had in advance chosen to fight not only one but two wars, all under the umbrella of a third: war on terrorism – endless war.

Subsequently, instead of leaping forward, America slid backward, losing connections to its humanitarian impulse, the Constitution and International Law. That we were unable to resist the shrewd machinations of those in command and let ourselves be used, confirms the analysis offered above with respect to our psychological and spiritual state of development.

This is the exact opposite of what should have been our course, for nothing, not even the invocation of "National Security" ever justifies abandoning our ethical principles, much less our humanity. Now that it has occurred, let us, however, not miss the opportunity to learn from it. Let what has come to pass be a warning to never again follow corrupt leaders onto such a catastrophic path. In fact, in the future we ought to require of every elected officer a pledge to adhere to guidelines articulated by that grand political genius, Thomas Jefferson, who counseled: "If you just give the people the truth, the Republic will be safe."

Genuine security does not rest in overwhelming defense systems and devastating weapons, but in honesty, authenticity and good will toward others. That was the lesson we so badly needed and so sadly missed.

The world's judgment

In light of our government's conduct post 9/11, how did the world perceive us? On June 3rd the Pew Research Center released its *Views of a Changing World 2003*. According to the 44-nation poll, the war with Iraq widened the rift between Americans and Western Europeans and further inflamed the Muslim world. Favorable opinions of the US steeply declined in nearly every country.

Interestingly, while the poll paints a mostly negative picture of America, its people and policies, it shows wide support for the vital economic and political values that the US has long promoted. Not surprisingly, US policies toward the Middle East come under especially heavy criticism. Pluralities or majorities believe the US favors Israel over the Palestinians too much. This opinion is shared in Israel itself. Only Americans, the poll indicated, are unable to see it that way. Why, one must ask again, are Americans so poorly educated about the most crucial issue of our time?

The data further reveal that in the eyes of the world, the US has become identified with self-absorption, isolationism, hypocrisy and arrogance. Yet, despite soaring anti-Americanism and, at that time, substantial support for Osama bin Laden, there is considerable yearning in the Muslim world for democratic freedoms. The Arab uprisings of 2011 would certainly confirm this.

Another interesting finding revealed by the poll is that Americans are more individualistic and favor a less compassionate government than do Europeans and others; i.e., Americans care more about personal freedom than governmental assurances of social justice.

Finally, there is broad global acceptance of the increasing interconnectedness of the world.

Reflecting on the results of the survey, especially with respect to the aspirations of the Earth's people, there are reasons to be hopeful. It seems humanity is ready for a quantum leap in consciousness. However, as for the US, we should be deeply concerned. The taking of the planetary pulse shows that it is high time for precisely what we discussed earlier: the need for introspection that we might become more authentically ourselves. Again, columnist Steve Chapman: "It's a dangerous delusion to think that our...[policies are] unpopular abroad only because everyone else in the world is cowardly...or blind. ... If even your friends disapprove of what you're doing, maybe you're doing something wrong."

Pausing to contemplate our attitudes and ways of relating to the rest of the world may help open our eyes, better yet, our hearts, to the fact that there is plenty of room for improvement.

Fear controls, distorts, disempowers and ultimately destroys everything – relationships, people, countries. That we could not manifest moral courage when it was most needed is, I believe, a devastating loss, one that cannot be mourned deeply enough.

Paying the price

The USA Patriot Acts I and II should by now have convinced us that the price we paid in liberties for the sake of security has been far too high. This development presents the most serious domestic hazard to our Republic since its inception. There is irony in this, because first terrorism and later

Saddam Hussein were sold to the public as grave threats. As developments have shown, however, our violent military conquests since 9/11 have turned out to be a far greater peril, not only to world peace and our own cherished liberties, but to our very essence as a people.

Clearly, much more has been lost since that ill-fated day than terrorists could ever have hoped to achieve. And that's where we are right now: a people living under truncated liberties and controlled by clever forces of deceit.

We shall stress in some of the chapters that follow how corporate media failed the American public following the tragedy of 9/11, thus contributing to both the state of ignorance and the degree of exploitation/domination we are experiencing unto this day. Sadly, that failure did not start on the day of the attack, but had been in the making for years, with events from around the world being registered as mere blips on the television screens of most US households.

Americans have been poorly informed and often misinformed for a very long time. Being without knowledge is a serious deficiency in the life of any person, but it can be fatal for a democracy. For when ignorance rules, people become either phobic and submissive or counter-phobic and domineering.

As to the pundits that rose to prominence in our country during a bewildering post 9/11 climate, their divisive words still echo across the airwaves today: absolute right and wrong, absolute winners and losers, endless scare tactics, war as the only means of solving conflict. When ignorance and arrogance cohabit, their offspring inevitably turn malevolent. This is how politics in America became toxic and fraught with pitfalls and dangers.

Meanwhile, a majority of us are living a life, which on the whole, and on the surface, can be considered rather comfortable, even satisfying for most. We can say, in fact, that most of the 300 million American citizens enjoy what a large percentage of the world's people would consider an enviable standard of living. But below that smooth and seemingly solid surface, we are riding atop a volcano: there is churning and boiling and shifting beneath our feet.

This metaphor allows for underscoring a vital point: we need to wake up from our slumber and become aware of the dangers lurking beneath our feet in order to find ways of dealing with something that has the potential of becoming immeasurably worse than 9/11. We must indeed strive to take our country back – our laws, our values, our very humanity. As I have sought to emphasize in my writings, we presently live in the most perilous time in all of human history. We are standing at a crossroads of the most profound and enormous consequences ever. Under such conditions, not a single individual can afford, or even be permitted, to stay asleep.

Until we recognize the urgency of that situation and respond en masse, our moral vigor will further decline, while our losses shall mount.

Chapter 3

BEATING THE WAR DRUMS

We speak to the rest of the globe in the language of violence.
                                        ~Chris Hedges

War is too important a matter to be left to the military.
                                        ~Georges Clemenceau

The 'war on terror' is a 'war of terror.'
                                        ~Edward S. Herman

By think tanks, I mean the people who are paid to think by the makers of tanks.

                                        ~Naomi Klein

On October 27, 2010, shortly after the death of President Nestor Kirchner of Argentina, *Democracy Now!* featured excerpts from an interview the president had with filmmaker Oliver Stone. In it, Kirchner recounts a conversation with then President George W. Bush on war and the economy.

"We had a discussion in Monterrey. I told Bush that a solution to the problems right now is a Marshall Plan. And he got angry. He said the Marshall Plan is a crazy idea of the Democrats. He said the best way to revitalize the economy is war and that the United States has grown stronger with war."

Oliver Stone, incredulous: "Was he suggesting that South America go to war?"

President Kirchner: "Well, he was talking about the United States ... All of the economic growth of the United States has been encouraged by the various wars. He said it very clearly."

Then Kirchner inquires, "President Bush is – well, he's only got six days left, right?"

Oliver Stone: "Yes."

Nestor Kirchner: "Thank God."

Wandering in a spiritual wilderness

On September 11, 2001, the opinion reigned that we must do something: we must get *even!* Was bombing another country and its people the only option? Could there have been ways to handle this tragedy other than causing so many more deaths and inflicting such devastation on an already war-ravaged land and people who were not responsible for 9/11? Though photos of that destruction were off-limits (see below), we can be sure that death in Afghanistan has meant not only uncounted combatants, but also tens of thousands of civilians. And today, after more than a decade, the carnage continues, having now spread into Pakistan.

Imagine if every group of people who have ever been wronged throughout history would have reacted the way the US did after the attacks. What kind of world would there be left to inhabit?! We would be looking at a scorched Earth, indeed. Which leads one to ask: Why did we go on this brutal rampage lasting seemingly forever? Is it because, to use Bill Clinton's notorious phrase, *we could?* And if so, is that not the worst, the most arrogant, abuse of power when emanating from a government?

On 9/11 and weeks beyond, the whole world mourned with and for us. Yet, the administration, acting like an impetuous adolescent, immediately projected the image of a tough unilateralist. Ruthless vengeance became its modus operandi.

This is how the government, skillfully employing the art of deception, took advantage of the widespread incredulity and anger of our citizens to commit acts of aggression, both domestic (the trashing of constitutional rights) and foreign (global war on terror). Moreover, it appears those crafty manipulators exploited the situation by using it as a pretext for implementing a Middle East policy outlined on paper long before that fateful day provided a reason and a perfect cover to put it into action.

With every day and every deed, we thus moved deeper into a spiritual wilderness where no rules applied and no one was held accountable. We were, in fact, returning to an era that preceded international law, the United Nations charter and the Fourth Geneva Convention.

To entice the American public into blindly going along, the Bush/Cheney/NeoCon administration made sure that the war against Afghanistan was essentially a conflict without visual documentation, a war without pictures. The government purchased the satellite photos showing the damage inflicted on cities and villages, on valleys and mountains, on people and animals. The government did not permit them to be published, claiming "national security" for the adamant restrictions. Have you noticed how national security trumps everything these days, especially truth and the right of the people to know?

Now, if Washington believed our actions were justified and just, why not show the results – as proof to our friends and foes alike that the power of "good" always triumphs over "evil", and as a further warning to our enemies, that our response to acts of terror will be swift and merciless! Or is there perhaps something we must hide from the eyes of the world, from the inherent goodness of the human heart, which does not believe that two wrongs make a right? In fact, might it be that the damage inflicted by the military was so ferocious its impact amounted to a World Trade Center attack multiplied a hundred, a thousand times – a devastation so shocking it must never be broadcast to the citizens of this world?

Still, Scott Simon of NPR, reporting from Afghanistan, was not hesitant to state what he observed in an interview several months after the first missiles plowed into the land and the people. The country, he exclaimed, is so utterly destroyed it looks "worse than Hiroshima." Can we, who are living in the most comfortable, untouched-by-war place on the planet, even begin to imagine what such utter destruction with its ensuing despair really means? For a native German like myself, it certainly exemplified George Orwell's reaction when seeing Germany after WWII. "To walk through the ruined cities of Germany," he lamented, "is to feel an actual doubt about the continuity of civilization."

The United States hit 700 targets a day in Afghanistan

until running out of missiles and so-called "smart bombs." I shudder to think not only of the humans but the inhabitants of the natural world that were subject to such deadly assaults. And I shudder for the sake of our own people, for when a nation fights an alleged evil with evil in such a terrifying manner – with carpet bombing, with 15,000-pound bombs – we not only increase the very hate we claim not to comprehend, but do great damage to that which is human in us. We simply cannot dehumanize another without diminishing our own humanity.

And with each day the news grew more disturbing. March 4, 2002, brought a particularly shocking revelation when for the first time America lobbed a still-experimental bomb so fierce it can crush an enemy's internal organs even when hiding far beneath the surface of the earth. The warheads are reportedly designed to suck the oxygen out of a cave or tunnel, followed by a horrendous explosion which kills even earthworms deep underground. Weighing a ton, they are called "thermobaric."

In my view, "thermo" should be renamed "bar" to accurately describe these hideous weapons: bar-baric. Barbaric bombs dropped in the name of the American people on those that have been demonized! Excuse me, but were we not supposed to be the "good" side in this struggle?

Battle du jour

In faraway places armies thrash
monsters du jour
strike them with ghastly weapons
pound them with iron grit:
a killing machine
unleashed to batter the enemy
annihilate evil
as apocalyptic assaults
rattle the earth, blacken the skies
pulverize mountains and people –
fighting for the good, battling for civilization…

RC - Nov. 2001

Do we really believe that destroying "the enemy" will solve our problem? How many enemies and monsters have we been fighting over the last hundred years alone, and still they raise their fearsome countenances? In addition, if we are so outraged about the atrocities and terror committed by them, how can we believe that killing and terrifying in response will make us less of a monster? In fact, maybe we are the monster all along and when we call another a "terrorist", we are merely looking into the mirror! In brief, we project onto others what is darkest in us.

There is something primitive in all humans, something rooted in fear, which, when allowed to have free reign, can drive us to commit irresponsible acts. This is why we need laws to restrain at least the majority of us. And that restraint applies especially to governments. Is that not the principle on which our country was founded – a nation based on laws rather than the will, much less the grudges or hubris of leaders?

In the end, lashing out and causing horrendous devastation neither diminished threats nor increased our security. And we can be sure that nothing will, troop surges included, until we address root causes. Yet, that has been made extraordinarily difficult by a major psychological blockage: On September 11, 2001, the United States of America became a victim. And as we have learned, the defining feature of those who see themselves as a victim is that a victim can do no wrong. This is why our country is having such a difficult time realizing what we are doing to others.

Or maybe not. For if we didn't, how does one account for a headline such as this one in the *Arizona Daily Star*, proclaiming in bold letters on its front page, October 10, 2001: "US owns Afghan skies". US owns Afghan skies? Since when is the sky anyone's possession?

Appealing to the conscience of America

Hamid Karzai, the President of Afghanistan, a man with direct experience of our military actions, attempted four years into the war to speak to America's conscience. During a commencement address at Boston University in May of 2005, he warned against an extended version of narcissistic self-interests perpetrated in the name of a nation. "I urge you," he pleaded, "to question the notion of national interests, especially when it is narrowly defined and pursued at the expense of other people, when it justifies the inflicting of pains on others, and where it allows the neglect of human suffering."

These words, spoken without judgment or anger, should have given us pause. In response, we should have asked ourselves, and our government, how decimating a people and their land can ever lead to peace or awaken goodwill. Does not such behavior ultimately reduce us morally and spiritually, no matter how successful we might be militarily or how good we feel about "getting even"? Today, eleven years into the war, and a year after an extrajudicial execution eliminated Osama bin Laden, we must ask: getting even with whom? The whole of the Afghan people, perhaps?

Considering the merciless warfare, the carnage, the Special Forces operations and hundreds of billions of dollars spent, Americans should insist on knowing what this fighting is *really* about, and for how long US and NATO forces will be engaged in such futile, inane conduct. Has it not occurred to any of our generals that the longer we occupy a country and systematically kill anyone who does not like our presence, the more enemies we make?

Even more to the point, are the Pentagonists and their moneymen interested in *ever* ending this longest of wars fought in US history? Or is the enormous profit that comes with such "projects", not to mention the guinea pig testing of new weapons, a temptation too enticing to resist? With such enormous benefits serving the military/industrial complex, how can we expect the charade to end?

There could exist, of course, a far more sinister reason for all that destruction, all those deaths, all those tortured detainees. In fact, more astute observers have long suspected that this so-called war *on* terror is actually a war *of* terror – a barely disguised physical and psychological crusade against the very religion of Islam and its adherents, perpetrated by a power-addicted clique craving global dominance.

47

As if to confirm the conjecture, the former Muslim chaplain at Guantanamo, James Yee, made a chilling revelation on *Democracy Now!* in May of 2006. Among the many methods used by interrogators to debase and break detainees, he said, was a particularly odious one. It consisted of drawing "a satanic circle" around the prisoner, and then forcing him to "bow down to Satan" by pressing his forehead to the ground, mocking the Islamic practice of touching a prayer rug with the brow in a gesture of surrender to God. Such callous conduct on the part of interrogators must indeed have been a moment of utter terror for the detainee.

Islam is a strong religion and a vital presence, with 1.4 billion followers worldwide. Spiritually grounded and knitted together by a powerful sense of community, as well as permeated with a strong sense of equality and justice, Islam is clearly an enormous impediment to those who desire Total Spectrum Dominance. This is because, generally speaking, Muslims place their relationship to the Divine far above submission to any opportunistic schemes perpetrated by human beings.

Christianity, on the other hand, no longer presents the same rampart against the powers of the world, having been weakened by criticism, revisionism and privatization during the last decades. A privatized religion, no longer energetically committed to the transformation of society, and no longer a force to reckon with when it comes to issues of justice and humanitarian principles at home and abroad, presents no threat to those who seek control. But, as stated, Islam does, and this would explain the hateful attitude and sadistic behavior toward Muslims since 9/11.

The above profile of Islam would also explain the massive surveillance by the New York City Police Department of the Muslim population as revealed by the Associated Press during an exposé in 2012. Not only in New York City, but all over the Northeast, paid informers infiltrated businesses, mosques, schools and universities to keep track of the conversations and activities of Muslim citizens. This occurred despite willing cooperation with the NYPD and the FBI by the leaders of the Islamic community since 2001.

Those police tactics were confirmed by one of the hired men who now regrets his work as an informant. The story appeared in an article by the AP on October 10, 2012, and documented the activities of Shamiur Rahman, a 19-year-old American of Bengali descent who was part of a wide-ranging program by the New York Police Department's intelligence unit to monitor life in the Muslim community.

As a paid informant, he was under orders to "bait" Muslims into saying inflammatory things as he lived a double life, snapping pictures inside mosques and collecting the names of innocent people attending study groups on Islam, he told the Associated Press.

He revealed that the police told him to embrace a strategy called "create and capture", which involved starting a conversation about jihad or terrorism, then capturing the response to send to the NYPD. For his work, he earned as much as $1,000 a month and goodwill from the police after a string of minor marijuana arrests.

To these disturbing developments we must add how copiously peppered with fear mongering about Islam our language has become as we are constantly reminded of "the threat of radical Islam", "a militant Islamic group", "Islamic terrorist organizations", "the worldwide threat of Islamic fundamentalism", "Islamofascism", etc. If nothing else, this certainly gives a sense of the scope of the vilification. And, as history shows, vilification is an essential first step in preparing for war on real or perceived enemies.

Finally, should any reluctance remain to accepting the real story behind this perpetual war being so relentlessly waged by Washington, a news item on *Democracy Now!* April 26, 2012, should remove any remaining scales from the eyes of those in persistent denial. The report is blunt: "The Pentagon has suspended a course at the Joint Forces Staff College in Norfolk, Virginia, that taught senior officers the United States is at war with Islam."

It may have escaped some that for once the American military has admitted the truth behind the war on terror, and though that has now been "suspended", one can only hope that, in the process, enough citizens have been awakened that they will not be brainwashed by lies again.

Hanging on a cross of iron

On January 16, 2002, several months after our attack on Afghanistan, I shared my response about the misery we were causing mostly innocent people via a letter published in the *Arizona Daily Star*: "I have listened intently to the various voices of this world since September 11," I wrote, "and I have concluded with heavy heart that there is no difference between the terror experienced in New York and Washington and the continued terror visited upon Afghanistan. Terrorism by any other name is still terrorism, and when it is perpetrated by one's own country, it makes of us all accomplices to horrific crimes. We have reminded the German people of this for over 50 years now."

"9/11 could have been a major turning point, an awakening to the interconnected web of life, but it seems after the initial shock too many have simply gone back to sleep. Thus the way of fear and hatred, and of ever more terrifying ways of destruction, goes on. And it will no doubt continue until human beings discover that true strength and protection do not lie in weapons but in being compassionate and just."

The most surprising response came from a retired military officer. In a letter to me personally, he confessed: "As an Air Force Colonel I once endorsed, and helped carry out, the concept of solving world problems through military power. Now, it has become very obvious to me that war and retaliation will never, ever bring peace to the world, and as a permanent solution to world problems, is fatally flawed. The nations of the world suffer the delusion of, and are besieged by, a military-might-equates-to-national-security mentality. The opposite is true. The more the world has armed itself over the years, the greater the danger has become!"

This from an officer who served in three wars – WWII, Korea, and Vietnam. I was deeply touched and contacted him immediately – and Bill and I have been friends ever since.

There is an ironic aspect to this, for he could have been

the airman who piloted the plane that nearly caused my demise at the age of five.

I had been out in the meadow by myself on a lovely summer day when I heard an airplane approaching. My natural inclination would have been to wave to the men in those amazing machines that could fly. But I suddenly realized the plane was descending rapidly. In fact, it was coming right at me!

I was terrified, and being very close to a potato field, instinctually threw myself into the first row, seeking a hiding place. With an ear-splitting sound, the plane passed over me.

When it had disappeared, I rose, dazed and shaking. Yet, in the end, I only needed to spit the dirt out of my mouth and brush off my face and clothing, while approximately 1 kilometer up the road, a farmer and his ox, working in his field, were not so fortunate. Both were gunned down.

The story came back to me upon meeting Bill, who had been assigned to the skies over Germany and told me that toward the end of the war, the command was to "shoot anything that moves on the ground" including people, horses and other livestock. This is when questions about war and its brutality first surfaced in his conscience.

Dwight D. Eisenhower, WWII general and President of the United States, admonished the country in 1953: "Every gun that is made, every warship launched, every rocket fired, signifies, in the final sense, a theft from those who hunger and are not fed, those who are cold and are not clothed. This world of arms is not spending money alone. It is spending the sweat of its laborers, the genius of its scientists, the hopes of its children. This is not a way of life at all in any true sense. Under the cloud of war, it is humanity hanging on a cross of iron."

While President Eisenhower was clearly aware of the massive military-industrial complex, now grown into the largest economic venture in the US, imagine what his response would have been to the rise of unfettered American militarism and the scope and power of its influence in the wake of 9/11!

Meanwhile, the bloated budget of the Pentagon and the deployment of US forces to overpower and bring under control two Muslim countries, are having a potent effect on national and international peace activists. Their conviction that war is an anachronistic, obsolete way of solving conflict, is growing no less exponentially, attracting an ever-increasing number of people worldwide.

The gathering storm

Rather than the citizens of our country welcoming such an encouraging development toward a safer, saner future, they found no objection to the belligerent mood emanating from Washington. For by 2002, bombing and killing in Afghanistan were no longer sufficient for willful autocrats at the Pentagon and White House. Thus, even as those attacks continued, another "threat to our security" was brought to the attention of the American public, raising fear and warmongering to new heights. The target of that campaign was none other than Saddam Hussein.

During the following months, President Bush uttered unequivocal pronouncements that Saddam possessed weapons of mass destruction, that he was a bloodcurdling menace to the world. "The danger to our country is grave," he intoned. "The danger to our country is growing," he later warned. "The Iraqi regime possesses biological and chemical weapons...The Iraqi regime continues to conceal some of the most lethal weapons ever devised," he charged darkly.

He raised the specter of 25,000 liters of anthrax, tons of chemical weapons, and a mad dictator on the brink of possessing a nuclear bomb, and willing to employ it. In fact, various members of the administration, interviewed on popular news shows, spoke as though with one set of larynges about the possibility of a "smoking gun" coming in the form of a "mushroom cloud".

Once again the ominous sound of war drums could be heard throughout the land, this time louder and more menacing than before, even as every attempt was made to link Saddam to both 9/11 and the al-Qaeda network – all of which, as some pointed out from the start, was pure fabrication.

Along those lines, there was an unusual development wherein former US Ambassador Joseph Wilson was sent to Niger to ascertain the validity of those infamous "yellowcake" documents showing Saddam's purchase of uranium to build a bomb. He found them to be a fraud.

But never mind the truth. In his provocative State of the Union message of 2003, President Bush repeated the false claims and Congress, wildly applauding, rose to its feet in support of the president's threat to bring such illegal activities by Saddam Hussein to an end.

There was one among the gathered, however, who did not join in the acclamations. Instead, Rep. Dennis Kucinich of Ohio, faithful to the Constitution, strongly, eloquently sounded the alarm. "The question is not whether or not America has the military power to destroy Saddam Hussein and Iraq," he declared. "The question is whether we destroy something essential in this nation by asserting that America has the right to do so anytime it pleases."

And then there was Ambassador Wilson himself. Listening to the State of the Union address, he could not believe what he heard the president say. A true patriot, he reported to the press what the real situation was. Highly displeased by Mr. Wilson's candidness, "Scooter" Libby of the Vice President's office, in a reckless display of vindictiveness, "outed" the Ambassador's wife Valerie as an undercover CIA agent, thereby effectively ruining her career.

And how did the rest of the country react? Distressingly, with barely a question or doubt, the American public accepted the lies disseminated by the President, and relentlessly repeated by the corporate media, to the point that the great majority actually succumbed not only to the falsehood that Saddam Hussein possessed nuclear weapons, but that he was involved in the crime of 9/11 itself!

It has been stated that American citizens tend to trust their government. Regrettably, relentless agitating for war with Iraq proved the point. But why was it made so incredibly easy? The answer is not hard to find: this country is not only ruled by some very ruthless men, but it no longer has a free press.

Those who usurped the US government knew that they could never succeed without control of the corporate media.

Napoleon's Foreign minister Talleyrand once famously uttered the obvious: "Without freedom of the press, there can be no representative government."

Having written at length in my previous book, *Envisioning a New World*, about the media's willingness to be a mouthpiece of propaganda, I shall merely repeat the conclusion then drawn, namely that the media was shamelessly complicit in the attack on Iraq. And once the war started, it was, no doubt, that terribly tempting embeddedness, this "being-in-bed-with" to use Michael Moore's sarcastic phrase, which fully cemented the unholy alliance. It goes without saying: in a democracy, media without an investigative arm and an independent voice is far more of a threat than any hyped-up danger from "terrorists".

Now, while the buildup to the invasion of Iraq was chiefly a NeoCon "project" with assured support from pundits on the right, many on the left consented as well. Among them were influential figures like David Remnick at *The New Yorker*; Bill Keller, then a columnist at the *New York Times*, now its executive editor; George Packer and Peter Beinart of the *New Republic*; Tom Friedman of the *New York Times;* and dozens of other well known journalists of the so-called liberal persuasion. They all backed the war, some of them advocating for it more zealously than others. A rather stark example of that was Michael Ignatieff from Harvard's Carr Center for Human Rights, now the head of the Liberal Party in Canada.

Years later, Robert Fisk, long-time Middle East correspondent for *The Independent*, would speak caustically on *Democracy Now!* (5.7. 2013) of the "parasitic, osmotic relationship between journalists and power, our ever-growing ability, our wish, to rely on these utterly bankrupt comments from various unnamed, anonymous intelligence sources." He then asked in what sounded like utter frustration, "Why are Americans tolerating these garbage stories with no real sourcing except for very dodgy characters indeed, who won't give their names?" Caring individuals everywhere need to ask themselves the same.

When media executives no longer permit in-depth discussion of crucial contemporary issues, falsehood freely flourishes. And in our time it has, in fact, done so profusely. As a result, unbeknownst to most citizens, propaganda rather than facts rules the airwaves and the printed pages.

Anyone daring to speak truth under such circumstances will be savagely attacked, labeled and silenced.

Granted, such individuals are presently not sent to Soviet-style gulags – except for those who are actually branded a "terrorist" – but they are put out of commission nonetheless. They cannot get tenure at universities, publishers turn them down, their opinions will not be printed in newspapers or magazines; they are, in essence, marginalized, ignored, and no longer "in the news". Thus, many who could make a difference are muzzled.

How could this possibly happen in our country? Newspaper mogul William Randolph Hearst gave at least part of the answer a number of years ago. "People," he observed rather cynically, "would rather be entertained than informed." Which, not surprising, makes the life of truth-tellers a rather difficult one. A similar and more recent observation comes from former war correspondent for the *New York Times*, Chris Hedges. "We prefer to amuse ourselves with trivia and gossip that pass for news rather than understanding," he lamented.

How different by comparison is the vision of another successful newspaper publisher, the renowned Joseph Pulitzer, who advocated the view that "a newspaper should have no friends." By that, he meant that a newspaper's only commitment should be to truth and its dissemination.

Pros and cons grow sharper

This concept leads us back to our topic at hand, campaigning for a preemptive attack on Iraq. While the moral compass of the United States had seemingly been buried in the rubble and debris of two fallen towers, not all was lost of democratic principles, especially in the US Senate.

When H.J. Res. 114, the resolution that authorized the Bush administration's war against Iraq came up for a vote, a group of Senators, in an act of true patriotism, voted against it.

These are the men and women of courage and honor: Senators Akaka, Bingaman, Boxer, Byrd, Chafee, Conrad, Corzine, Dayton, Durbin, Feingold, Graham, Inouye, Jeffords, Kennedy, Leahy, Levin, Mikulski, Murray, Reed, Sarbanes, Stabenow, Wellstone, Wyden. It was later reported that Sen. Graham, Democrat from Florida, who chaired the Senate Select Intelligence Committee, looked at privileged information about Iraq, and after reading it, changed his mind and voted against the decision to invade the country.

Robert Byrd named those voting against the war "The Immortal 23", while adding that his own vote was the most important he ever cast in 48 years in the Senate and more than 17,000 roll calls.

Meanwhile, some European countries, Germany and France in particular, continued to respect the cherished principles articulated by our own Founders in 1776, and gratefully adopted by the traumatized populations of Western Europe after 1945. They refused to travel the road of illegality.

Soon Donald Rumsfeld could be heard speaking disparagingly of those unwilling to support the administration's Iraq plans, calling them "Old Europe". This in contrast to the "New Europe", meaning the supposedly more contemporary countries willing to send their young soldiers to fight and die for stripping Saddam of nuclear weapons. (As an aside, this was also the time when some Congresspersons, in the throes of adolescent patriotic fever, went so far as to rename French fries "Freedom fries".)

Regrettably, not everyone in Europe was anti-invasion, most notably the government of British Prime Minister Tony Blair. His eagerness to march to war with his comrade George W. Bush became legendary.

Blair's book, *A Journey: My Political Life,* published in September of 2010, gives first-hand insight into the kind of administrations over which Blair and Bush presided. Particularly startling is the additional revelation that Dick Cheney had placed Damascus on his hit list, with the implicit agreement of both Bush and Blair. The latter wrote, "He [Cheney] would have worked through the whole lot, Iraq, Syria, Iran, dealing with all their surrogates in the course of it – Hezbollah, Hamas, etc. In other words, he thought the whole world had to be made anew, and that after September 11, it had to be done by force and with urgency."

Now, where had we heard echoes of such bellicose language before? Those interested in history should have had no problem locating the setting: the ultra-nationalist fervor of the 19th and 20th centuries, when colonial powers carved up countries to suit their imperial designs, and *my-country-right-or-wrong* made super-patriotic men march blindly to their graves. Indeed, largely because of ultra-nationalism, the world was thrown into the hell fires of war not once but twice in the span of 21 years! It seems to me, in an age when planet Earth is being reconfigured into a global village, the threat of "terrorism" from single individuals or small groups of radicals is minor compared to the haughty nationalism which employs carpet-bombings for the purpose of subduing entire countries.

Meanwhile, in France and Germany, where the governments boldly refused to be accomplices to an illegal military invasion, strong voices of disagreement could also be heard. As reported by long-time Israeli civil rights lawyer/activist Felicia Langer, for instance, the then president of the Central Council of Jews in Germany, Paul Spiegel, vehemently denounced the German opposition to the war as articulated by Chancellor Gerhard Schroeder and the Green Party.

And, of course, the same disapproval was relentlessly echoed by the US government and press, as the haughty voice of unilateralism became more shrill. The US would act alone, we were told, if the security of "our friends in the region" (read Israel) and our own were further compromised by that dark and dangerous figure residing with his WMDs in Baghdad!

Speaking of the crucial role of the press, two important items of more recent development should give us pause. One came to light with the unexpected death of Alexander Cockburn, longtime journalist, columnist and publisher. It is reported that in a 2007 interview with C-Span he expressed the view that liberal US media pundits who backed the invasion of Iraq should go to Baghdad to hear from the war's victims. "This country is gone ... millions of lives destroyed."

I fully support Cockburn's proposal, though I am not

sure any of those journalists would allow their hearts to be touched by the necessary remorse and compassion. Their cool and imperious intellects, it can be safely presumed, have long ago self-justified their words, be they written or spoken.

The second item is another example of the exceptional power certain media moguls have over politicians and their policies. No one epitomizes this more than Rupert Murdoch and the inordinate pressure he placed on the British Prime Minister, Tony Blair, over the Iraq war.

While in the US, the media followed the government's prompting, in the UK the opposite seemed to have occurred. In an exposé of June 15, 2012, titled "Blair aide: Murdoch pressed UK chief over Iraq war", the Associated Press reports on the diaries of Tony Blair's ex-communications director, Alastair Campbell, as excerpted by *The Guardian* newspaper. In them, Campbell reveals that media tycoon Rupert Murdoch warned the British leader over the dangers of delaying the 2003 US-led invasion as he made efforts to press the U.K. to support the conflict. In fact, Murdoch had pledged that *News International* – the division which runs his British newspapers – would support Britain if it backed the United States on the issue. Blair himself acknowledged during a media ethics inquiry that he and Murdoch had spoken by phone three times in the immediate run-up to the war, and that he had explained Britain's likely course of action. So much for the role of the Fourth Estate!

A quick and inexpensive "regime change"

Simultaneously, another reason for invading Iraq was being introduced. Overnight, "regime change" became part of the American vocabulary. Even if UN inspectors could find not a single trace of those lethal weapons, Saddam was such a horrible dictator that it became incumbent upon the US and "the coalition of the willing" (more accurately described as the coalition of the willful and the coerced) to liberate the people of Iraq from his iron grip. To that end, the vilification process was cranked into high gear. Saddam became another Hitler.

Though the Bush/Cheney administration sought by various means, including a high-profile act at the UN Security

Council by Secretary of State Colin Powell to seduce members of that exclusive club into legalizing its aggressive intentions, the overture was rebuffed. Representatives of France, Russia and China voiced courageous opposition.

Meanwhile, "experts" filled the airwaves, claiming that victory would be swift and the overthrow of Saddam Hussein inexpensive.

Dick Cheney opined that "It'll go... quickly. Weeks rather than months." This after a Pentagon official had already predicated the operation to be a "cakewalk".

As for the cost, no problem! Paul Wolfowitz, second in command at the Pentagon, estimated that the entire enterprise would not exceed one or two billion dollars, with revenues from Iraq's oil soon able to "finance its own reconstruction". The president himself assured the American public that "we would be greeted as liberators" and that the removal of Saddam would result in a democracy designed to be "a beacon for a new Middle East."

Media commentators also chimed in. Fox News' Bill O'Reilly was convinced that "military action will not last more than a week" – for which he was willing to wager "the best dinner in the gaslight district of San Diego." Fred Barnes of Fox News also voiced his opinion, saying that while war may be hard, it gets easier thereafter. "I mean, setting up a democracy is hard, but not as hard as winning a war," he explained. Topping them all was Bill Kristol, editor of the *Weekly Standard*, the supreme propagandist for the war.

People around the globe, alarmed by the lies and the spin, mobilized. Spirited worldwide protests included the largest anti-war rally ever held as three million marched through the streets of Rome in February 2003. In fact, it has been estimated that from January 3 through April 12, 2003, thirty-six million people around the globe took part in demonstrations against the invasion of Iraq! Humanity was waking up.

Thunder and lightning

For the people of Iraq, what may have been the waking up of millions came too late. On March 19, 2003, an attack took place that shook the conscience of the world – or should have. On that day, the oldest democracy in existence abandoned the principles of International Law, the UN Charter, multilateralism and the emerging global consciousness, and preemptively struck a sovereign nation – unprovoked and unjustified.

Soon, amid a hail of Tomahawk missiles and high explosive bombs, Baghdad, the ancient city by the banks of the Tigris, lay burning. Like colossal fireworks, the threatened "Shock and Awe" of the American war machine illumined the night skies while shattering buildings and lives in a brazen barrage of staggering firepower.

US militarists were displaying unrestrained aggression even as they tested their newest weapons on an essentially defenseless country and its sanctions-exhausted men, women and children. And each of the deadly weapons carried the label, "Made in the USA."

In the end, all the reasons so cleverly put before a reluctant international community and gullible American public proved to be, in Senator Robert Byrd's words, "a house of cards built of deceit." Iraq was being invaded by the full force of the most colossal military power in the history of the world.

Although many worked tirelessly to prevent this devastating attack, in the end it could not be stopped, prompting media critic, Norman Solomon, to conclude, "We are living today in a warfare state."

Obviously, the consciousness of the citizens of this country was not awakened enough to be able to see through the travesty and halt the administration's aggression. Consequently, as is the case with any form of blind acquiescence, once sucked into such a moral black hole, we must go through the entire cycle before arriving on the other side. What will we have learned once we get to that point?

"Your democracy is a sham"

The Nuremberg Tribunals established that preemptive war is a crime under international law. In fact, experts have called such a war "a supreme international crime". It is war unleashed when no immediate danger exists; it is a war of aggression. Nazi leaders were judged, condemned and executed by those standards. In 2003, the Bush administration committed such a crime against Iraq with impunity.

Along with many others, acclaimed Canadian author, Margaret Atwood, expressed disenchantment and alarm. In her *Letter to America* of April 2003, Atwood minced no words: "I think your recent Iraqi adventures have been an ill-advised tactical error," she wrote. "Let's talk, then, not about what you're doing to other people, but about what you're doing to yourselves…If you proceed much further down the slippery slope, people around the world will stop admiring the good things about you. They'll decide that your city upon the hill is a slum and your democracy is a sham."

The illegal and immoral act of invading Iraq not only rained death and destruction on a people, but placed the entire region in the gravest of perils. After all, the Middle East is not exactly a place for a militaristic cabal to wage war without running the risk of making the whole vicinity explode in flames, jeopardizing the peace of the world.

Witnessing what was unfolding, one could not help but ask: Can the terror acts of 9/11 even be compared with the war crimes committed against Afghanistan, Iraq and the Muslim world in general? Has not the war *on* terrorism turned into a war *of* terror, destroying, maiming and disrupting many thousand times more lives than the event of 9/11? Moreover, how could we have condemned the attacks on the Twin Towers of New York as terrorist acts, and yet insisted that the "shock and awe" bombardment of Baghdad was an act of liberation?

Speaking of war crimes, historian Howard Zinn said, "There was scarcely a photograph of a single dead Iraqi child, or a name of a particular Iraqi, or an image of suffering and grief to convey to the American people what our overwhelming military machine was doing to other human beings."

Instead, a Pentagon spokesperson, after the Iraqi army's "liquidation", chillingly admitted: "(We) count destroyed tanks, artillery pieces and missile launchers. (We) count captured weapons. (We) do not count people, civilian or military."

Upon hearing these words, every decent human being should have immediately paused and pondered: What's wrong with a picture in which the highest leadership in the Pentagon is focused only on the loss of military hardware and has not the slightest interest in knowing what those weapons are doing to human beings?

They may have been "the enemy", but beware a government that divides humankind into people that matter and those who don't. In the end, it may turn out that no life really has significance to such callous operators, but they perceive every person merely through the lens of opportunism – of who is useful and who expendable for their grand schemes.

The man in charge of life and death in Iraq was Secretary Donald Rumsfeld. His performances during news briefings were in a class by themselves; in fact, his war updates were dubbed "The Existential Poetry of D. H. Rumsfeld." Here is a sample: "We are not doing that well/ and of course, the reason is/ it's not an even playing field/ we are a democracy/ and they are a dictatorship/ so they control their ground/ and they manage the press/ and they lie repeatedly/ and we don't manage the press/ we don't lie –/no, we don't at all."

Resistance commences

With that kind of arrogant and self-deluded leadership, it should come as no surprise that even after the conquest of Iraq, there were continual headlines such as: "Iraqi resentment palpable to US, British troops"; "Analysts warn of open revolt from Iraqis"; "New attacks kill 3 US soldiers, wound dozens."

Thus the insurgency was inaugurated, the US having stirred a hornet's nest of resentment. While all this created hell for the Iraqi people, the revolt continued throughout the long years of occupation, led by the charismatic cleric, Muqtada al-Sadr with his intense anti-occupational stance and fierce Shi'a militia.

Commenting on the disastrous aftermath in the wake of the military's brutal assault and occupation of both Afghanistan and Iraq, *New York Times* columnist Paul Krugman offered this assessment: "The Bush people have a habit of conquest and malign neglect, a slash and burn approach to governing. The rest of the world has to live in the wreckage they leave behind."

To this, Steve Chapman, columnist for the *Chicago Tribune*, added his own touch of sarcasm, saying, "In the months leading up to the war in Iraq, the Bush administration gave the impression that bringing down Saddam Hussein would be like hitting a piñata ... Turns out it was Pandora's box."

Surveying the tragedy of the situation, Senate Majority Leader Harry Reid lamented in 2007, "It will take generations to undo the damage the war has done to Iraq, the region and the reputation of the United States."

In stark contrast to those critical remarks, it was sobering to read in the *Jerusalem Post* on January 9, 2008, of a short verbal exchange at the Ben-Gurion Airport Terminal. As President George W. Bush was about to depart, Chief Ashkenazi Rabbi Yona Metzger thanked the President for the US's military intervention in Iraq. "I want to thank you for your support of Israel and in particular for waging a war against Iraq," Metzger told Bush, according to the chief rabbi's spokesman. Bush reportedly answered that the chief rabbi's words "warmed his heart."

Imagine the heart of the President of the United States being "warmed" by the expression of gratitude from a religious leader in response to having brought carnage and chaos into the life of another people!

Meanwhile, those who want to understand more fully the true motivations behind the aggression against Iraq can find various experts on the subject. One such critic is Avi Shlaim, professor of international relations at St. Antony's College, Oxford, and author of *The Iron Wall: Israel and the Arab World*. He offers the following reflections.

"The premise behind American policy was that Iraq was the main issue in Middle East politics and that regime change in Baghdad would weaken the Palestinians and force them to accept a settlement on Israel's terms. The road to Jerusalem, it was argued, went through Baghdad. This premise was wrong. Iraq was a non-issue; it did not pose a threat to any of its neighbors, and certainly not to America or Britain. The real issue was Israel's occupation of the Palestinian territories and America's support for Israel in its savage colonial war against the Palestinian people ... The neoconservatives who drove American policy were interested in overthrowing Saddam Hussein and in nothing else."

This assessment was seconded by none other than Tom Friedman of the New York Times, who told an interviewer in 2005: "Iraq was the war the neoconservatives wanted, the war the neoconservatives marketed. I could give you names of twenty-five people [here in Washington], who, if you had exiled them to a desert island in 2001, the Iraq war would not have happened."

There you have it, not democracy but destabilization and regime change had been the goal from the start. Sept. 11 was the perfect pretext for bringing it about. And it continues to be pretext for all manner of governmental deception!

Calculated and unintended consequences

Whether it is Prof. Shlaim or other astute observers of the international political scene, the Israeli occupation is central to the question of war and peace in our world today, starting with the deep resentment and resistance of people in various Muslim countries. Many of them experience the suffering of the Palestinian people as a deep ache in their own hearts. Let us recall that justice is of paramount importance in Islam, and feeling solidarity with other Muslims is part of its all-inclusive communal spirit. To aid those who suffer oppression is, in fact, a sacred requirement of their faith.

As for the idea of democratizing the political landscape in the Arab world, it did not materialize with the arrival of US troops. Every new development merely proved that promises of "democracy" were empty words. The ensuing disappointment underlined for citizens of the region that representative governments will only be permitted if they are explicitly pro-US and pro-Israel.

This was confirmed especially by the surprise victory of Hamas in the Palestinian legislative election of 2006 and the subsequent and ongoing vicious attempt to destroy not only its effectiveness, but its very existence. At the same time, those Arab countries which Washington and the US media had been fond of calling "moderates" proved to be ruled by autocrats supported by ruthless security forces, as the events of 2011 known as the Arab Spring would demonstrate.

In the end, those who haughtily ruled Washington post 9/11 chose to fight not only one but two wars, all under the umbrella of a third: war on terrorism – continuous war. Yet, years after the first missiles struck, instead of winning, our people have been on the losing side – losing our constitutional rights, our humanity and our moral standing in the world.

As this is unfolding, we need furthermore to keep in mind that these wars are executed by a volunteer army supported by enormous contingents of highly-paid private contractors fighting far away on the soil of another people. Our citizens at home, meanwhile, are never exposed to the menacing sounds of heavy bombers or deafening artillery fire; never must endure the panicked screams of fleeing women and children, much less inhale the nauseating stench of death. War, in other words, is something that happens to other people.

One could easily imagine that under such conditions, combat abroad could go on forever.

In addition, during April 2007, as the number of dead and injured in Iraq soared, as the country was ripped apart and many of its intelligentsia were assassinated, as millions were made homeless, or escaped to other countries to stay alive, there came news from Wall Street that the Dow Jones average was climbing into the 13,000s – an all-time high. How disturbing that companies and individuals should be raking in huge profits because war is raging in distant countries, inflicting death and misery on innocent civilians!

Did we say: government of the people, by the people, for the people? Try: government of special interests, by special interests, for special interests! Lobbyists rule Congress and to a large degree governmental offices, from the American Israel Public Affairs Committee (AIPAC) to the makers of weapons, from the powerful moneymen of Wall Street to various mammoth business enterprises.

Addicted to oil for an entirely different reason

A brief observation about the much-vaunted hypothesis that the war against Iraq was motivated by a desire for oil. We all remember the sea of placards at every anti-war demonstration, proclaiming, NO BLOOD FOR OIL. As I pointed out in my book, *Envisioning a New World,* the idea is so groundless that one has to wonder how it ever took hold as a reason for a war that destroyed a culture, murdered hundreds of thousands of people, tainted the image of our country, and lasted nine devastating years.

As we have learned with regard to other unsubstantiated claims in general, if repeated often enough, especially by supposedly knowledgeable people, it will eventually be accepted as true. And once it has reached that point, woe unto those who seek to dislodge it! This, I regret to say, applies as much to people on the left as to those on the right.

Before analyzing the proposition of a war allegedly fought for oil, let us begin by looking at a basic misconception concerning US imports of oil from the Middle East. This particular fallacy seems to have served well those parties and pundits who benefit from keeping the focus on oil rather than on inconvenient facts and troublesome implications.

According to the U.S. Energy Information Administration, the US consumes 19.2 million barrels of petroleum products per day. Of that amount, a net 49% is produced domestically. The rest is imported. Only a small amount of this comes from the Middle East, and that quantity has been *declining*. For example, in 2011, imports from the Persian Gulf region made up 9.8% of total petroleum supplied to the US, down from 14.1% in 2001.

The final data shows that the United States is twice as dependent on petroleum from Canada and Mexico as it is on imports from the Middle East. If this is combined with the oil produced domestically, then the majority of petroleum consumed in the US comes from North America.

Now, while Iraq sits on the world's third-largest known oil reserves, its production has been far below its potential due to decades of war, UN sanctions and lack of foreign investment. None of that has changed much since the invasion in 2003, despite claims that this was a war for oil.

In addition, oil companies do not see conflict and the resulting instability as their preferred climate of operations. That's why none of them lobbied for war with Iraq. Of course, they were not disinclined to gain some of the usual spoils of war. But that booty never materialized, either. Instead, the price for a barrel of crude oil rose from $26 before the invasion to nearly $140 four years later, thanks to speculators and futures trading.

If there was, in the end, one beneficiary from those developments, it was the makers of small fuel-efficient foreign cars, which became quite popular, saving those who purchased them a goodly amount of money at the gas pump.

Today, Iraq, lying largely in ruins and experiencing continual turmoil, is no longer a threat to Israel or "our friends in the region", but it has certainly been a high-priced affair for our country – a *Three Trillion Dollar War,* according to a book by Nobel Prize winning economist, Joseph Stiglitz! Imagine the amount of oil we could have bought with that kind of money, especially from Saddam Hussein, who was eager to sell it, had it not been for those stifling sanctions. In addition, if this very bloody, very costly Iraq war was fought for oil, why is the United States government so doggedly determined to become oil self-sufficient – and is, in fact, succeeding?

Finally, the concept that the US invaded Iraq to establish control over its vast oil reserves was addressed by political journalist Alexander Cockburn in the August 30/September 6, 2010 issue of *The Nation*. He recalls that during auctions in December 2009 and August 2010, the most lucrative of the multi-billion-dollar contracts "that will shape the Iraqi oil industry for the next couple of decades" went to two countries which bitterly opposed the US invasion – Russia and China. US firms, it turned out, were the losers in the majority of bidding as the Iraqi Oil Ministry awarded licenses to a broad range of international companies, with scarcely an American firm included.

Cockburn concludes by saying, "Either the all-powerful US government was unable to fix the auctions to its liking or the all-powerful US-based oil companies mostly decided the profit margins weren't sufficiently tempting. Either way, the "war for oil" isn't in very good shape."

Perilous times

Among genuine patriots concerned about the disturbing trends of the Bush/Cheney administration was former Nebraska Senator Chuck Hagel, since March 2013 Secretary of Defense after a bruising, but not surprising, battle during Senate hearings. In a book published in 2008, he revealed that his standing as a Republican was called into question because of his opposition to what he regarded as "a reckless foreign policy ... divorced from a strategic context."

Hagel concluded in *America: Our Next Chapter* that the invasion of Iraq was "the triumph of the so-called neoconservative ideology, as well as the Bush administration's arrogance and incompetence."

I agree with his assessment though I would differ with the last part of his statement. Arrogance, yes, but incompetence is, in my view, not a correct characterization. From what I know and intuit about the forces that coerced the US to invade Iraq, there is not the slightest indication of either miscalculation or incompetence. Rather, everything that happened unfolded according to well-laid plans intent on creating chaos and bloodshed, division and despair. The shock and awe assault on Iraq and its people was, after all, not a humanitarian mission; in fact, it was as far to the other end of the spectrum as one dares to imagine.

What is missing in the life of a people when such appalling crimes can be committed in their name with barely a shrug of the shoulders, and absolutely no change in the preferred lifestyle, which must (of course) include a large dose of "having fun"? It pains me to say it, but it is a lack of spirituality, a lack of recognizing and operating from the realization of life's Oneness and the inherent worth and dignity of every person.

Today America is in peril, not because of terrorist threats, but because of the state of our inner being. Yes, we are outwardly powerful, a giant among the nations, but we are frail within. This is why we so easily succumbed to fear and manipulation, to the point of sacrificing what is most precious – our rights and liberties – in order to feel safe.

Invisible wounds

A decade after the first assaults, and an administration later, we are still stuck in Afghanistan, which no patriotic speech about "national security" or a surge in troops can whitewash of its insanity and waste. Think of it: A country devastated, a people subjugated, our own soldiers killed or maimed by the thousands, and more than one trillion dollars spent on the Afghan war alone! And for what? For wanting to destroy a small band of al-Qaeda fighters and a contingent of a few thousand Taliban in sandals and turbans with outdated or improvised weapons – a group of insurgents much like the one which drove the occupying Soviets from their country. With our help, no less!

Why is Congress still funding this? And why are so many of our citizens still compliant/complacent and silent about such irrational behavior? How can we be so devoid of empathy for the suffering we inflict, not least on our own young men and women?

Speaking of suffering, one of the tragic features of the war of 1914 was the damage done to the psyche of soldiers, known as "shell shock", the result of the unbearable horrors of trench warfare. In today's conflicts, instead of shell shock, soldiers return from combat with Post Traumatic Stress Disorder.

PTSD is an occupational hazard associated with subduing another country, and the sustaining of concussions and other forms of brain injury inflicted by resistance forces. This syndrome is marked by a wide range of physical and psychological symptoms, frequently leading to chronic handicaps such as depression, being unable to find or keep a job, and severe relational difficulties.

Recently, a new category was added to the list of invisible wounds (AP, February 23, 2013). It is known as "moral injury", so named because it tortures the conscience with an overwhelming sense of shame, guilt and rage. These emotions arise as a consequence of what a soldier has done or witnessed others do in combat, leading to an intense inner conflict vis-à-vis personal values. If such a psychic injury is not addressed, it can lead to serious mental health problems.

These are tragic figures indeed, and they are telling us what inhumane acts soldiers are asked to endure or commanded to engage in, acts which can lead to a breakdown of the person's psychological makeup. As a result, they sometimes take their own lives; more frequently, however, they are involved in domestic violence, to the point of occasionally torturing and killing members of their own families. Moreover, those who, in their despair, choose to die by their own hands, presently outnumber the ones who perish in combat.

Clearly, war is so dehumanizing and barbaric that it can no longer be seen even as an option by civilized humanity.

Perhaps this is what has prompted Afghan President Hamid Karzai more than once to question the motives of our government, especially in view of the continual killing of civilians by Special Forces, air strikes and drones. In 2011, for example, he likened US forces to occupiers, saying they were not in Afghanistan to help Afghans but were present "for their own purposes, for their own goals, and they are using our soil for that."

Now, what exactly did he mean by that? If we had a free investigative press, perhaps we would receive the eye-opening answers we deserve.

Three trillion dollars and an enemy later

Over the last twelve years, the American people have financed a military adventure that has led to the agonizing death of uncounted human beings and unimaginable suffering, including the killing and maiming of our own soldiers abroad. In counting the cost of war, we must not, however, overlook a separate $667 billion defense budget, the highest military expenditure in the world, and a sum nearly as large as the defense spending of all other countries combined. At the same time, the infrastructure of the "homeland" is badly in need of repair, the government in Washington is outrageously in debt, the social support systems of many states are in crisis, and Social Security and Medicare are being strained. The list of items in need of urgent attention is long indeed.

So who and what has dimmed our light, has made our country a place of such spiritual darkness that many inhabitants of this Earth resent, reject, and even curse us? Through Washington's warring ways and people's inability to change them, the hopes of those who have looked to us to be exemplars and defenders of human rights and dignity have been betrayed. This is not only their loss but ours as well. Whether as individuals or a nation, we simply cannot abandon others and their aspirations without doing harm to our own being.

In fact, the discord occurring in the political arena of our own country, the war of words, the battle of ideologues, is surely a sign of something disturbingly out of alignment. Seen through a spiritual lens, it may well be the price we are paying for our lack of empathy for the war victims created by us, and other unjustly treated, even vilified, people of this world.

Meanwhile, a number of years ago, another "dangerous" character entered the international scene and soon found himself in the crosshairs. By now, Mahmoud Ahmadinejad has fully replaced Saddam Hussein as the most vilified man on the planet. As Israel's enemy du jour, he has been depicted as the latest Hitleresque figure to threaten not only Israel and the US, but "the peace-loving citizens of the world".

Thus, like Iraq a decade ago, Iran presently stands accused of developing nuclear weapons, which is, of course, an unacceptable prospect to the so-called "international community". Heavy sanctions, reminiscent of Iraq, and some even more severe, are cemented in place and constantly "upgraded".

(As an aside, when Madeleine Albright was US Ambassador to the UN, she was questioned by Lesley Stahl on *60 Minutes*, May 12, 1996, about the effect of those US-led sanctions on Iraq: "We have heard that a half million children have died. I mean, that's more children than died in Hiroshima. And, you know, is the price worth it?" Albright responded matter-of-factly: "I think this is a very hard choice, but the price – we think the price is worth it.")

Today, with a cynical propaganda machine in high gear, and an always obliging media eager to generate the needed fear and fervor for an attack on Iran (while most recently also advocating for US military aid to the Syrian rebels), the present scenario strongly resembles the grand farce of 2002/03.

Will the American public once again fall for the bait, even after former press secretary Scott McClellan, in the wake of his departure, had characterized the shenanigans of the Bush White House as "a culture of deception"?

To their credit, some have recognized that we are dealing with not only stale but dangerous reruns. This was exemplified by the reaction of Mikhail Leontyev, a Russian TV commentator, as reported by the Associated Press on April 8, 2008. Brushing aside the unrestrained fear-mongering concerning Iran's alleged nuclear weapons program, he said, "There is no such thing as a threat from Iran; don't take us to be idiots. The political and military doctrine of the United States is complete domination ... of the entire world."

That there is indeed no Iranian threat was confirmed by Mohamed ElBaradei, for twelve years the director-general of the International Atomic Energy Agency (IAEA) and a Nobel Peace Prize laureate. Now retired, he declared, "I don't believe Iran is a clear and present danger. All I see is the hype about the threat posed by Iran." (*Democracy Now!* June 3, 2011)

But to return to Mikhail Leontyev's blunt response. His accusation that our government desires world domination should give us pause. We ought to ask ourselves: Is this really what we, the people of the United States, desire, complete domination of the world? Is this *really* who we are? If not, then we must insist that our government do away with the most obvious sign of it by beginning to close down some of the 700-plus military bases we have erected all over the globe.

Nick Turse, managing editor of TomDispatch.com and a fellow at the Nation Institute, gives a vivid account of the US military profile abroad. Speaking of a reach that is global, he writes, "Its soldiers, commandos, trainers, base builders, drone jockeys, spies, and arms dealers, as well as associated hired guns and corporate contractors, can now be found just about everywhere on the planet. The sun never sets on American troops conducting operations, training allies, arming surrogates, schooling its own personnel, purchasing new weapons and equipment, developing fresh doctrine, implementing novel tactics, and refining their martial arts."

This, then, is the picture. The US has soldiers on the ground in every strategically placed country, employs submarines and aircraft carriers across the seas, has drones and manned airplanes patrolling the skies, and spy satellites circling the planet, keeping an eye on friend and foe alike.

Clearly, all this is so thorough and immense, it literally shouts: "We are the rulers of the world!"

Again, if that is not reflective of who we are, or what we truly desire, then we the people must demand major changes, because, as Nelson Mandela discovered through direct experience, "The authorities do not undergo changes of heart because they have suddenly become kindly men. Every concession they have made is under pressure of one sort or another." America ought to listen and take heed.

NeoCons and NeoLibs

I have more than once spoken about the stranglehold on the American system of governance by the neoconservatives, known as NeoCons. It is not fair, however, to hold them alone responsible for the quagmire into which our country has sunk. Contributing equally, though in a more subtle way, are the neoliberals, or NeoLibs. NeoLibs are not the same people as NeoCons, but their marching orders originate from the same source. That's why even when the American people elected a Democratic majority to both houses of Congress in 2006, Representatives did nothing to end the government's anti-democratic measures such as warrantless wiretapping and other such invasions of privacy.

These developments serve as a disturbing reminder that the so-called war on terror was simultaneously an attack on the civil rights of American citizens. And while there was some criticism in Congress of the administration's behavior, in the end, it remained only words sans action; that is to say, it amounted to nothing more than posturing. Is it any wonder, then, that one observer despairingly concluded that when it comes to politics in America, hypocrisy is a prerequisite for both running and staying in office? And that regardless of political affiliation!

This is how, during eight years of the Bush/Cheney administration, Republicans were reduced to counterfeit conservatives, and Democrats to bogus liberals. I know of no other such pathology in recent history except in cases where a country is under foreign occupation and a puppet government is doing the bidding of the conqueror.

Yet, despite a severe psychological concussion called 9/11, which made the American people stupendously compliant, even subservient, it is encouraging to note that surveys today indicate a high percentage of citizens are dissatisfied with the direction the country has embarked upon. This indicates that a substantial portion of the populace is regaining consciousness and raising some serious questions.

Let none assume, however, that answers will be easily forthcoming. The forces aligned against change in Washington are formidable. This is why, despite stirring campaign promises in 2008, the president has been unable to truly deliver. And since he is prevented from fulfilling his destiny, America too is unable to rediscover and recommit to its true purpose.

Additionally, because few citizens suspect that there are cunning behind-the-scenes operators, the majority of Americans assume that Mr. Obama is to blame for reneging on his promises. This is not only a clever way to undermine a country's trust in its highest elected leader, but it also results in citizens becoming ever more apathetic and cynical about politics and politicians. The most dangerous aspect to such a development, however, is the fact that disenchanted masses are easily manipulated.

Asking questions

On Oct. 7, 2010, the war in Afghanistan entered its 10th year. In an article, Deb Riechmann of the Associated Press made a surprising disclosure. "Looking back at the first years of the war," she writes, "the effort was underfunded from the start. When the Bush administration's attention shifted to Iraq in 2003, the Taliban began to regroup."

What happened here? Why was there no greater effort made to win the war against what had been claimed to be the group granting safe haven to Osama bin Laden, the alleged mastermind of 9/11? What game did Washington play with Afghan and American lives alike? And what are we still doing in Afghanistan all these years after the start of the assault, now using drones routinely even in Pakistan to shamelessly snuff out the lives of those who resist occupation? Clearly, our war enterprise goes beyond what were once presented as "legitimate" reasons, drawing not only our country, but all the members of NATO, into continual combat now for 11 years.

To help us understand the folly committed by an imperial presidency and a militaristic mindset, here is a response which permits a glimpse into a far more evolved, diametrically opposed, consciousness. It occurred at the end of a talk by the Dalai Lama when someone asked, "Why didn't you fight back against the Chinese?" After a pause, the revered teacher said with a gentle smile, "Well, war is obsolete, you know."

Then, after a few moments, his face grave, he said, "Of course the mind can rationalize fighting back...but the heart, the heart would never understand. Then you would be divided in yourself, the heart and the mind, and the war would be inside you."

Based on the present erratic pulse of our country, its polarized politics and the irate behavior of noisy groups of ultra-conservative Americans, it seems safe to say that today the war is indeed inside of us. And it is tearing us apart.

Harry Patch, the last surviving WWI soldier, who died at the age of 111 in 2009, said it from firsthand experience and thus said it best: "War isn't worth one life."

A visionary American statesman, former US Secretary of State Charles Evans Hughes, would certainly have agreed, considering his radical proposal during a speech in 1923: "War should be made a crime, and those who instigate it should be punished as criminals."

Eighty-seven years later, on June 12, 2010, in Kampala, Uganda, history was made when the International Criminal Court established waging aggressive wars as a prosecutable crime. The resolution declared the use of force, including invasions, bombardments and blockades against another country, to be a violation of the Charter of the United Nations. It empowers the Court to try future political and military leaders who plan, prepare, initiate or execute illegal wars, and to hold them criminally responsible. (The highly significant event receives greater in-depth treatment in my book, *Ultimate Choices: Armageddon or Awakening*.)

Donald Rumsfeld and his obedient warriors unleashed their "Shock and Awe" campaign on the defenseless people of Iraq. Shock was, undoubtedly, the reaction to America's ferocious military offensive. And shock also entered the lives of American soldiers and people here at home, as war dragged on and death tolls mounted, while revelations of moral depravity stunned the country with photographs of torture and brutalities. This included, last but not least, the appalling conditions and disgraceful treatment of injured soldiers in hospitals for veterans.

It is doubtful that the defenseless people of Iraq were "awed" by the brutality visited upon them. One could, however, foresee a time when the world and especially the United States will be amazed by the final results of this pitiless war: the self-emancipation of Iraqis, not through NeoCon style "democracy" but by shaking off the yoke through which outside forces sought to single-mindedly subdue and control them.

Imagine what a twist of fate it would be: a group of ideologues acting as though entitled to rule the world by decree and military force rushes to crush a third-world country – and turns the vanquished into winners and the victors into losers. Surely, there is nothing minor about this war and its seemingly endless aftermath. Instead, it is a seminal event setting the stage for the fate of our country and the Islamic world for generations to come.

In the meantime, let us contemplate a powerful call to vigilance and participatory democracy issued by The Reverend

William Ellery Channing, grandson of William Ellery, one of the signers of the Declaration of Independence. Channing was the principal Unitarian theologian of the United States during the early 19th century, and a man known for sounding a cautionary note concerning the relationship between government and governed vis-à-vis the issue of war.

He passionately writes, "We should teach our present and all future rulers that there is no measure for which they must render so solemn an account to their constituents as for a declaration of war; that no measure will be so freely, so fully discussed; and that no administration can succeed in persuading this people to exhaust their treasure and blood in supporting war, unless it be palpably necessary and just. In war, then, as in peace, assert the freedom of speech and of the press. Cling to this as the bulwark of all your rights and privileges."

Having totally ignored the voice of wisdom, we let war drag on even as sabers are rattling for yet another confrontation in the Middle East. Suddenly, there hangs over our world an ominous cloud, with menacing lightning and rumbling thunder disturbing the peace. Humanity stands at a fateful crossroads, and close to an abyss. May those who care see in Albert Einstein's famous words a call to action, considering the immense peril surrounding us: "I do not know what weapons World War III will be fought with, but World War IV will be fought with sticks and stones."

Chapter 4

BECOMING THE EVIL
WE DEPLORE

Power that is not constrained by humanity is not constrained at all.

~Leonard J. Pitts, Jr.

Forgiving no enemy, forgiven by none, we live the death of liberty, become what we have feared to be.

~Wendell Berry

One finds evidence of the powerfully tunneling impact on clarity of moral vision when a people become convinced that an act of monstrously evil proportion is in defense of their interest.

~John Thomas Didymus

In the same manner an alcoholic cannot dominate a bottle of booze by will power, a power-drunk nation cannot subdue its terror by practicing torture.

~Phil Rockstroh

On October 13, 2010, I watched spellbound on live stream the gripping drama and astonishing rescue of the last six Chilean miners trapped for 69 days deep beneath the Earth. Cameras were set up to give viewers around the globe a glimpse of both the people and activities below and above the ground. I responded to each emerging individual with shouts of joy.

The daring operation turned into a record-setting triumph of faith, hope, endurance and love on the part of many: the persevering miners, the team that worked to save them, the families that held vigil as they waited in an improvised camp near the collapsed mine, and the people of Chile, who stood heart and soul behind those below and those above the ground. Last but not least, moral support came from concerned citizens around the globe, as they anxiously participated in the process via the media's extensive coverage. And all the focus was on one goal: to save lives, to give life back to those who had been lost, and traumatized.

Thus, a small country in South America, with the help of several international equipment suppliers, managed what had not been done before: to rescue 33 miners, one by one, entombed for over two months in the bowels of the Earth at 2,200 feet.

It was, by any measure, a victory for a great team and a tribute to all of humanity, underlining what can be accomplished when intelligence, resourcefulness and compassion are combined to serve life and the living. And it showed the strength of the human spirit, anchored in faith, to weather the most trying of circumstances and emerge triumphant, though surely forever changed.

While it was riveting to follow the skillful execution of the rescue procedure, it will undoubtedly be equally engrossing to learn of the ways the miners' lives will unfold from this time forth. In the meantime, we all received what is becoming an ever more rare gift: a reason to celebrate being a member of the human race.

Black sites – a journey into darkness

I chose to open this chapter with a narrative that for an extended period held millions around the planet in its electrifying grip, a story that would allow us to feel fully what human beings are capable of when rightly motivated, before contrasting it to what occurs when they are taught to hate, to demonize, to dehumanize – when the journey is not into the depth of the Earth to save a human being, but when it ends in the Heart of Darkness to destroy one, or ten or ten thousand.

The latter capability was painstakingly compiled in a report, "Secret detentions and illegal transfers of detainees involving Council of Europe member states", by the Swiss lawyer Dick Marty. It was issued after he interviewed scores of intelligence officers, prisoners, attorneys and guards in connection with what is perhaps the darkest chapter in the history of the

United States: the treatment of detainees in the wake of 9/11 in so-called "black site" prisons. Subjected to "extraordinary rendition", that is, being kidnapped and illegally incarcerated, they were held with no charges filed. He estimated that the CIA has kidnapped about a hundred persons on European territory alone and subsequently outsourced them to various countries for torture.

In an editorial, "US Justice, Euro Prisons", *The Nation* of July 2, 2007, stated that in exchange for increased influence in NATO, Washington persuaded "the highest state authorities in Poland and Romania" to turn over detention facilities to US operatives who established what can only be described as torture shops. Prisoners were kept naked for weeks, chained to walls and often condemned to "solitary confinement and extreme sensory deprivation in cramped cells, shackled and handcuffed at all times, sometimes at temperature extremes so hot one would gasp for breath, sometimes freezing cold." The report confirms the CIA's reliance on "enhanced interrogation techniques" such as waterboarding, sleep deprivation and other tactics condemned as torture by human rights organizations as well as the United Nations.

The editorial concluded by saying: "In 2005, when the *Washington Post* caught the scent of CIA secret flights and 'black site' prisons for terrorism suspects in Eastern Europe, the Bush Administration managed to intimidate the paper into keeping the names of the host countries out of its stories. Now, thanks to a report from the Council of Europe, we know why: not national security but sordid criminality."

Here was Dick Cheney's infamous remark, "We will have to go to the dark side." Here was displayed the true nature of the cabal that became the supreme rulers of Washington on 9/11. This is as low as human beings can fall while rising as high as possible on the ladder of worldly power. This is, indeed, the most abysmal chapter in the history of our country – a total dismissal of the Constitution, our democratic values and moral principles.

Yet, black site prisons were only a small part of the atrocities committed with impunity by those who exercised extraordinary arrogance of power and savage abuse during the reign of George W. Bush and his scheming NeoCons.

Subsequently, as one might expect, such deeds raised alarm around the globe as to who we had become as a country and people. Wrote James Rubin, professor at Columbia University School of International and Public Affairs, in the July/August 2008 issue of *Foreign Affairs*: "The average European has come to doubt whether the United States is a responsible member of the international community."

The United Nations Convention Against Torture, Article 1, describes torture as: "Any act by which severe pain or suffering, whether physical or mental, is intentionally inflicted on a person for such purposes as obtaining from him … information or a confession, punishing him for an act he … has committed or is suspected of having committed, or intimidating or coercing him."

Today America is still the most powerful nation on Earth, the strongest in every way, except morally. This is because, among those who call themselves a democracy, our nation ranks lowest along with Israel due to our willingness to inflict cruelty and suffering on other human beings for entirely self-serving purposes, also known as "national security". And both countries do so in the face of international criticism – and obviously in violation of international law and that which human beings consider decent, and yes, civilized.

A cache of defilement and shame

One of the most unexpected and stunning developments of 2010 was the release by WikiLeaks of a huge cache of official reports and cables recording the day-by-day operations of the wars in Afghanistan and Iraq, as well as cables from the diplomatic corps to the State Department in Washington.

All of these have made clear that there have been ongoing fraud and corruption, a massive cover-up of civilian deaths, falsified reports by military personnel and deception by political leaders regarding the US-led wars, not to mention the hypocrisy and conniving of Arab leaders. (To be discussed specifically in Chapter 6, "Wiki and Other Leaks.")

Meanwhile, here are but a few of the grim revelations, dealing with crimes by both US forces and the Iraqis themselves, and undoubtedly with consent of the US military:

- The story of a prisoner who said he was hog tied and beaten with a shovel as part of a days-long torture ordeal at the hands of the Iraqi army.
- An Iraqi detainee being covered in bruises and a scar from being bludgeoned with a pickax.
- The use of electric drills, of acid, of inflicting various mutilations.
- Detainees being scalded by boiling water, having their fingernails pulled out, the soles of their feet smashed with electrical cables and their genitalia subjected to electric shocks.
- US interrogators clearing detainees for questioning, despite signs that they had suffered abuse from Iraqi security forces (considered a violation of the Geneva Conventions).

Five years earlier, *The New York Times* (Jan.12, 2005) reported about similar events having taken place at Abu Ghraib prison. Quoting testimony by former abused detainees, the paper described various forms of torture, among them:

- Urinating on detainees
- The blaring of uninterrupted, full-volume music
- Sleep deprivation
- Jumping on a detainee's wounded leg with such force that it could not thereafter heal properly
- Continuously pounding a detainee's wounded leg with a metal baton
- Pouring phosphoric acid on detainees
- Sodomizing detainees with a baton
- Tying ropes to the detainees' legs or penises and dragging them across the floor

Former Brig. Gen. Janis Karpinski, in charge of the military police unit at Abu Ghraib and other prisons when the abuses were committed, was accused of negligence, relieved of her duties and discharged. On July 3, 2004, however, she told BBC Radio 4's Today program, that she had been made a "convenient scapegoat" for abuse "ordered by others".

One of the elements of her interview was a story that sheds light on the peculiar torture methods used by US soldiers. She relates that during a visit to an intelligence center with a senior coalition general, she met a man who claimed to be an Israeli. "I saw an individual there that I hadn't had the opportunity to meet before, and I asked him what did he do there, was he an interpreter – he was clearly from the Middle East," she emphasized in the interview. "He said, 'Well, I do some of the interrogation here. I speak Arabic but I'm not an Arab; I'm from Israel.'"

Reports that Israeli torture experts participated in the abuse of the detainees under the control of the American military at Abu Ghraib should come as no surprise. The sadistic ways of inflicting pain were too similar not to be related. In fact, what Janis Karpinski revealed on the BBC, she also disclosed on *Democracy Now!* with Amy Goodman following the pictorial revelations of midnight torture at the infamous prison. She cited the time she met a couple of men in blue jeans. When asked who they were, they replied, "Israelis".

As far back as June 1977, Ralph Schoenman, executive director of the Bertrand Russell Foundation, wrote in *The Sunday Times of London*: "Israeli interrogators routinely ill-treat and torture Arab prisoners. Prisoners are blindfolded or have a stifling, foul-smelling sack placed over their heads, hung by their wrists for long periods and subjected to loud music. Most are struck in the genitals or in other ways sexually abused. Most are sexually assaulted. Others are administered electric shock." (Incidentally, the significance of this special report lies in the fact that up to that point there had been scant mention of Israel's torture practices. By publishing the information, the *Sunday Times* broke a taboo, one which, incidentally, also put the human rights community to shame, because with few exceptions such torture was not so much unknown as simply ignored.)

Later, *The Washington Post* made identical accusations

about Palestinian detainees tortured in Israeli prisons. "Upon arrest, a detainee undergoes a period of starvation, deprivation of sleep by organized methods and prolonged periods during which the prisoner is made to stand with his hands cuffed and raised, a filthy sack covering the head. Prisoners are dragged on the ground, beaten with objects, kicked, stripped and placed under ice-cold showers."

The New York Times of January 24, 1999, reported that none other than a government lawyer, Shai Nitzan, confirmed these reports when he deliberated before the Israeli Supreme Court on the methods used by the Shin Bet security forces while interrogating Palestinian prisoners. *The Times* called the testimony "extraordinary" since it dealt, after all, with methods considered as torture by the United Nations, Amnesty International and other human rights organizations. Nitzan testified that typically, suspects are held for many hours between interrogations on miniature chairs that tilt forward. And during questioning, some are grabbed by the collar and violently shaken, causing their heads to whip back and forth.

Amnesty International, having conducted its own investigation, concluded "there is no country in the world in which the use of official and sustained torture is as well established and documented as in the case of Israel." Those methods were supposed to have been outlawed by the Supreme Court in 1999, but the release of Palestinian prisoners in 2011 in exchange for the captured Israeli soldier, Gilad Shalit, brought to light many stories of continued abuse.

Losing one's humanity

While the US may have received instructions from Israeli torture teams on how most effectively to break the spirit of "the Arabs", stories have emerged about how these methods were executed as detainee and torturer alike descended into an abyss of malevolence.

To get a feeling for the terrifying fate of some of those hapless victims, here are a number of them.

In the infamous torture chambers of Abu Ghraib, Hashem Muhsen, one of the naked men in the scandalous human pyramid photo, said he and others were made to crawl around the floor naked and that US soldiers rode them like donkeys. One prisoner, Manadel al-Jamadi, died as a consequence of such abuses, a death the military ruled a homicide.

There are several direct quotes from a prisoner who was fortunate to be released from his chamber of torment. Ameen Saeed Al-Sheik, detainee No.151362 reported: "They said 'we will make you wish to die and it will not happen' … They stripped me naked. One of them told me he would rape me. He drew a picture of a woman to my back and made me stand in a shameful position holding my buttocks."

At another time, they asked him, "Do you pray to Allah?" I said yes. They said, '[expletive] you. And [expletive] him.' One of them said, 'You are not getting out of here healthy, you are getting out of here handicapped. And he said to me, 'Are you married?' I said, 'Yes.' They said, 'If your wife saw you like this, she will be disappointed.' One of them said, 'But if I saw her now she would not be disappointed now because I would rape her.'" … "They ordered me to thank Jesus that I'm alive." … "I said to him, 'I believe in Allah.' So he said, 'But I believe in torture and I will torture you.'"

In a video diary, one female prison guard said that prisoners were shot for minor misbehavior, while venomous snakes were used to bite prisoners, acts that sometimes resulted in their deaths. By her own admission, she was "in trouble" for having thrown rocks at the detainees.

At the same time, in the documentary film *Ghosts of Abu Ghraib* (2007), former US Justice Department counsel John Yoo can be heard claiming that although he does not think the Geneva Conventions covered the prisoners at Abu Ghraib, he believes the soldiers and their commanding officers felt the interrogation techniques used were within the parameters of the Conventions. Today this same official, never having been held accountable, retains a teaching position in law at the University of California in Berkeley. This is how our country lost its moral moorings.

That loss must surely include the cynical and tactically cunning appointment of female officers in charge of the worst kind of abuse in prison facilities in Afghanistan and Iraq by the Rumsfelds and Wolfowitzes of the Pentagon.

Besides Janis Karpinski in charge of the detainee facilities in Baghdad, there was Captain Carolyn Wood, responsible for the notorious Bagram prison in Afghanistan. In August 2002, nine interrogation techniques not included in Army field manuals were added after the detention unit in Bagram was turned over to the 519th Military Intelligence Battalion of which Wood was the commanding officer.

Reports indicate that in December 2002 two inmates were tortured and beaten to death in cells down the hall from her office. They were hung by their arms from the ceiling and beaten so severely that, according to a report by Army investigators later leaked to the *Baltimore Sun*, their legs would have needed to be amputated had they lived. The Army's Criminal Investigation command launched an inquiry, but few people outside Afghanistan took notice.

A former Bagram interrogator told a *Knight Ridder* journalist that at the time of the two deaths, screams and moans would easily have been heard from interrogation rooms, and that there can be little doubt that Wood was aware of the abuse, as the interrogation rooms were near her office.

Reports show furthermore that starting in December 2002, interrogators were removing clothing, isolating people for long periods of time, using stress positions, exploiting fear of dogs and implementing sleep and light deprivation.

As for Abu Ghraib, Major General Antonio Taguba, who authored the investigative report of abuses in the prison in 2004, has stated that there is photographic evidence of rape being carried out by American military personnel. Among the evidence cited is an Iraqi teenage boy being raped by a uniformed man while photos of it were taken by a female US military police. Another photo shows an American soldier apparently raping a female prisoner. Other photos show sexual assaults on prisoners with objects including a truncheon, wire and a phosphorescent tube. In Major General Antonio Taguba's own words, "These pictures show torture, abuse, rape and every indecency."

The cavalier way in which the Pentagon sought to dismiss the devastating revelations of the Taguba report was demonstrated during an interview on *Face the Nation*, May 2, 2004, when the Chairman of the Joint Chiefs of Staff, General Myers, claimed that he had not yet seen the report, although its publication was then nearly a month old.

Four years after he issued his findings, General Taguba accused the Bush administration of war crimes in a preface to a report by Physicians for Human Rights on detainee abuse and torture in American military prisons in Abu Ghraib, Guantanamo and Bagram. He wrote: "There is no longer any doubt that the [Bush] administration committed war crimes. The only question is whether those who ordered torture will be held to account."

The tragedy is that so far no one has. And all indications are that the Obama administration is either morally unwilling or politically unable to issue charges.

As to the fate of General Taguba, he knew that the report would make him unpopular with his superiors, and said so: "If I lie, I lose. And if I tell the truth, I lose."

Such a fatalistic statement requires a brief reply. From a spiritual perspective, telling the truth can never make anyone a loser, no matter the consequences. Nonetheless, considering the ways of our world, for an honest general, speaking truth did result in a loss: He was instructed to retire the following January (2007). Taguba believes that his forced retirement was ordered by civilian Pentagon officials in retaliation for his report on prisoner abuse. He thus became yet one more victim of a power-intoxicated clique without conscience.

It's been a long time since Patrick Henry insisted that the rack and screw have no place in the New World. Half of the American public today still resonates with that core belief of human decency. However, according to a Pew Research Center survey in 2009, the other half, 49 percent, still believes – despite detailed reports, complete with shocking photographs – that waterboarding, shackling people to walls or floors while defecating on them, or otherwise brutalizing them can be justified. The number was still higher in the case of religious affilia-

tion, peaking in fundamentalist circles where the struggle between good and evil is seen in cosmic terms.

A haunting legacy: becoming the evil we deplore

The concept of the United States as a force for good
was thoroughly shattered by its attack on and occupation of
Iraq, although after Dresden, Hiroshima and Vietnam, and
other such terrors, our citizens should have recognized long
ago that the idea was pure myth. Native Americans, in fact,
have for generations been disabused of that notion.

Meanwhile, post 9/11, in a shadow government somewhere underground in the environs of Washington, ideologues
single-mindedly worked to implement an agenda alien to basic
American values – a throwback to a consciousness that had the
feel and smell of things totalitarian, that was obsessed with the
idea of enemy and the accompanying dehumanization and brutal treatment of those it had named a threat. No "quaint" Geneva Conventions applied, no Bill of Rights, no half century of
work and progress on human rights.

This is why during the Bush/Cheney/NeoCon administration we became the evil we deplored. Or perhaps more accurately, we became the evil we had projected onto others –
and then had to abhor and fight because evil is too potent a reality to ignore.

This is how rulers declare war on that which has been
declared "evil", not knowing that in reality they are fighting
their own and their country's shadow. Think of the "War on
Terrorism", "the fight against terrorists" and see what it is doing to us. Look to the war in Afghanistan, the war in Iraq; look
to Guantanamo, Abu Ghraib, Bagram. It's *our* shadow, not that
of the abused, and it will continue to destroy our moral fiber
unless we recognize it as such and do the spiritual work which
alone can stop further self-injury.

We can begin the painful journey into greater self-
knowing by returning for a closer look to the notorious places
of inhuman and degrading treatment already mentioned above
– places of staggering torment and suffering.

Bagram, Afghanistan

The official Bagram Theatre Internment Facility lies in a sprawling US military complex, about 25 miles northeast of Kabul, as part of Bagram Air Base. The military detention center was built by the Soviets and used as an aircraft machine shop during the Soviet invasion and occupation of Afghanistan, 1980–1989. A concrete and sheet metal facility, it was retrofitted with wire pens and wooden isolation cells. The prison holds "enemy combatants" captured in the so-called war on terror. The inmates have never been charged with a crime, yet they allege abuse at the hands of their captors, ranging from sleep deprivation to brutal beatings.

Andrew Wander, who is a media fellow for Reprieve, a legal charity based in London, which represents more than 30 prisoners in Guantanamo Bay and investigates US secret prisons worldwide, reports on Bagram prison in an article of August 22, 2009, titled, "Guantanamo's 'more evil twin'?"

Wander points out that Bagram prison had been operating entirely in the shadows until the first announcement of detentions was made in January 2002, coinciding with the US renditions program. After that, the site became a key location in a global network of prisons. In fact, it was often used as a holding site for detainees on their way to Guantanamo Bay. However, the number of individuals incarcerated remains an official secret, but it is assumed to be almost three times as many as were kept in Guantanamo at the time of the article's publication. Journalists are not allowed to visit and lawyers are banned from the premises.

Wander quotes a former inmate, Omar Deghayes, who described being held in Bagram in 2002 before he was transferred to Cuba as "terrifying."

"Lying on the floor of the compound, all night I would hear the screams of others in the rooms above us as they were tortured and interrogated," he says. "My number would be called out, and I would have to go to the gate. They chained me and put a bag over my head, dragging me off for my own turn. They would force me to my knees for questioning, and threaten me with more torture."

The New York Times appears to have given credence to those testimonies in its reports that prisoners held at Bagram were made to stand for up to 13 days with their hands chained to the ceiling, naked, hooded and unable to sleep. *The Washington Post* too claims that prisoners at the same airbase were "commonly blindfolded and thrown into walls, bound in painful positions, subjected to loud noises and deprived of sleep" while kept "in black hoods or spray-painted goggles."

Based on numerous first-hand accounts of excessive maltreatment, human rights campaigners soon referred to Bagram as "Guantanamo's more evil twin".

"There are serious concerns that Bagram is another Guantanamo – except with many more prisoners, less due process, no access to lawyers or courts and reportedly worse conditions," says Melissa Goodman, staff attorney with the ACLU National Security Project.

With access and identification of the prisoners denied, lawyers cannot obtain the necessary authorizations to begin proceedings on behalf of the abused.

Wander reports that in response to the uncovered mistreatments, Reprieve announced it was suing the UK government in an effort to obtain the identities of two Bagram prisoners that British forces captured in Iraq in 2004 and handed to the US military. The two were transferred to Afghanistan and have been held in Bagram ever since. After years of denying involvement, the British government finally admitted its role in their capture earlier this year and apologized. However, in an act of hypocrisy and callousness, the government, citing the men's "privacy rights", refused to release their names! Of course, without having their identification disclosed, lawyers cannot act for the detained men.

In the US, meanwhile, the ACLU has filed requests under the Freedom of Information Act in a bid to obtain details about the inmates. So far all queries have been refused.

Shortly after the information was disseminated by Andrew Wander on behalf of Reprieve, *The New York Times* published a column on November 29, 2009, by Alissa J. Rubin, titled, "Afghans Detail Detention in 'Black Jail' at U.S. Base."

Rubin describes the site, known to the prisoners as the "black jail", as consisting of individual windowless concrete cells, each illuminated by a single light bulb burning 24 hours a day. In interviews, former inmates said that their only human contact was at twice-daily interrogation sessions.

The black jail is separated from the larger Bagram detention center, which, according to the article, holds about 700 detainees, kept mostly in cages of about 20 men apiece.

"The black jail was the most dangerous and fearful place," said Hamidullah, a spare-parts dealer in Kandahar who said he was detained there in June. "They don't let the ICRC [International Committee for the Red Cross] officials or any other civilians see or communicate with the people they keep there," he added.

Other former detainees interviewed by Rubin complained of being held for months after the intensive interrogations were over without being told why. One detainee said he remained at the Bagram prison complex for two years and four months; another was held for 10 months.

Rubin points out the detainees said the hardest part of their detention was that their families did not know whether they were alive. "For my whole family it was disastrous," said Hayatullah, a Kandahar resident who said he was working in his pharmacy when he was arrested. "Because they knew the Americans were sometimes killing people, and they thought they had killed me because for two to three months they didn't know where I was."

Ten months after his initial detention, American soldiers came to the group cell where he was then being held and told him he had been mistakenly picked up under the wrong name. "They said, 'Please accept our apology, and we are sorry that we kept you here for this time.' And that was it. They kept me for more than 10 months and gave me nothing back."

All of the former detainees spoke of being hooded and handcuffed when they were taken for questioning at the black jail, so they did not know where they were or anything about other detainees.

The article underscored that the secrecy continued even

after a new administration was installed in Washington, eliciting a strong response from Jonathan Horowitz, a human rights researcher with the Open Society Institute. "Holding people in what appears to be incommunicado detention runs against the grain of the administration's commitment to greater transparency, accountability, and respect for the dignity of Afghans."

Scandalous deaths

In January 2010, the American military released the names of 645 detainees held at the main detention center at Bagram, reversing its long-held position against making such information public. This list was made available under a Freedom of Information Act lawsuit filed in September 2009 by the ACLU, whose lawyers had also demanded detailed information about conditions, rules and regulations.

The names of those 645 detainees may not mean much to the average citizen. Yet, becoming informed about the fate of some, and especially those who died a miserable death in that dark place of lawlessness and loneliness, might stir America's conscience and compassion.

Habibullah

Habibullah expired on December 4, 2002. Several US soldiers hit the chained man with so-called "peroneal strikes", or severe blows to the side of the leg above the knee. This debilitates the leg by hitting the common peroneal nerve. According to *The New York Times*, by Dec. 3, Mr. Habibullah's reputation for "defiance" had made him the target of at least nine peroneal strikes from two MPs.

"When Sgt. James P. Boland saw Mr. Habibullah on Dec. 3, he was in one of the isolation cells, tethered to the ceiling by two sets of handcuffs and a chain around his waist. His body was slumped forward, held up by the chains. Sergeant Boland ... had entered the cell with [Specialists Anthony M. Morden and Brian E. Cammack] ... kneeing the prisoner sharply in the thigh, "maybe a couple" of times. Mr. Habibullah's limp body swayed back and forth in the chains." When medics arrived, they found Habibullah dead.

Dilawar

Dilawar expired on December 10, 2002. He was a 22-year-old Afghan taxi driver and farmer who weighed 122 pounds and was described by his interpreters as neither violent nor aggressive.

When beaten, he repeatedly cried "Allah!" The outcry seemed to have amused US military personnel, and they struck him just to hear him cry "Allah!" This became "a kind of running joke," as one of the MPs put it. "People kept showing up to give this detainee a common peroneal strike just to hear him scream out 'Allah,'" he said. "It went on over a 24-hour period, and I would think that it was over 100 strikes."

The *Times* reported that on the day he died, Dilawar had been chained by the wrists to the top of his cell for much of the previous four days. "A guard tried to force the young man to his knees. But his legs, which had been struck by guards for several days, could no longer bend. An interrogator told the prisoner that he could see a doctor after they finished with him."

When he was finally sent back to his cell, the guards were instructed only to chain the prisoner back to the ceiling. "Leave him up," one of the guards quoted Specialist Claus as saying. Several hours passed before an emergency room doctor finally saw Mr. Dilawar. By that time he was dead, with his body having begun to stiffen.

After months of inquiry into the case, Army investigators learned a final horrific detail: Most of the interrogators had believed Mr. Dilawar was an innocent man who simply drove his taxi past the American base at the wrong time.

(A documentary made about the incident, *Taxi to the Dark Side*, claims that Dilawar was not captured driving past Bagram air base, but while passing through militia territory. He was stopped at a roadblock and handed over to the US Army for a money reward. The militia said he was a terrorist.)

The enigmatic/tragic case of Dr. Aafia Siddiqui

Dr. Aafia Siddiqui, a Pakistani neuroscientist, was suspected of the attempted assault and killing of US personnel in Afghanistan. She mysteriously disappeared in 2003 with her three children, and was allegedly detained for five years at Bagram, where she was the only female prisoner. She was known to the male detainees as "Prisoner 650" and has been labeled by the media as the "Mata Hari of al-Qaeda" or the "Grey Lady of Bagram".

In addition to former detainees of Bagram, Yvonne Ridley maintains that Siddiqui is the "Grey Lady of Bagram" – a ghostly female detainee, who kept prisoners awake "with her haunting sobs and piercing screams". In 2005, male prisoners were so agitated by her plight, Yvonne said, that they went on a hunger strike for six days. Siddiqui's family maintains that she has been abused.

Siddiqui was convicted in an American court on Sept. 23, 2010. Judge Richard Berman, US District Court Judge of a Federal Court in Manhattan, stated, "It is my judgment that Dr. Siddiqui is sentenced to a period of incarceration of 86 years." This for the *attempted* murder of US officers in Afghanistan!

Dr. Aafia Siddiqui herself denounced the trial saying, "An appeal would be a waste of time. I appeal to God."

In the meantime, it has been reported that 12-year-old Ahmed (Dr. Aafia's son) was handed over to his aunt Fauzia Siddiqui in September 2008, after years of being incarcerated in a US military base in Afghanistan. It was later reported that a small girl named Fatima was dropped off in front of the home of the sister and the girl's DNA matched that of Ahmed. One outraged Pakistani Senator, Talha Mehmood, sharply criticized the US "for keeping the child in a military jail in a cold, dark room for seven years."

The abuse of Binyam Mohamed

Mohamed came to the UK from Ethiopia in 1994, seeking asylum. In 2001, he converted to Islam and traveled to Pakistan and later to Afghanistan, to discover, as he said, whether Taliban-run Afghanistan was "a good Islamic country". Considered by US authorities as a would-be bomber, he was arrested at the airport by Pakistani officials in April 2002 on his way back to the UK. Mohamed insists the only evidence against him was obtained using torture in Pakistan, Morocco and Afghanistan between 2002 and 2004 before being secretly rendered to Guantanamo.

He accuses his captors of having beaten, scalded, cut and confined him to a black hole at the "Prison of Darkness", where he was deprived of sleep, blasted with sound, starved, and hung up.

Then, in October 2008, the US dropped all charges against him. While US authorities had been reviewing his case, Mohamed became very ill as a result of a hunger strike in the weeks before his release.

In an interview in February 2009, Mohamed confirmed to fellow Bagram detainee Moazzam Begg that the woman he and the other male detainees saw at Bagram, named "Prisoner 650", was Aafia Siddiqui. The confirmation occurred when Begg showed him a picture of her.

Extrajudicial incarceration: Mohammed Sulaymon Barre

Mohammed Sulaymon Barre, a Somali refugee who worked for a funds transfer company, described his Bagram interrogation as "torture." He had been living at home with his wife when the Pakistani authorities arrested him in the middle of the night in November 2001, soon after the US invasion of Afghanistan. It is believed he was sold to the United States for a bounty. At the time, the US military offered large sums of money – $5,000 or more – to anyone who handed over alleged "terrorists". The promises of "wealth and power beyond your dreams" or "enough money to take care of your family, your village, your tribe for the rest of your life" were made in numerous leaflets dropped over Afghanistan and Pakistan.

At Bagram prison, Barre said he was thrown around the interrogation room when he wouldn't confess to a false allegation. He was then put into an isolation chamber that was maintained at a freezing temperature for several weeks. He said he was deprived of sufficient rations during his time in isolation. As a result of this treatment, his hands and feet swelled, causing him such excruciating pain he couldn't stand up. Though no charges were filed against him, he was transferred to Guantanamo and remained imprisoned for nearly eight years. In December 2009, Mr. Barre was released and returned to his family in Somaliland.

Finally, abuse was not only committed in the war prisons of the US Army, but in jails seemingly under the control of Afghan officials. Thus we learn on June 13, 2008, that Kandahar Jail was the scene of a mass hunger strike by hundreds of inmates a month earlier, during which 47 of the prisoners sewed their lips shut after complaining they had been tortured and denied fair trials.

There is nothing normal about the stories and descriptions above. Rather, all are windows into warped minds and hearts consumed by hatred; all are the deeds of power-intoxicated sadists. While some of those soldier-torturers have been charged for their criminal acts, their commanding officers, and above all, those who usurped our country on 9/11 and whose malevolent obsession with Islam led to those crimes, have not. Can a democratic nation allow such violations of human rights and decency and not call for investigations and trials? In fact, can a people ignore such abuses without further spiritual harm to themselves?

Abu Ghraib, Iraq

A year after the fall of Baghdad, in the spring of 2004, Abu Ghraib, which had previously been the notorious prison where Saddam Hussein's henchmen tortured opponents of the regime, was, in a case of grotesque irony, suddenly thrust into the limelight. The event was a broadcast on ABC news of April 28, showing a collection of photos taken by US soldiers participating in the torture and dehumanization of Iraqi prisoners. Viewing those now iconic pictures stunned friend and foe alike and filled millions across the globe with disgust and outrage.

An article by investigative reporter, Seymour M. Hersh, in *The New Yorker* – posted online on April 30 and published in the May 10 issue of the magazine – reported the gruesome details of the story.

The revelations were almost beyond belief, striking the

viewer like a warp in time, like a trip back to the dungeons of Medieval Europe. Those photographs, like no verbal descriptions previously, illustrated the twisted and cruel methods of the NeoConian culture occupying Washington while horrifying and sickening observers.

There were naked humans on chains being dragged across cement floors like dogs; there were naked humans smeared with excrement; there were naked humans piled into a pyramid of sexual degradation; there was a single blindfolded, hooded prisoner wearing a fringed cape, standing on a narrow box, his extended arms and fingers connected to "wires", having been told that if he were to move he would be electrocuted.

Here were utterly dehumanized figures, and inflicting agonies and obscenities on them were grinning American male and female soldiers.

I have in my documents a photo of a detainee being tortured at Abu Ghraib, which is both revolting and heartrending. It shows a hapless prisoner strapped into a contraption resembling two metal gurneys, one on the bottom and one on top of his naked body. His arms are swollen grotesquely and blood can be seen spilling out of his nose and mouth. A tall, maybe 250-pound, American soldier sits nonchalantly on top of the already flattened prisoner. An appropriate title for such a scene would certainly be, "When men turn into monsters."

It is reported that after General Miller, commander of Guantanamo, visited Iraq in September 2003, commander General Ricardo Sanchez ordered Guantanamo-style abuse at Abu Ghraib prison. Professor Alfred McCoy of the University of Wisconsin–Madison reviewed the 1,600 still-classified photos taken by American guards at Abu Ghraib. According to him, they "reveal not random, idiosyncratic acts by 'bad apples', but the repeated, constant use of just three psychological techniques: hooding for sensory deprivation, shackling for self-inflicted pain, and, to exploit Arab cultural sensitivities, both nudity and dogs." He commented further, "It is no accident that Private Lynndie England was famously photographed leading an Iraqi detainee leashed like a dog."

And now, like others before us, we must ask ourselves

what in our national character prepared the way for such abhorrent behavior, what in us and our culture fostered such moral bankruptcy?

Lamentation

America so tall, so proud
so full of confidence and future
has slipped
disgraced
despised
from its pedestal
among the nations.

In Bagram, Abu Ghraib, Guantanamo and other
hubs of malevolence and torture
captives chained and hooded
hang beaten and bleeding
from ceilings by hooks
in scenes reminiscent of medieval dungeons.

Here the vision of a virtuous people evaporates
as honor is trampled and values are mocked
while copies of the Rules of Engagement
lie soiled in blood and excrement
and the disfigured image of a once great nation
grins grotesquely through perverse pyramids
of sexual humiliation
degradation
shame…

America so tall, so proud
so full of confidence and future
has shown its dark and cruel side
has shocked the world
with callous crimes
and staggering
human rights abuses.

Oh, God! When did we

so completely
forsake ourselves?!

RC - March 2004

Crime and punishment

After the bombshell of 2004 exploded the myth of the American military abiding by international law in the treatment of detainees, the Department of Defense removed seventeen soldiers and officers from duty, while eleven soldiers were charged with dereliction of duty, maltreatment, aggravated assault and battery. Between May 2004 and March 2006, eleven were convicted in courts martial, sentenced to military prison, and dishonorably discharged from service. In trials ending on January 14, 2005, and September 26, 2005, Specialist Charles Graner was sentenced to ten years, and his former fiancée, Specialist Lynndie England, received a three-year prison term.

At that time, the commanding officer of all Iraq detention facilities, Brigadier General Janis Karpinski, was also reprimanded for dereliction of duty and then demoted to the rank of Colonel on May 5, 2005, allegedly for a pending misdemeanor shoplifting charge filed years earlier. Col. Karpinski has denied knowledge of the abuses, claiming that the interrogations were authorized by her superiors and performed by subcontractors, and that she was not even allowed entry into the interrogation rooms.

The United States of America, that once shining beacon on the hill, illegally and shamefully bombarded a country so relentlessly that the Air Force ran out of Tomahawk missiles, and the Army nearly out of bullets because it had shot billions of them! After that, revengeful young Americans who had been made to believe that Saddam Hussein was involved in 9/11, were given free rein to "soften up" detainees at midnight in windowless cellars of torture.

When, we must ask, will outraged citizens of this country demand accountability from the officials responsible for the nightmarish scenes visited upon other people, and indeed for this insane rush toward moral self-destruction?

Guantanamo

As more details emerged from that other prison of shame at Guantanamo Bay, in, of all places, part of Fidel Castro's Cuba, it once again sent shock waves through the hearts and minds of those whose moral compass is still functioning even after heavy propaganda and fear campaigns. America undoubtedly encountered its darkest shadow in the torture chambers it created to break the spirit of Islamic resisters, conveniently vilified as "terrorists".

When listening to accounts of the brutal methods employed by interrogators against what were mostly innocent people, one must constantly wonder what sinister force had infiltrated our country, and, in fact, occupied its highest offices.

That there are people willing to inflict on others such degrading, reprehensible acts is nearly incomprehensible. This is the United States of America?! This is done in the name of the American people?! Into what evil web have we blundered? And what sinister forces wove those poisonous threads? The answer is obvious: 9/11 gave certain individuals in Washington carte blanche to do anything they wanted, with no restrictions placed on ruthless minds or heartless selves.

This spiritual pathology was furthermore evidenced by members of the medical profession, both physicians and psychologists, in their collaboration with the torturers. As such, they advised them on the most effective methods of breaking the spirit of a detainee, while leaving as little physical evidence as possible on the body of the abused.

Voices of conscience

Investigative reporter and author Jane Mayer is a Washington based staff writer for *The New Yorker*. She has authored several articles exposing the treatment of prisoners at Guantanamo. In 2008, she published a defining work, titled: *The Dark Side: The Inside Story of How the War on Terror Turned Into a War on American Ideals.*

The Dark Side addresses the origins, "legal" justifications and possible war crimes liability, with respect to interrogation techniques to break down detainees' resistance, and the subsequent death of detainees under such interrogations.

Soon after the publication of her work, Bill Moyers invited the author for an interview on *Bill Moyers' Journal*. Referring to the Congressional hearings about the treatment of detainees she had been attending, Moyers wanted to know, "Are you certain that the witnesses who came from the government knew they were talking about torture?"

Mayer replied, "Well, I think they knew they were being asked about torture. I mean, they danced around the question. They've redefined the term 'torture' so that what was torture before 9/11 they say has not been torture since."

When Moyers asked, "Why?" she gave a most revealing answer. "Because they wanted to interrogate people in completely brutal ways," she said. "And they wanted to avoid being accused of war crimes. So one of the witnesses there, Doug Feith in particular, who was the number three in the Pentagon, argued right after 9/11 that the Geneva Conventions should no longer apply to anybody that was picked up in the war on terror, that was a terrorist suspect. And so they took away the rules of war, which were the Geneva Conventions, which America really pioneered in many ways. And they also said that the criminal laws didn't apply to the same suspects. So they were left with kind of a legal limbo. And they made up the laws as they went along on it."

When made aware of the depth of the betrayal of democratic values by members of the Bush administration, especially its brutal treatment of detainees, former CIA officer Ray McGovern, who once gave daily briefings on national security to President Bush the Elder, suggested on August 31, 2009, that "this is not the CIA in which I served for 27 years. There were abuses before the Bush/Cheney administration, but Bush and Cheney thoroughly corrupted both substance and operations, and enlisted creeps and charlatans to do their bidding."

Of course, none can say we weren't warned. Many probably can recall how Vice President Dick Cheney set a chilling tone just five days after 9/11, when he told Tim Russert: "We also have to work, though, sort of the dark side, if you will. We've got to spend time in the shadows in the intelligence world. A lot of what needs to be done here will have to be done quietly, without any discussion, using sources and methods that are available to our intelligence agencies ... and so it's going to be vital for us to use any means at our disposal, basically, to achieve our objective."

The image that comes to mind when reading these words is that of dungeons of torture where the institutionally "disappeared" are mercilessly maltreated.

Shadow at work or shadow work?

We must inquire of the present administration why there are no plans to bring the individuals who were the architects of carnage, chaos, and torture before a court of justice. Is there no one in the halls of Congress or the White House itself who can speak to the fact that by not confronting such perversity, the malignancy could metastasize, causing yet greater and more unpredictable damage? What occurred and those responsible must be subjected to the laser beam of truth to allow for in-depth healing. This is necessary not only for the many who have been shattered by acts of brutality, but for the future of our country.

Still, on April 16, 2009, President Barack Obama declared that "Nothing will be gained by spending our time and energy laying blame for the past." To which one might reply, "Justice, Mr. President, is greater than blame, and if not justice in the traditional sense, how about a Truth and Reconciliation process? To brush aside such brutal crimes as torture not only means that victims are essentially abused a second time, but so too are the American Constitution, International Law, the American people and humanity itself."

In fact, the UN's chief official on torture, Manfred Nowak, reminded the President that in compliance with international agreements, Washington was actually *obliged* to investigate possible violations of the Convention Against Torture.

Clearly, how else except through open hearings can we break the cycle of deceit that took hold of our country on 9/11 and its aftermath?

Only such an uncovering of the facts can awaken the American people from their trance and make them realize what is occurring in their name, and expose the real powers that are occupying the seat of governance in our capitol.

Beyond that, in order to move on, our people must squarely face the heavy baggage of our national shadow, must acknowledge how our dark side has permeated political aspirations and actions at home and abroad. There is much negativity to be transmuted. We need a potent catharsis to cleanse our soul of all this accumulated pollution. And truth is the only agent for achieving it.

What we need to learn is that as the most powerful nation on Earth, we are presently the heavyweight who can push the ship of humankind in any direction we choose. Under the right leadership, this could be of great benefit to all. Under delusional leadership, it could bring about the biggest disaster ever to befall the planet and its inhabitants.

Will Americans awaken in time to realize the moral degradation that has taken place? Will a once naïve and gullible citizenry, frightened into compliance, begin to open its collective eyes before the country is duped into yet another war? Years ago I heard a sage say that the psyche of America contains a large amount of repressed toxic energy, and that one day, this must come to the surface so that people can acknowledge and work on it, in order to be cleansed and healed. Only then, the lecturer said, will this country be free to become a truly progressive nation.

If one accepts the premise, then what is happening is occurring for an unavoidable reason, and we must generate the fortitude to remove the mud and muck to get back to the light and purer air. America must meet and wrestle with its shadow, must do "shadow work", in order to be free.

Have they no shame?

The question is a familiar one: "Have they no shame?" Unfortunately, the answer is once again the same: They have none. When someone has no reservations about inflicting extreme suffering or bringing death en masse to others, what in

103

life can move him or her to have a conscience, much less a heart? Look to the hell those warlords have spawned by their ruthless invasion of Iraq and you get an idea about the character of the individuals that hijacked our government.

The threat to human existence is at an all-time high not only because of vast stockpiles of WMDs, but because the forces of darkness have cloaked themselves in (artificial) light. They have deceived the many with their superior intellect and ability to manipulate the human heart. They know that when emotions are fully aroused, and especially when fear and vengeance are added at a high voltage as they were on 9/11, it is difficult for human beings to step back and analyze a situation critically. Crafty propagandists know about the phenomenon and apply the principle in the cleverest of ways.

When syndicated columnist and author Norman Solomon (*War Made Easy: How Presidents and Pundits Keep Spinning Us to Death*) wrote that "The human spirit cannot be killed, but it can be sedated," he must have had in mind such states as the anesthetizing or deadening of the spirit. One should think that repeated waterboarding, severe beatings, being placed under ice-cold showers in an ice-cold room or being sodomized with a baton can definitely lead to such a state. Yet, does not being made fearful repeatedly or being fed lies continually have the same effect, lead to the same numbing of the spirit, and a deep tiredness of the soul?

Ideologues know how to lure us into a wilderness from which return is never easy. If we don't want to fall into the traps which are part of the landscape of those who rule by divide and conquer, we must be willing to reject lies and let truth, no matter how painful, be our guide. Nothing more is required – and nothing less will do.

Finally, the crimes against humanity which have been committed in the torture chambers of the US military, or subcontracted to some of the world's darkest places – places utterly devoid of empathy or ethics – cannot be judged disconnected from 9/11. For that event changed not only the skyline of lower Manhattan, but the moral profile of America. What emerged is both a frightened and frightening visage that bears little resemblance to the self-confident and hopeful people we thought we were before calamity struck.

Will a duped citizenry, stampeded into fear and compliance, one day gain the courage to open to the voices of its truth-tellers and comprehend the extent of its subservience and acquiescence?

Behavior contrary to our proclaimed values has diminished both us and our effectiveness in the world. Through our conquest of Muslim countries, due to a loss of moral vision, we are not only expanding the size of our shadow, but are becoming a mere shadow of ourselves. That is our self-created fate and it will continue to worsen until we decide to listen to painful but ultimately liberating truths.

On June 3, 2011, *Democracy Now!* featured an extensive interview with one of those not afraid to utter truths, Seymour Hersh. He was interviewed on the subject of one of his then upcoming articles, "Iran and the Bomb: How Real is the Threat?" (*The New Yorker*, June 6, 2011 issue). At the end of the conversation, Amy Goodman asked: "You made headlines a few years ago when you said President Bush operated an executive assassination ring. Has that policy continued under President Obama?"

Hersh replied: "What I said was that in the early days under Cheney … there was a direct connection between the vice president's office and individuals getting hit. That got institutionalized later in a more sophisticated way. There's no question that … look, there's an enormous military apparatus out there that isn't seen. That's what I'm writing about. We're not seeing it. We don't know it exists. Cheney built up a world that still exists. And it's a very ugly, frightening world that has not much to do with what the Constitution calls for."

The Rev. William Sloane Coffin admonished, "When a government betrays the ideals of a country, it is an act of loyalty to oppose the government." As though immobilized, too few of us are responding to that patriotic call. Morally and spiritually, this is an American tragedy.

In closing this chapter, I shall give the last word to one of the wrongfully imprisoned men at Guantanamo, Mohammed Sulaymon Barre. When he was released after eight years of incarceration, he appealed to President Obama and the American people to close that "prison of shame".

Calmly and without bitterness he implored, "Is it not time that you should awaken from your slumber? Is it not time that you should realize what you are doing, acknowledge the mistakes you have made? The thing you fear is the very thing you cause by your wrongful actions. This is what constitutes the real threat to the United States, not the closing of this prison."

In the midst of all that has gone fundamentally wrong in our country since 9/11, each one of us must finally ask of self a question of enormous consequence: Would I rather lose my life or my humanity?

Chapter 5

TORTURE – WHEN HUMANS MORPH INTO MONSTERS

Hostis humani generis (enemy of all humankind)
~Modern legal term for torturer

Verschärfte Vernehmung (enhanced interrogation)
~Gestapo Chief Heinrich Müller

The United States of America does not torture.
~George W. Bush; George Tenet

Psychology is an important weapons system.
~Kevin Kiley, Army Surgeon General

Even victors are by victories undone.
~John Dryden

     The fact that the United States of America, at the beginning of the 21st century, reverted back to a time devoid of human rights protections by officially reinstating torture must be seen as an absolute low point, a nadir, in the history of our country. In a brazen act displaying arrogance of power, the Bush administration contemptuously discarded both international and domestic law. It was a blow not only to the American Constitution, but also to the aspirations of the world community.

     This disgraceful development must neither be underestimated nor hastily removed from our conscience. Horrific crimes were committed by a government that self-righteously issued threats to the rest of the world on behalf of the American people – and felt no hesitation to carry them out. This means we collectively share responsibility. However, unless we know some of the details of those atrocities, we can neither fully feel their impact nor strive for the moral awakening necessary to prevent them from reoccurring.

It is for that reason that this chapter needed to be written. In addition, all that is said herein will take on even greater significance in view of chapter 7, "September 11th Revisited."

Background

Throughout history, torture has been used as a means of intimidation and for interrogation in an effort to obtain information or a confession. It has also been a tool of punishment or political re-education. Official use of torture means that the state uses these methods to terrify or eliminate its enemies. It is authorized violence and the attainment of power through brute force.

Beyond state-sponsored torture, there may be individuals or groups who are motivated to inflict torture on others for reasons similar to those of a government. But torture can, in certain instances, also be for the sadistic gratification of the torturer.

Specifically, torture means an act committed with the intention to inflict severe physical or mental pain and suffering upon another person within someone's custody or physical control. While physical torture means inflicting acute and tormenting pain on the body, psychological torture, directed at the psyche, is designed to inflict deep damage to inner structures, especially the breaking down of beliefs that ensure normal sanity. Thus, psychological torture needs no physical violence to be effective, and the torturer(s) can inflict acute pain, suffering, and trauma with no visible effects.

Torture, Inc. in the 21st century

In our time, even in countries where the government permits severe interrogation techniques, torturers prefer methods that leave victims alive and unmarked. This is because someone who shows no detectable injury would have a more difficult time proving claims of being tortured than those whose eyes or fingernails are missing.

For that reason, today's professional torturers use extreme stressors such as extended solitary confinement, mock execution, shunning and violation of deep-seated social or sexual norms and religious taboos, heat, cold, noise, and sleep deprivation. Rape and other forms of sexual abuse are often included for interrogative and punitive purposes.

Although the aim is to use methods that have a maximum psychological impact while leaving only minimal physical or visible evidence, in some cases torture ends in horrific mutilation or death.

In practice, many torturers prefer to inflict both physical and psychological torment on a victim in order to achieve the maximum effect. As a consequence, having been severely tortured often leads to lasting mental and physical health problems, from chronic muscular or skeletal difficulties, injury to the brain, post-traumatic epilepsy and dementia, to unremitting pain syndromes—effects that are deep and unrelenting.

Yet, since some victims inevitably die from such cruelties and the associated extremes of stress, death can be certified via an autopsy as having simply been from "natural causes" like a heart attack, inflammation, or an embolism.

Even when returned to their previous life, daily living for the cruelly abused will never be the same. Most victims suffer disability of one form or another, the most prevalent being post-traumatic stress disorder (PTSD). Symptoms displayed are flashbacks, insomnia, nightmares, severe anxiety, powerlessness, depression and memory lapses. This is compounded by feelings of guilt and shame caused by the humiliation they had to endure. In addition, the victim frequently experiences a sense of self-betrayal or of having betrayed friends and/or family. While such symptoms are normal human responses to abnormal and inhuman treatment, they disrupt any attempt at "normal" living, especially with respect to intimate relationships.

Beyond post-traumatic stress and depression and anxiety disorder, the worst imaginable loss is the absence of any desire to connect with others or to find meaning in life. It is a psychological condition known as psychic deadness, whereby torment has been so acute that any kind of goodness, hope and being in relationship with another are experienced as immaterial and are actively blocked. Victims display a kind of self-deadening behavior whereby they live as though "to prove death itself."

These are the signs of the deepest post-traumatic injury, and as such, a mark of the most malevolent human-rights violations.

Universal Declaration of Human Rights

An extraordinary milestone in the history of humanity was the establishment of the UN Universal Declaration of Human Rights in December 1948, which created rights for the individual vis-à-vis political institutions and governments.

The broad and far-reaching steps leading to its establishment were reflective of a strong desire by the international community to promote equality and justice for the people of the world. Various national constitutions which came into being after WWII have, in fact, drawn practical inspiration from those joint declarations.

Fundamental to the UN's human rights law is the prohibition of torture. Article 5 of the Universal Declaration of Human Rights declares that "no one shall be subjected to torture or to cruel, inhuman or degrading treatment or punishment." The passage of that law, known as the Convention Against Torture, is the most important UN treaty for controlling, regulating, and banning torture and related practices. Torture is described as "any act by which acute pain or suffering, whether physical or mental, is intentionally inflicted on a person ... with the consent or acquiescence of a public official or other person acting in an official capacity."

In addition, signatories of the Third and Fourth Geneva Conventions have officially agreed not to torture prisoners in armed conflicts. Torture is also prohibited by the United Nations Convention Against Torture, which has been ratified by 147 states.

The Convention Against Torture furthermore holds countries responsible for taking "effective legislative, administrative, judicial and other measures to prevent acts of torture."

Now, despite the clear consensus of the international community, the perennial problem is the weakness of these principles in practice, with the United Nations facing certain institutional limitations which restrict enforcement. This is due to the fact that certain governments still insist on the "necessity" to have recourse to the use of violence.

Aware of those enforcement deficiencies, international nongovernmental organizations started to be involved in worldwide campaigns against torture, with Amnesty International, in 1961, being the most significant to emerge. AI's focus on members' participation for individual victims via letter writing campaigns was highly innovative, contributing greatly to the development of a grassroots-based global initiative to support and complement the work of the United Nations. Consequently, Amnesty International's early monitoring of torture worldwide was instrumental in generating the interest, pressure and support for more governmental initiatives.

Addressing complaints

Investigating any complaints of violations of the UN's Convention Against Torture falls under the jurisdiction of the Committee Against Torture. However, for various administrative reasons, the Committee's effectiveness is both hindered and flawed; that is, it does not have the capacity to act when help is most urgently needed.

For example, weakening its effectiveness is a six-month deadline for a state's response to an individual's report of torture. Such a delay lends itself to the disappearance or extrajudicial execution of a victim willing to talk and expose what has happened.

In 1985, to strengthen its capacity to respond, the UN Commission on Human Rights established the office of the Special Rapporteur on Torture. Such an expert can examine questions of torture in all states which are parties to the Convention, UN member states, and states with observer status.

The formation of the office of Special Rapporteur was another determined effort to combat torture. Unfortunately, the Rapporteur shares the Committee's staggering workload and lack of funding. Thus, while the structures created by the UN provide symbolic importance, global accountability for torture has not yet been attained, due to political constraints and obstructions on the part of governments.

Developments post 9/11: "Enhanced Interrogation"

The first mention of the term "enhanced interrogation" appears to have been made in a 1937 memo by Gestapo Chief Heinrich Müller, in which he coined the phrase "Verschärfte Vernehmung," German for "sharpened interrogation," "intensified interrogation," or as euphemistically adopted by the Bush administration, "*enhanced* interrogation."

(It should be noted that in 1948, Norway prosecuted German officials for the practice of "Verschärfte Vernehmung" which included subjecting detainees to extreme cold, sleep deprivation, repeated beatings and deliberate exhaustion.)

Enhanced interrogation techniques or alternative sets of procedures were used by US military intelligence and the Central Intelligence Agency to obtain information from individuals captured in the "War on Terror" soon after September 11, 2001.

Author/activist George Monboit writes in *The Guardian*, December 18, 2006: "After thousands of years of practice, you might have imagined that every possible means of inflicting pain had already been devised. But you should never underestimate the human capacity for invention. The United States interrogators, we can discover, have found a new way of destroying a human being."

While many in the international press regard these techniques as torture, both the *Washington Post* and *New York Times* (and the US media in general) avoid the word, using instead the description "harsh" or "brutal" and most frequently, the cynical "enhanced interrogation".

Regardless of how the administration or corporate media have labeled the technique, what it means for the detainee is being subjected to such inhumanities as waterboarding, sleep deprivation, isolation, exposure to extreme temperatures, enclosure in tiny spaces, mock executions, bombardment with agonizing, high-decibel sounds, and religious and sexual humiliation, as we saw in the last chapter.

When Major General Geoffrey Miller was named commander of Guantanamo in 2002, it became known that he believed strongly in breaking detainees down. Miller would later be assigned to Abu Ghraib to "Gitmo-ize" the prison by giving advice on detainee treatment, where, according to one general, he told subordinates that detainees "should be treated like dogs."

This led, for example, to the story of Mohammed al-Khatani, the supposed "20th hijacker". After becoming a detainee, an army psychologist helped interrogate him. Some of the techniques used included stripping him naked, giving him intravenous fluids to force him to urinate on himself, exercising him to exhaustion, and making him perform dog tricks.

Another form of torture, perhaps better described as sadism, was to restrict an individual for years to a totally sense-deprived environment. This meant being confined to a blackout cell, unable to see or hear anything, while being periodically subjected to "walling," that is, having one's head slammed against a cell wall by interrogators. The prolonged isolation and relentless mistreatment can result in "lobotomizing" a person. Not literally but psychically: a human having lost his mind.

The APA and its searing ethics

In August of 2006, Kevin Kiley, the Army Surgeon General, addressed the governing council of the American Psychological Association (APA) on the subject of psychology in the war on terror. He argued for keeping psychologists on the offensive against "sworn enemies" of the country, letting it be known how essential they were for the process. As he put it, "Psychology is an important weapons system."

The organization's leadership was fully behind him at a time when many members wanted the participation of psychologists in interrogations officially banned. Among them was Dr. Steven Reisner, who reminded those present of their Hippocratic oath of 'do no harm', adding, "It does not say 'measure harm and see if it is the correct amount.'"

These words were spoken in response to a paper on "21st Century Ethics" presented at the same New Orleans conference by board member Gerald Koocher (who would take over the APA presidency the following year). His distilled message was this: "The dictum of 'do no harm' has evolved to 'do as little harm as possible.'" In other words, psychologists who were participating in harsh interrogations – thereby having betrayed their oaths as health care professionals – were liberally exonerated.

Not by Arthur Levine, however, who is a contributing editor to the *Washington Monthly*. In an article titled "Collective unconscionable: how psychologists, the most liberal of professionals, abetted Bush's torture policy" (Jan-Feb 2007), he writes, "Why was the leadership of the APA, an organization representing one of the most liberal professions imaginable, so willing to essentially acquiesce with a conservative administration's efforts to torture prisoners? The answer is that it fell into a classic Washington trade-group dilemma: It became so enmeshed in the gears of the federal machine that it could be influenced by a determined administration and ended up supporting policies that many of its own members opposed."

Appalled by the participation of some members of the organization, psychologists such as Stephen Soldz, Steven Reisner and Brad Olson realized how the techniques against detainees mimicked what was taught in the SERE-program. SERE is the military's "Survival, Evasion, Resistance, and Escape" program that trains US Special Operations Forces, aviators and others at high risk of capture to evade being taken prisoner and to resist breaking under torture.

Subsequently, in June 2007, they wrote a letter to the president of the APA, Sharon Brehm, expressing their alarm about both the program and members of the Association participating in it. The letter voices their main concerns. "First, we believe that SERE interrogation methods constitute torture and cruel, inhuman, and degrading treatment and should be prohibited, as should any involvement of psychologists in their use." They then referred to a report by Mark Benjamin in the online magazine, *Salon*, "CIA's Torture Teachers: Psychologists helped the CIA exploit a secret military program to develop brutal interrogation tactics – likely with the approval of the Bush White House", which documents the central role of psychologists from the Department of Defense's SERE program in implementing abusive interrogation tactics for the CIA.

The letter to Brehm also mentions that these psychologists relied heavily on experiments done by American psychologist Martin Seligman in the 1970s known as "learned helplessness". During those experiments caged dogs were exposed to severe electric shocks in a random manner in order to completely break their will to resist. In 2002, after the capture of suspected al-Qaeda facilitator Abu Zubaydah, psychologists Jim Mitchell and Bruce Jessen flew to a secret CIA prison in Thailand and personally subjected the prisoner to brutal interrogations. (More about them and their methods in a moment.)

At the time of Zubaydah's capture, many of the interrogation techniques used in the SERE program, including waterboarding, cold cell, long-time standing, nudity and sleep deprivation, were considered illegal under US and international law (see the UN Convention Against Torture as well as the European Convention on Human Rights). In fact, the United States prosecuted Japanese military officials after World War II for waterboarding, as well as American soldiers post Vietnam. In addition, since 1930, the United States has defined sleep deprivation as an illegal form of torture.

The brutal assault on a human being's psyche under the severe trauma of torture is the reason why, in a heated debate on August 19, 2007, the APA finally voted to prohibit participation of its members in a wide variety of interrogation techniques, including "mock executions, simulated drowning, sexual and religious humiliation, stress positions or sleep deprivation," as well as "the exploitation of prisoners' phobias, the use of mind-altering drugs, hooding, forced nakedness, the use of dogs to frighten detainees, exposing prisoners to extreme heat and cold, physical assault and threatening the use of such techniques against a prisoner or a prisoner's family."

"They sought to render the detainees vulnerable – to break down all of their senses. It takes a psychologist trained in this to understand these rupturing experiences," one official told author Jane Mayer, who has done her own investigative work on such issues.

As we shall learn later, despite all of the horrifying revelations of ill treatment, a majority of the participants at the August conference did not insist that there would be automatic repercussions for those guilty of degrading other human beings and causing them unspeakable suffering.

Descent into darkness

To get a fuller sense of the degree of acute pain and torment inflicted on detainees (most of them, as it turned out, innocent victims), specifics are needed. Here are three as revealed by former and current CIA officials as they relate to authorized interrogation techniques:

- Long Time Standing: This technique is described as among the most effective. Prisoners are forced to stand, handcuffed and with their feet shackled to an eyebolt in the floor, for more than 40 hours.
- Cold Cell: The prisoner is left to stand naked in a cell kept near 50 degrees Fahrenheit (10 degrees Celsius), while being regularly doused with cold water.
- Waterboarding: The prisoner is bound to an inclined board, feet raised with the upper body slightly below the feet. The head and body are immobilized and material is wrapped over the prisoner's mouth and nose while an interrogator pours water onto the cloth in a controlled manner. As the airflow is restricted for 20 to 40 seconds, the gag reflex gets activated and the person experiences an uncontrollable terror of impending death by drowning and suffocation.

Now, since waterboarding has raised contention among some US officials as to whether it constitutes torture, it is important to note that the cruel method dates back to the Spanish Inquisition. First documented in 1478, it was used to force confessions from people accused of heresy. It should be added that besides causing extreme pain, the procedure can injure the lungs, lead to brain damage from oxygen deprivation, and result in other physical harm including broken bones due to struggling against restraints, as well as lasting psychological impairment, and actual death. We can be certain that the numerous human beings who have experienced its terror over the years would surely not consider it anything other than torture.

This, then, is how, with the help of high-paid psychologists, the CIA was able to administer some of the world's oldest as well as most advanced forms of torture.

As referenced above, among the most prominent of psychologists accused of "reverse engineering" the SERE program were Jim Mitchell and Bruce Jessen. After retiring in 2001 from the military, Mitchell started a training company called Knowledge Works. Shortly after 9/11, he asked Air Force psychologist Jessen to allow him to examine a top-secret document, believed to have been an interrogation program for high-value al-Qaeda members. Based on its contents, Mitchell wrote a proposal for a torture interrogation program, which he and Jessen offered to run for the CIA as private contractors, to be paid "more than $1,000 a day" plus expenses, tax free.

In April 2002, with high-value al-Qaeda prisoner, Zubaydah, held at a CIA safe house in Thailand, the CIA took Jessen and Mitchell up on their offer and invited them to try the methods on the prisoner.

Mitchell, eager to apply what he had learned, flew to Thailand, and announcing to the FBI interrogators that he was now in charge, ordered that Zubaydah be confined "like a dog" to a small box. When he ceased cooperating with interrogators, Mitchell ordered waterboarding and other torture. He reportedly videotaped the proceedings and submitted daily reports to Alberto Gonzales, then the President's personal lawyer. The prompt replies he received made him feel authorized to continue and even accelerate the torture.

In 2004, Mitchell's Knowledge Works program was certified by the American Psychological Association as a provider of continuing professional education training. In 2005, the partners formed a company called Mitchell, Jessen and Associates, which, by 2007, employed approximately 60 people. In

2008, however, after the "enhanced interrogation" techniques they pioneered had become extremely controversial, the APA cancelled Knowledge Works' certification; and in April 2009, the CIA ended its contractual relationship with Mitchell and Jessen.

Then, on December 27, 2010, Matt Lake of the *Daily Mail*, UK, posted an article titled "The CIA secretly agreed to pay over five million dollars to shield the architects of its waterboarding programme." In it he writes: "Psychologists Jim Mitchell and Bruce Jessen are well-known to have invented the brutal interrogation programme, now classed in the US as torture. [...] They are now facing a federal investigation over their exact roles in the simulated drowning tactic. It is the first time those who carried out the waterboarding have been publicly identified."

Referring to the military's SERE program, Lake underscored that those had always been training sessions, never actual interrogations. That changed in 2002 with the capture of Abu Zubaydah.

(On July 10, 2010, AP News reported that Zubaydah told a military tribunal he suffered physical and mental torture and nearly died four times. Zubaydah claims that after many months of such treatment, authorities concluded he was *not* the No. 3 person in al-Qaeda, as they had long believed.)

In addition, Lake writes that former intelligence officials confirmed that the same psychologists waterboarded USS Cole bombing plotter Abd al-Nashiri as well as the accused 9/11 mastermind Khalid Sheikh Mohammed in Thailand. Moreover, the latter was subjected to waterboarding no fewer than 183 times in Poland in 2003! This occurred with the approval of the President of the United States, as admitted in his 2010 memoir, *Decision Points*, and subsequently repeated in media interviews.

Brad Olson, president of the Divisions for Social Justice within the APA, commented on what he named "the irony – and ultimately the tragedy – in the migration of SERE techniques," observing that "the program was specifically designed to protect our soldiers from countries that violated the Geneva

Conventions. The result of the reverse-engineering, however, was that by making foreign detainees the target, it made us the country that violated the Geneva Conventions."

Apropos torture by American agents, there seems to be no end to irony, for US law itself contains an important clause about it. Because our Constitution recognizes customary international law, we have the Alien Tort Claims Act to provide legal remedies for victims of torture in the US. In fact, the status of the torturer has become, like the pirate and slave trader of old, "hostis humani generis" – an enemy of all humankind.

Abu Ghraib encounter

Tonight the cries of the shackled
the moans of the caged
the screams of the brutalized
crash without pity
through the protective
membranes of my heart
torment my senses
ravage my thoughts.

A pain deeper than grieving
is assailing the very core of me
tossing me into waves of despair
and salty tears of compassion
and shame...

I could not
live with myself
were I to remain
unmoved
by the agonies
of the violently abused
the callously discarded
in places black as ink
and stripped of anything
civilized, humane, human.

RC

Torture made in USA, 2001

In 2009, an exhaustive report by the Senate Armed Services Committee reviewing torture under the Bush administration brought to light a number of previously hidden factors.

The information was compiled after studying hundreds of thousands of pages of documents and calling about 70 witnesses. Claims by officials of the Bush administration that they turned to coercive interrogations only after captured al-Qaeda suspects wouldn't talk, were not in alignment with the facts. Instead, evidence showed that torture had become a focus of the White House hours after 9/11, as it was used to "find" links between al-Qaeda and Saddam Hussein.

Planning for it began in earnest in December 2001, and a program to develop the interrogation techniques was in place by the next month, with the military and the CIA starting to train interrogators in coercive practices in early 2002. This occurred prior to having any high-value al-Qaeda suspects in detention or any trouble eliciting information from detainees.

Then, in April 2002, US Air Force psychologist Bruce Jessen (see above) drafted a paper, an "exploitation plan", in which he suggested the establishment of secret prisons not exposed to the scrutiny of the International Committee of the Red Cross. Abu Zubaydah was the first to be carted off to one of those CIA black sites in Thailand to be brutalized.

It is worthy of note that at this point the FBI, which had been present at the interrogations, distanced itself from the coercive techniques. Being a law enforcement agency, the goal and training of its personnel is to bring people to trial using interrogations that are allowed by the courts. It was decided that none of what its agents witnessed would ever be permissible under the law.

Then, in 2002, senior law enforcement agents with the Criminal Investigation Task Force started to complain that interrogation tactics used at Guantanamo were not likely to produce reliable information, and were probably illegal (told to MSNBC in 2006). Unable to get satisfaction from the Army commanders running the detainee camp, their concerns were finally brought to the attention of Navy General Counsel Alberto J. Mora.

General Counsel Mora and Navy Judge Advocate General Michael Lohr believed the detainee treatment to be unlawful, and demanded clear standards prohibiting coercive interrogation tactics. The upshot of this effort was new guidelines in 2003 written by John Yoo from the Department of Justice and signed by Jay S. Bybee, at the time Assistant Attorney General, and today a federal judge on the United States Court of Appeals for the Ninth Circuit. The outlined course of action would later become widely known as the "Torture Memos".

These secret memos from the Bush administration to the CIA, issued in 2003 and 2004, explicitly endorsed the agency's use of interrogation techniques such as waterboarding. The documents were prompted by worries among intelligence officials about a possible backlash if details of the program became public.

The memos revealed, among other secret information, that not only a select group of Republicans but also Democrats were privy to information about "harsh interrogation tactics" – all under the rubric of "classified." Which, in this case, meant that everyone was sworn to silence – in the name of "national security". A crafty move, indeed.

General Counsel Mora argued against the standards contained in the documents and confronted Yoo in person over the issue. His objections were overruled and the final report was signed and delivered to Guantanamo without the knowledge of Mora and others who had opposed its contents.

In 1898, when it became known that US troops were waterboarding Filipino guerrilla fighters, author Mark Twain remarked, "To make him confess what? Truth? Or lies? How can one know which it is they are telling? For under unendurable pain a man confesses anything that is required of him, true or false, and his evidence is worthless."

Today this knowledge remains alive in genuine experts on such matters, in individuals with a developed conscience and endowed with moral clarity. Alfred W. McCoy, Professor of History at the University of Wisconsin-Madison, and author of a number of books on torture and surveillance, expresses his overview of the subject in an article on June 25, 2009.

"Physical torture is a relatively straightforward matter of sadism that leaves behind broken bodies, useless information, and clear evidence for prosecution. Psychological torture, on the other hand, is a mind maze that can destroy its victims, even while entrapping its perpetrators in an illusory, almost erotic, sense of empowerment. When applied skillfully, it leaves few scars for investigators who might restrain this seductive impulse. However, despite all the myths, psychological torture, like its physical counterpart, has proven an ineffective, even counterproductive, method for extracting useful information from prisoners."

Contorted semantics

A February 2002 memorandum signed by President George W. Bush made it clear that the Third Geneva Convention guaranteeing humane treatment to prisoners of war did not apply to al-Qaeda or Taliban detainees, and a December 2002 memo signed by former Defense Secretary Donald Rumsfeld approved the use of "aggressive techniques" against detainees held at Guantanamo Bay.

Despite these revelations, the President repeatedly stated, "The United States of America does not torture."

Nonetheless, a report by Human Rights First and Physicians for Human Rights steadfastly declared that those interrogation techniques do indeed constitute torture. They also cited the Office of the Inspector General report, which concluded that SERE-type interrogations constitute "physical or mental torture and coercion under the Geneva Conventions."

Human Rights Watch furthermore pointed out that the US State Department itself has more than once condemned in its annual "Country Reports on Human Rights Practices" as torture or other inhumane treatment many of the techniques used by the CIA in Iraq, Afghanistan, and at secret detention sites in other countries.

Yet, there is always room in the US media for apologists for Washington's arrogance of power. In this case, it was

NPR and its controversial ban on using the word "torture". Ombudsperson Alica Shepard defended the policy by stating torture is illegal and that "calling waterboarding torture is tantamount to taking sides." Strange reasoning, indeed!

Since virtually all media around the world call these tactics torture, one can only assume that a lot of international journalists must be afflicted with an acute case of prejudice!

Glenn Greenwald, legal analyst, author and press critic writing for *Salon* in July 2009, would have none of this. In an article on the euphemisms invented by the American media, including NPR's stance, he discussed the "corruption of American journalism", saying, "This active media complicity in concealing that our Government created a systematic torture regime […] is one of the principal reasons it was allowed to happen for so long."

He explains, "The steadfast, ongoing refusal of our leading media institutions to refer to what the Bush administration did as "torture" – even in the face of more than 100 detainee deaths […] and the fact that media outlets frequently use the word "torture" to describe the exact same methods when used by other countries – reveals much about how the modern journalist thinks."

He sarcastically concludes, "We don't need a state-run media because our media outlets volunteer for the task: once the U.S. Government decrees that a technique is no longer torture, U.S. media outlets dutifully cease using the term."

For corporate media it was obviously adequate that George Bush, the president, and later, George Tenet, the head of the CIA, repeatedly declared, "The United States of America does not torture!" No need for further questions.

As to the effectiveness of brutalizing prisoners, Dick Cheney, an unembarrassed supporter of the technique, stated: "I know specifically of reports... that lay out what we learnt through the interrogation process and what the consequences were for the country."

And what were those reports? The only publicly released example was the statement that the waterboarding of Khalid Sheikh Mohammed helped prevent a planned attack on

Los Angeles in 2002. Unfortunately, the Vice President's veracity was seriously undermined when it turned out that Mohammed was not even captured until 2003!

Then there is the other frequently cited case of Ibn al-Shaykh al-Libi, an Iraqi prisoner who, after the Vice President's Office suggested waterboarding him, "confessed" that Iraq had trained al-Qaeda in the use of weapons of mass destruction. This "information" was subsequently used to justify the invasion of Iraq – a confession now known to have been utterly false. The story was reported on May 13, 2009, by former NBC News investigative producer Robert Windrem and confirmed by former Iraq Survey Group leader Charles Duelfer.

Then, on May 24, 2009, *Time* magazine reported that the same al-Libi, who famously confessed under torture a link between Saddam and al-Qaeda, but later admitted to Senate investigators to have lied, supposedly committed "suicide" in a Libyan cell.

Abettors right and left

As mentioned previously, according to records made available by the Obama administration, in 2002 and 2003, several Democratic congressional leaders were briefed on the proposed "enhanced interrogation techniques". Among them was Nancy Pelosi, the future Speaker of the House. Congressional officials have stated that the attitude in the briefings was "quiet acquiescence, if not downright support".

Furthermore, the 2007 report by EU investigator Dick Marty on secret CIA prisons not only pointed out that the phrase "enhanced interrogations" was a euphemism for torture, but spoke of documents which show that top US officials were intimately involved in the discussion and approval of the harsher interrogation techniques used on Abu Zubaydah.

And we now know that Secretary of State Condoleezza Rice would tell the CIA the harsher interrogation tactics were acceptable. Despite mounting concerns about the damage torture was doing to America's standing – a view shared by Colin Powell – Rice reportedly told agency officials "with the cool demeanor of a dominatrix": "This is your baby, go do it."

Then, in 2009, Rice, not surprisingly, claimed, "We never tortured anyone," while Dick Cheney self-satisfactorily admitted, "I signed off on it; so did others." During the discussions it was John Ashcroft who is alleged to have said, "Why are we talking about this in the White House? History will not judge this kindly."

Philip Zelikow, adviser to Secretary Rice, also opposed the harsher techniques. Reading the August 1, 2002, memo, which justified the torture, Zelikow drafted his own opinion in which he contested the Justice Department's conclusions, declaring them wrong both legally and as a matter of policy. He argued that it was unlikely that "any federal court would agree (that the approval of harsh interrogation techniques) ... was a reasonable interpretation of the Constitution."

In response, he was told by the administration to destroy copies of his own memo and ordered to collect and destroy other dissenting legal advice.

Jane Mayer, author of *The Dark Side*, quotes Zelikow as predicting that "America's descent into torture will in time be viewed like the Japanese internments," in that "fear and anxiety were exploited by zealots and fools."

Erasing the evidence does not wipe out the crime

In December 2007, it became known that the CIA had destroyed videotapes depicting prisoners being interrogated and brutalized. As was subsequently disclosed in 2010, it was Jose Rodriguez Jr., head of the directorate of operations at the CIA from 2004 to 2007, who supposedly ordered the evidence destroyed, concluding that what they showed was so horrific it would be "devastating to the CIA," and that "the heat from destroying is nothing compared to what it would be if the tapes ever got into public domain."

This desperate concern for secrecy and dread of discovery reveals two things: (1) the tapes did indeed show gruesome abuses, and (2) if the American people saw them, they would be outraged. The potential inherent in the latter would mean that there is still hope for our country.

On February 17, 2008, during *Democracy Now!*, evidence was presented that the US government routinely videotaped the 24,000 interrogations conducted at Guantanamo between 2002 and 2005. This information was made available by professors and students from the New Jersey-based Seton Hall University School of Law, citing internal reports from 2005 by Army Surgeon General Kevin Kiley and Lieutenant General Randall Schmidt.

Were there to be an inquiry into the CIA's secret detention program, *The New York Times* speculates, it "might end with criminal charges for abusive interrogations." Included in the evidence would certainly have to be Dick Marty's reports on "Secret detentions and illegal transfers of detainees", in which he cites cases of individuals kidnapped by the CIA on European territory and subsequently rendered to specific countries for the purpose of torture. (See previous chapter.)

Responding to the destruction of the tapes, Tom Kean and Lee Hamilton, chair and vice chair of the 9/11 Commission, in an op-ed for *The New York Times*, observed: "As a legal matter, it is not up to us to examine the CIA's failure to disclose the existence of these tapes. That is for others. What we do know is that government officials decided not to inform a lawfully constituted body, created by Congress and the president, to investigate one of the greatest tragedies to confront this country. We call that obstruction."

Echoing their view is Scott Horton, a human-rights expert, who chairs the International Law Committee at the New York City Bar Association, and who, additionally, is a legal affairs and national security contributor to *Harper's* magazine. He has called attention to the fact that the authors of the so-called "torture memoranda" who counseled the use of lethal and unlawful techniques, could face criminal culpability themselves.

In 2008, nearly seven years after the "enhanced interrogation" tactics had been implemented, fifty-six House Democrats asked for an independent investigation because of concerns that the interrogative techniques of detainees constituted torture or otherwise violated the law. The letter, addressed to Attorney General Mukasey, further stated: "Because apparent 'enhanced interrogation techniques' were used under cover of Justice Department legal opinions, the need for an outside special prosecutor is obvious."

Mukasey rejected the idea. According to the *Washington Post*, he saw no justification for it because he felt that officials acted in "good faith" when they sought legal opinions, and that the lawyers who provided them used their best judgment. He also warned that criminalizing the process could cause policy-makers to second-guess themselves and "harm our national security well into the future."

Jordan Paust, a respected Professor of Law, criticized the Attorney General's refusal to investigate and/or prosecute, saying that just "following orders" is no defense.

It is important to note that requests to investigate and prosecute have not only come from domestic sources but also from foreign ones. Many have reminded the Obama administration that under the UN Convention Against Torture, to which the US is a signatory, this country is in fact obligated to prosecute those who have committed egregious crimes.

In May 2006, the UN Committee against Torture issued a report stating the US should stop its "ill-treatment" of detainees, since such treatment violates international law.

And in January of 2009, the UN Special Rapporteur on torture, Prof. Manfred Nowak, observed on German television that, following the inauguration of Barack Obama, George W. Bush has lost his immunity as head of state, and under international law, the US is now obligated to start criminal proceedings against all individuals involved in violations of the UN Convention Against Torture. Clearly, both under US and international law, the former president is criminally responsible for adopting torture as a tool of extracting information.

Despite these strong judgments, President Obama has tenaciously vetoed the idea of prosecution, claiming that the country needs to move forward rather than look back. Can this possibly be his personal opinion? After all, he is a Constitutional scholar, and a man of principles who knows that when laws, national and/or international, are broken, there must be consequences. Politically, however, he was probably prevented from serving justice the moment he assumed the presidency.

Of course, despite what the President says or is obliged to say, the constructive way of moving forward is to face the crimes of the past so that we can create a clean slate and lay the foundation for a more just future. Otherwise, we merely dump the toxicity of our misdeeds into the subconscious arena. Since it is known that everything which remains intentionally hidden has a tendency to grow hideous, it becomes even more urgent to address past crimes. In a word, we cannot indefinitely postpone the necessary self-examination and moral purification we need as a people, and the longer we wait, the more difficult will be the inevitable hour of reckoning.

There is another, more encouraging side to this, reported by the meticulous Jane Mayer. She revealed that during the transition period for then President-elect Barack Obama, his legal, intelligence, and national-security advisers had met at the CIA's headquarters to discuss "whether a ban on brutal interrogation practices would hurt their ability to gather intelligence." Among the consulted experts, there was unanimity that to change the practices would not in any material way affect the collection of intelligence.

Consequently, on January 22, 2009, President Obama signed an executive order requiring the CIA to use only the 19 interrogation methods outlined in the United States Army Field Manual on interrogations "unless the Attorney General with appropriate consultation provides further guidance."

Ethical arguments regarding torture

Torture has been criticized for humanitarian and moral reasons on grounds that evidence extracted by torture is unreliable, and because torture corrupts individuals and institutions that tolerate it. In fact, organizations like Amnesty International argue that the universal legal prohibition is based on a philosophical consensus that abuse and torture are "repugnant, abhorrent, and immoral." Since post 9/11, however, a debate has taken place in the United States about whether torture is justified in some circumstances. People such as Professors Alan Dershowitz and Mirko Bagaric have argued that the need for information outweighs the moral and ethical arguments against torture.

This is contrary to the moral progress humankind has made, a reality confirmed especially by the UN's human rights law with its prohibition of torture and other inhumane treatment. When influential voices with considerable media exposure can make statements dismissive of those principles, it would be advisable to examine the background that encourages such individuals to see themselves and their opinions as above national and international law.

In the meantime, Robert Mueller, FBI Director since July 5, 2001, has pointed out that, despite former Bush administration claims that waterboarding has "disrupted a number of attacks, maybe dozens of attacks", there is no evidence gained by the US government that enhanced interrogation has disrupted a single attack, and no one has come up with a documented example of lives saved thanks to these techniques.

On June 19, 2009, the US government announced that it was delaying the scheduled release of declassified portions of a report by the CIA Inspector General that allegedly cast doubt on the effectiveness of the "enhanced interrogation" techniques employed by CIA interrogators.

In his 2007 book, *Beyond the Law: the Bush Administration's Unlawful Responses in the "War" on Terror,* Jordan J. Paust, Professor of International Law at the University of Houston, and a Fulbright Professor at the University of Salzburg, Austria, (see above) details the War on Terror from an international lawyer's perspective. Paust shows that the Bush Administration repeatedly and intentionally violated international law. He argues that many of these violations constituted war crimes, relative to both international and domestic law.

His evaluation is candid: "The role that several lawyers played directly in a dreadful process of denial of protections is particularly disturbing. Not since the Nazi era have so many lawyers been so clearly involved in international crimes concerning the treatment and interrogation of persons detained during war." His detailed charges show how the Bush administration is unique in American history regarding its multiple violations of laws and human decency, including the president authorizing systematic denial of the treatment of detainees as prescribed by the Geneva Conventions. Those policies were approved by lawyers at the highest levels of the US government, as well as by the Secretary of Defense and top generals.

He subsequently denounces the Bush administration's "unprincipled plan to evade the reach of law ... while seeking to avoid criminal sanctions."

Records indicate that 50,000 individuals have been detained at various times in Guantanamo Bay, at twenty-five sites in Afghanistan and seventeen in Iraq. It is safe to assume, Paust writes, that most would have been subjected to at least the cruel and inhumane treatment of captured human beings and the forced disappearance of various detained persons, though all such acts are absolutely prohibited under several treaties of the United States and customary international law.

In September 2006, President Bush publicly admitted that he had approved 'tough' interrogation tactics and a 'program' of secret detentions and secret renditions. Prof. Paust responded, saying, "The claim that the President has authority to violate international laws of war, human rights law, and domestic legislation is patently unconstitutional and unacceptable."

Truly, here is one of the strongest voices indicting a haughty group of individuals who became the absolute rulers of the United States of America and masters over life and death. Their sadistic deeds have taken us into a spiritual wilderness, into a maze of staggering crimes and horrifying inhumanities, from which no person or country can return without soul-searching, moral cleansing and regeneration.

Chapter 6

WIKI AND OTHER LEAKS

Unthinking respect for authority is the greatest enemy of truth.

~Albert Einstein

The crimes of the United States have been systematic, constant, vicious, remorseless.

~Harold Pinter

In war, the powerful never investigate their own crimes.

~Noam Chomsky

Washington is waging a war against truth.

~Julian Assange

"There has been so much growth since 9/11 that getting your arms around that – not just for the DNI (Director of National Intelligence), but for any individual, for the Director of the CIA, for the Secretary of Defense – is a challenge," claimed Defense Secretary Robert Gates in an interview with *The Washington Post.* "I'm not aware of any agency with the authority, responsibility or a process in place to coordinate all these interagency and commercial activities," he awkwardly admitted. "The complexity of this system defies description."

Growing a monster

What bloated, oversized creature is Secretary Gates referring to? What monster defying description does he have in mind? You guessed it, it's *Top Secret America,* and it can be found in *The Washington Post* under "Intelligence Investigation", the result of a two-year research project by reporters Dana Priest and Bill Arkin, published in July of 2010. Through a painstaking series of revelations, a door has been opened to a hidden world that has by all measures grown beyond control.

We are being made aware that the top-secret intelligence network the government created in response to the terrorist attacks of Sept. 11, 2001, has become "so large, so unwieldy and so secretive that no one knows how much money it costs, how many people it employs, how many programs exist within it or exactly how many agencies do the same work."

Available figures seem to confirm such statements. To get an idea of the scope of the operations as they relate to counter-terrorism, homeland security and intelligence, consider these statistics:

- 1,271 government organizations and 1,931 private companies work on the various programs.
- The network is embedded in 10,000 locations all over the continental US.
- 854,000 individuals have top-secret security clearance.
- 265,000 government contractors are doing top-secret work.
- The program devours tens of billions of dollars per year, with no real accountability.
- 33 building complexes for top-secret intelligence work are under construction or have been built since 9/11 in Washington and the surrounding area. This is the equivalent of almost three Pentagons or 22 US Capitol buildings – about 17 million square feet of space!

All that space, all those employees and all that money spent, yet, ironically, none of the "security threats" of recent years, such as would-be bombers, was captured by the vast net supposedly designed to do just that. Still, according to the ACLU's newsletter, Summer 2012, "Every day, the National Security Agency intercepts and stores *1.7 billion* international e-mails, phone calls, texts, and other electronic communications." Should it come as a surprise, then, that cavernous buildings are needed to store all that information?

At the same time, it is particularly disconcerting to learn how domestic and foreign intelligence gathering has been outsourced to private companies for profit. There is a stunning symbiotic relationship between the government and non-governmental contractors. The *Post* points out that what had been introduced as a temporary fix activated after the crimes of 9/11, has turned into such a dependency that it raises the question whether (a) the federal workforce includes too many people obligated to shareholders rather than the public interest, and whether (b) the government is still in control of its most sensitive activities.

Hundreds of thousands of private contractors working for for-profit companies are given access to top-secret documents on a daily basis. Experts have warned that the Pentagon should be much more concerned vis-à-vis any corporations that are potentially sharing classified information with other clients than they are about whistleblowers, "because the real threat to US national security is more likely to come from contractors with access to such secret information, especially since they simultaneously work for *other governments* and other corporations." (emphasis mine)

All these aspects are of vital importance because, since the war began in Afghanistan in 2001, and a second front was opened in Iraq in 2003, the reality is that "Contractors kill enemy fighters. They spy on foreign governments and eavesdrop on terrorist networks. They help craft war plans. They gather information on local factions in war zones. They are the historians, the architects, the recruiters in the nation's most secretive agencies. They staff watch centers across the Washington area. They are among the most trusted advisers to the four-star generals leading the nation's wars." (All quotes are from *Top Secret America,* Washington Post, July 2010.)

Such heavy presence of the private sector in the affairs of the Federal government is judged by most experts to be unhealthy, unmanageable and shamefully inefficient. In addition, many security and intelligence agencies do the same work, creating redundancy and waste.

Individuals who analyze documents and conversations obtained by foreign and domestic spying publish about 50,000 reports each year – a volume so large that many are routinely ignored. Indeed, one ironic fact to emerge from the investigation is that agencies are collecting so much data that they don't have enough translators or researchers to analyze it. Simultaneously, only a few officials in the Department of Defense have access to all of the top-secret activities and information.

How do all these elements combine to make the program a useful one? "We can't effectively assess whether it is making us more safe," admits Defense Secretary Robert Gates.

Perhaps you are right, Mr. Secretary. It does, however, do one thing: it quite effectively leaves one speechless. This is why, in my research concerning the topic, I was impressed with an insightful comment a reader left on one of the websites that carried the story.

"... It's absolutely appalling, and I use "appalling" because I'm not permitted to use the adjectives I'm really thinking. The objectives are suspect, the secrecy is unprecedented, the spending is outrageous, the accountability is non-existent and the accomplishments are negligible. Worst of all, it's clear that no one – absolutely no one, not the commander in chief himself – holds sufficient security clearance to be able to access all of this information and get a complete picture of what's really happening. ... You simply have to be appalled at how our tax dollars are being taken from our pockets and misused. ... This is absolute insanity on a massive scale such as the world has never seen."

Did you hear that, Mr. Orwell? Your scary *1984* is minor in comparison to the objective and size of this undertaking. Wish you were here to outline for us what life would be like in, say, 2024 – unless people wake up and reclaim their sanity, their life, and their country.

It is noteworthy that, except for a few, Americans have been almost blasé about the "breaking news" quality of this story. They seem to shrug their shoulders as if to say: After all, this is what our country needs, national security, isn't it? To which one can only reply, oh, how clever, and successful, they have been, those peddlers of disinformation and threat! And of course, the corporate media can be counted on to be a major part of the great sale. Tucson's rather large-circulation daily made only scant mention of the report and not a single letter was published in response to the shocking revelations.

In German there is a rather appropriate word for that kind of tactic: totschweigen – death by silence, or to strangle information and revelations by totally ignoring them. We can be sure that those who thrive on controlling others are adept in the art of totschweigen. (As an aside, this was also obvious in the way the *Post's* exposé was brought to the awareness of a national audience. Shortly after the publication in the summer of 2010, reporter Bill Arkin said during an interview on *Democracy Now!* that PBS would feature the story on "Frontline" in the fall. Fall came and went without the promised presentation. Then, on January 20, 2011, the producers ran a 20-minute segment, with the assurance that more would be presented "in the fall". No explanation as to why the delay.)

Meanwhile, in December of 2010, new details emerged about the "growing monster", the vast intelligence apparatus collecting data on American citizens. In another article published by *The Washington Post*, it was revealed that by using local police, state homeland security and military criminal investigators, the FBI is operating a huge database known as "Guardian". This file contains information on citizens and residents who have never committed a crime but were reported as acting "suspicious" by local police or other citizens. The file presently contains 160,000 names. Despite its large size, the FBI admitted that it has led to only five arrests and no convictions.

The *Post* further states that the FBI has stored 96 million fingerprints in Clarksburg, West Virginia, and that local law enforcement offices have started to utilize surveillance instruments, such as military-grade infrared cameras, designed for war zones.

We were introduced previously to Jane Mayer's 2008, *The Dark Side: The Inside Story of How the War on Terror Turned Into a War on American Ideals*. The exposé by *The Washington Post* makes chillingly clear that we are witnessing not only a war on American ideals, but a *secret* war on Americans.

A postscript is in order. On October 3, 2012, the Associated Press published an article on a multi-billion-dollar information-sharing program created in the aftermath of 9/11. It was written in response to a Senate report that found "improperly collected information about innocent Americans [which] produced little valuable intelligence on terrorism."

Placed under surveillance were, among others, supporters of Rep. Ron Paul, the ACLU, war protesters and advocates of gun rights. Reports on the activities of US Muslims were also widespread, and included information about books recommended by a Muslim community.

As it turned out, these reports contained no evidence of criminal activity or terrorist threats.

The lengthy, bipartisan summary is a scathing evaluation of the Department of Homeland Security and of a program that the department had held up as a crown jewel of its security efforts. Instead, it devolved into an enterprise that ballooned far beyond anyone's ability to oversee.

In the end, this program was as useless as it was costly. The DHS, meanwhile, having determined the information to be improper to disseminate, nonetheless considered it acceptable to keep the material indefinitely. The Senate panel wanted to know why, since doing so is a clear violation of the prohibition against the federal government storing information about First Amendment activities not related to crimes. Thus the civil rights of our citizens continue to be violated or ignored in what can only be called a bogus security offensive.

As this book is being readied for publication, the continuing secret machinations of the government were once again highlighted with the June 2013 disclosure of a massive mining effort by the CIA and National Security Agency of private telephone and Internet data. A former employee of the CIA and contractor for the NSA, Edward Snowden, made a stunning exposé of a spy network of mind-boggling proportions. It appears that under the rubric of "PRISM" and in the name of "security", the NSA issued a death warrant for privacy rights.

Here is Admiral Poindexter's *Total Information Awareness*, first developed after September 11, and now metastasized into *Total Spectrum Dominance*, as the US secretly monitors and mines all planetary communications.

For example, a top-secret NSA "global heat map"

shows that in March 2013 alone the agency collected 97 billion pieces of intelligence from computer networks worldwide. NSA's most frequently targeted countries appear to be Iran, Pakistan, Jordan, Egypt, Germany and India. Furthermore, the so-called "Boundless Informant" documents show that the agency collected almost three billion pieces of intelligence from US computer networks over a single 30-day period ending in March of 2013.

According to columnist Richard Silverstein, and confirmed by author James Bamford, NSA hired two secretive Israeli companies, Verint and Narus, to wiretap the US telecommunications network, which allowed for backdoor access to Microsoft, Google, Verizon, Facebook, Apple, Yahoo, Skype, AOL and YouTube.

The scope of the program is not only all-encompassing, but its sheer physical dimensions are staggering. For instance, the result of collecting billions upon billions of pieces of data has been the creation of a storage facility in Utah comprising an area of a million square feet and costing an estimated two billion dollars. The electricity required is equivalent to running a city of 66,000 on a daily basis while using 1.5 million gallons of water to cool down the system. This enormous energy is needed because the computing power necessary to process such a vast amount of information is beyond anything previously required.

"We make the East German Stasi state look like the Boy Scouts," exclaimed former *New York Times* reporter Chris Hedges in response to those mind-numbing numbers. He added, "What the security and surveillance state is doing is playing on fear and using that fear to accrue to themselves tremendous forms of power that in a civil society, in a democracy, they should never have. And that's the battle that's underway right now, and, frankly, we're losing."

Hedges fears that if we don't gain back our right to privacy and the capacity to investigate what our power elite is doing, "we can essentially say our democracy has been snuffed out." (A better term for PRISM might then be PRISON!)

Daniel Ellsberg, himself accused of treason in 1971

with the release of the Pentagon Papers, showered high praise on Snowden and his courageous moral act. "There has been no more significant disclosure in the history of our country. And I'll include the Pentagon Papers in that," he stated in an interview, then drew a chilling conclusion: "I fear for our rights. I fear for our democracy, and I think others should too. And I don't think, actually, that we are governed by people in Congress, the courts or the White House who have sufficient concern for the requirements of maintaining a democracy."

Meanwhile, the vilification of Snowden has shifted into high gear. Yet, anyone who watched the interview with him by Glenn Greenwald, who first reported the story in *The Guardian,* experienced in reality a highly intelligent young man of moral clarity and extraordinary courage. He is, in fact, a compelling, even amazing, presence.

For those of us concerned with the future of our country and the fate of the world, a final question remains: Will the revelations of a spy network of totalitarian proportions be a wake-up call shrill and alarming enough to finally shake the American people out of their slumber? Or will our country descend ever deeper into a nightmare, an oppressive maze of secrets and lies from which an exit will be extremely difficult?

I am afraid, even as I ask this rhetorical question, the latest disclosures by Snowden reported in *The Guardian* on September 11, are in some ways even more disturbing than what had been revealed thus far.

Accordingly, the NSA routinely hands over intercepted communications to Israel as part of a secret intelligence-sharing agreement. On September 12, in an interview on *Democracy Now!,* Alex Abdo, attorney with the ACLU, explained further that "The NSA was sharing what they call raw signals intelligence, which includes things like who you are calling and when you are calling, the content of your phone call, the text of your emails, your text messages, your chat messages." He added, "It sounds as though the information sharing was indiscriminate, that they handed over large amounts of information."

This was a bombshell – or should have been – were it not for the fact that the corporate media in our own country uttered nary a word about it. And Americans, unaware of the truth, were once again deprived of the opportunity to act, to stand up for their rights and the Constitution.

WikiLeaks 2010: A bombshell of a different kind

After reflecting on the latest revelations regarding US spies and secrets, let us return to an earlier event and a bombshell of a different kind. For that purpose, consider the following two statements, the first from a young, 22-year-old soldier at the time, whose conscience compelled him to reveal what is taking place behind the scenes in our terror-obsessed, world-domineering political and military establishments, and the second from the woman politician in charge of State Department affairs with the governments of the world.

Army Pfc. Bradley Manning: *"I want people to see the truth … because without information, you cannot make informed decisions as a public. … God knows what happens now … Hopefully worldwide discussion, debates, and reforms, if not … then we're doomed as a species."*

Secretary of State Hillary Clinton: *"This disclosure is not just an attack on America's foreign policy interests. It is an attack on the international community: the alliances and partnerships, the conversations and negotiations that safeguard global security and advance economic prosperity."*

In the spring of 2010, WikiLeaks shocked the world and outraged the US government when it posted a war video taken by Army helicopters showing its crew brutally gunning down two unarmed Reuters journalists and ten other Iraqi civilians, while badly injuring two children.

Over a period of time, the organization leaked some 76,000 classified US war files from Afghanistan, 400,000 from Iraq, and then began the process of releasing 250,000 diplomatic cables sent to Washington by US ambassadors and/or staff stationed around the world.

Prior to its Internet transmission, WikiLeaks made the material available to several news sources simultaneously: *The New York Times* in the US, *Der Spiegel* magazine in Germany, *The Guardian* in the UK and for the Iraq files, *Al Jazeera*, Qatar. It raises the fateful and alarming question: When and how did our country, and the US-controlled world per se, become such a breeding ground of lies, hypocrisy and deception?

A tsunami of secrets

Saturday, October 23, 2010, 3 a.m. Tucson time. I am tuned to the BBC World Service when the announcement is made that WikiLeaks founder Julian Assange is about to hold a press conference in London. The reason? WikiLeaks, his organization's website, has just begun to release some of the 400,000 classified documents dealing with US military activities in Iraq from 2004 through 2009, the largest trove of such secret files ever to be made available. He and his colleagues have done so in order to reveal the truth by publishing details of that war from the US perspective. "We hope to correct some of [the] attack on the truth that occurred before the war, during the war and which has continued on since," Assange declared.

The late Senator Daniel Patrick Moynihan, in a final letter to his constituents after 50 years of illustrious service to the nation, divulged, "The great fear I have is the enveloping culture of government secrecy. Since the end of the Cold War, the secret side of government just keeps growing." And that concern was voiced a year *prior* to September 11!

What would he say to us today in light of all those secrets and cover-ups that have marked life in Washington since?

As expected, the release of that vast collection of military documents about activities in Iraq was greeted by the Pentagon and White House with outrage. Outrage not by American citizens, but by the officials who are the perpetrators or apologists of those malevolent machinations!

Here was Assange, an extraordinarily courageous, charismatic young man, supported by an incredibly effective team, daring to take on the nearly unlimited power of the United States, unmasking lies and showing the barbaric reality of an illegal and immoral war.

Should one be surprised that officials – with Senator Joseph Lieberman leading the charge, and an always obliging press eagerly joining in – went into overdrive and spin to take attention away from the message by attempting to slay the messenger, for now, at least, metaphorically?

Apparently they see no other way to respond to the scandal. After all, denial is not an option considering that these documents are all *official* US military reports. And of course, today Pfc. Bradley Manning stands accused of being the whistleblower who passed the incriminating material on to WikiLeaks. His arrest and subsequent cruel treatment while incarcerated in solitary confinement in an Army prison, confirmed the culture of disdain for human rights prevalent in our country today.

The response of governmental and military officials has thus far made clear that secrets have been and continue to be the lynchpin of this government. According to investigative journalist Glenn Greenwald, their intense efforts to frighten challengers and whistleblowers into silence amount to saying, "Our power is unconstrained and unlimited."

Still, with WikiLeaks having released the largest trove of information about a war ever to be brought to the attention of the public, future conscientious historians will be kept busy deciphering these findings and their ramifications.

At this point, a sudden realization electrifies me: Suppose the world could have had this kind of access to documents about *all* of the wars fought in the 20th century, for instance. Surely lying and vilification was going on then as much as it is at the beginning of the 21st century with respect to Afghanistan and Iraq, not to speak of Vietnam earlier (see the Ellsberg/Pentagon Papers).

Imagine the wide-ranging benefits for humanity of such forced candor! Since truth is liberating, imagine additionally the boisterous sound of breaking chains as humankind is set free to comprehend the great issues of our time in a penetrating new light. As I have argued throughout my writings, the world is, mostly unknowingly, a prisoner of the Big Lie, a lie consisting of many branches, many roots – a network of fallacies that keeps humans entangled, unfree and in servitude.

The Afghan Logs

At the time of publication, David Leigh of *The Guardian* referred to the Afghan War Logs, saying, "The logs hold 92,000 field reports, many of them ugly and grim. The three [chosen papers] mined revelations about the cruel toll on civilians in the nine-year conflict, and about futile firefights which have cost the lives of so many western soldiers."

Official US Army documents confirm allegations previously revealed by independent correspondents and made available through alternative news sources. But beyond what was essentially already known, these logs also bring to light atrocities committed by a formerly undisclosed "black unit" of Special Forces, Task Force 373, which hunts down targets for death or detention without trial. There are more than 2,000 senior figures from the Taliban and al-Qaeda targeted on a "kill or capture" list. However, the killings, when executed, also include the deaths of numerous civilians, including children.

Details of deadly missions by TF 373 raise fundamental questions about the legality of the killings and of long-term imprisonment without trial, and especially the devastating impact on innocent bystanders. For example, one such secret raid by members of Task Force 373, designed to snag a high-ranking al-Qaeda commander believed to be running training camps in Pakistan's border region, exemplifies the method. Five rockets were launched into a group of buildings, and when forces moved into the destroyed area they found six dead insurgents and seven dead children. Al-Libi, the commander targeted, was not among them.

In 2008, the United Nations' special rapporteur for human rights, Professor Philip Alston, went to Afghanistan to investigate rumors of these extrajudicial killings. What he found was disturbing. He subsequently warned that international forces were neither transparent nor accountable and that Afghans who attempted to find out who had killed their loved ones "often come away empty-handed, frustrated and bitter."

Tom Parker, policy director at Amnesty International USA, said that the war in Afghanistan with its terrorist hit lists, counterinsurgency battles and high-tech battle gear, presents difficult questions. "It is really hard to know where assassination ends and war starts," said Parker.

The military's target list is different from a separate list run by the CIA. The two lists may contain some of the same names, but they differ because the military and CIA operate under different rules. While the military can only operate in a war zone, the CIA is allowed to carry out covert actions in countries where the US is not at war.

Despite these concerns, General David Petraeus (then head of the CIA), during a Congressional hearing in December of 2009, made it clear that the military, rather than curtail such activities, was going to increase its efforts to kill or capture enemy combatants. "There's no question you've got to kill or capture those bad guys that are not reconcilable," he insisted.

The situation was viewed quite differently by Jeremy Scahill, an investigative reporter for *The Nation* magazine, who has spent considerable time in Afghanistan on assignment. Focusing on accountability, he demanded to know in an August 30/September 6, 2010 article: "When you read in the documents [about] these assassinations, essentially of civilians, that are taking place, why is there no outrage about that? Why aren't there court-martials of the individuals responsible for these massacres? Where are the prosecutions for murder?"

In the same article, Scahill shares an email by then 22-year-old Army intelligence analyst Bradley Manning, who allegedly passed on official US documents to WikiLeaks.

As to what motivated Manning, Scahill observes: "Manning believed he was performing a public service by leaking what he did. In one chat, Manning and Lamo (the one who turned him in) are discussing Manning's passing of documents to WikiLeaks. Lamo asks Manning what his "endgame" is. Manning replies, "god knows what happens now," but then adds, "hopefully worldwide discussion, debates, and reforms, if not...then we're doomed as a species." (See above)

Citizens of the world, are you listening? These are powerful and profoundly disturbing words. "If not...then we are doomed as a species."

In a heroic act, Manning, recognizing the exceedingly dangerous situation in which humanity is caught, allowed the world a glimpse into a black hole of moral depravity. Showing the despicable wrongs committed in the course of endless war, he especially hoped to arouse the conscience of American citizens and consequently create an unstoppable wave of outrage that would result in the kind of in-depth change in Washington promised by then candidate Obama, but not yet delivered.

For that reason, let us turn once more to the beginning of his reflections when he states: "I want people to see the truth ... because without information, you cannot make informed decisions as a public." With that statement, Manning places himself in the midst of esteemed company, echoing as he does the view of the first President of the United States. In his *Farewell Address to the American People*, George Washington maintained that since the government has been created to enforce the opinion of the people, the opinion of the people should be informed and knowledgeable.

Those who choose to condemn Pfc. Manning for his action should contemplate how close this young American comes to fulfilling what Washington has described as essential: a well informed public. He did his best to bequeath us that gift in view of the deceit emanating from Washington, seat of the US government.

Beyond that, the Nuremberg War Crimes Tribunal is firmly on Manning's side since it makes clear that "individual citizens have the duty to violate domestic laws to prevent crimes against peace and humanity from occurring." Based on that statute, many young and older Germans lost their lives or received long prison terms after WWII in a process that was meant to radically expand accountability for violations committed during wartime.

Now, if we cannot prevent atrocious crimes from occurring, the next best thing is to report them so that they might be stopped and investigated. Moreover, so that citizens are informed of the schemes perpetrated by their government. This is what Manning has bravely done. We should be very grateful for such courage for our sake and the future of humanity.

A similar sentiment must have been influencing the thinking of Dallas Darling, author and correspondent for worldnews.com, writing in defense of WikiLeaks per se on Aug. 7, 2010: "Regarding the atrocities and illicit wars in Afghanistan and Iraq, we should all stand up for WikiLeaks, Assange and freedom of press and expression. This will not only help salvage a dying democracy but force America's war machine to stand down. There might someday even be a Truth and Transparency versus US Militarism and War."

Divide and rule: the death of civil society in Iraq

According to released documents, the US had received reports of more than a thousand allegations, many of them substantiated by medical evidence, of torture in Iraqi jails. Yet US authorities transferred thousands of prisoners to Iraqi custody, including almost 2,000 who were handed over to the Iraqi government as recently as July 2010. US military documents released by WikiLeaks have unanimously confirmed that such abuses against prisoners have indeed taken place.

By transferring military detainees to Iraqi control, the US appears to have knowingly violated the Convention Against Torture. The Convention proscribes signatory states from transferring a detainee to other countries "where there are substantial grounds for believing that he would be in danger of being subjected to torture."

These documents furthermore show how the US military deliberately sent Shi'a and Kurdish commandos into Sunni areas for torture, with some US officials even admitting that this strategy exacerbated sectarian violence. Concurrently, there was in effect an official military order directing US forces not to investigate cases of torture of detainees by Iraqis, an act which appears on the surface to show a pronounced lack of concern by our military about detainee abuse.

Yet, Gareth Porter, a historian and investigative journalist specializing in US national security policy, sees the matter differently. In an article first published on the Inter Press Service News Agency in November 2010, he argued that the deeper significance of the order was "part of a larger US strategy of exploiting Shi'a sectarian hatred against Sunnis to help suppress the Sunni insurgency when Sunnis had rejected the US war."

He notes that General David Petraeus was in fact a key

145

figure in developing the strategy of using Shi'a and Kurdish forces to suppress Sunnis in 2004-2005. In order to succeed, the strategy involved deploying Shi'a and Kurdish police commandos in areas of Sunni insurgency, knowing full well those commandos were torturing Sunni detainees, as documents released by WikiLeaks would eventually show.

The strategy backfired in that it contributed to the rise of al-Qaeda influence in the Sunni areas. "The escalating Sunni-Shi'a violence it produced led to the massive sectarian warfare of 2006 in Baghdad in which tens of thousands of civilians – mainly Sunnis – were killed," Porter maintains. Prior to those brutal killings, Petraeus created the first clearly sectarian Shi'a militia unit – the 2,000-man Shia "Wolf Brigade" trained by US forces – a key element of his police commando strategy. It did not take long for the Wolf Brigade to acquire its reputation for torture of Sunni detainees. The Associated Press reported the case of a female detainee in Wolf Brigade custody in Mosul who was whipped with electric cables in order to get her to sign a false confession that she was a high-ranking local leader of the insurgency.

After having driven the insurgents out of Mosul, the Wolf Brigade was deployed to Sunni neighborhoods in Baghdad, where the Association of Muslim Scholars publicly accused it of having "arrested imams and the guardians of some mosques, tortured and killed them, and then got rid of their bodies in a garbage dump…"

The war logs released by WikiLeaks include a number of reports from Samarra in 2004 and 2005 describing how the US military had handed their captives over to the Wolf Brigade for "further questioning". The idea was that the Shi'a commandos would be able to extract more information than US rules would allow.

General Martin Dempsey, who succeeded Petraeus as the commander responsible for training Iraqi security forces in September 2005, hinted strongly in an interview with Elizabeth Vargas of ABC News three months later that the US command accepted the Wolf Brigade's harsh interrogation methods as a necessary feature of using Iraqi counterinsurgency forces.

According to the documents released by WikiLeaks, the US military and the US Embassy were well aware of the grave risks that reliance on vengeful Shi'a police commandos entailed; how it would worsen sectarian tensions between Sunnis and Shi'a, and heighten the prospects of civil strife. In fact, in 2005, when John Burns of *The New York Times* asked an unnamed "senior American officer" whether the US might end up arming Iraqis for a civil war, the answer was a rather nonchalant, "Maybe."

As it turned out, the answer became a definite "Yes" as the US-sponsored Shi'a attack on the Sunnis led to al-Qaeda creating its own special unit, the Omar Brigade, to combat the Shi'a commando torture and death squads. That merciless clash led to the massive sectarian bloodletting in Baghdad in 2006, when thousands of civilians were dying every month and the country descended into chaos.

Sectarian strife or ruthless manipulation?

Before leaving this immoral, blood-soaked subject, I should add here an item gleaned from the investigative reporting of a very knowledgeable journalist. The information left me stunned, even as it confirmed long-held suspicions.

On April 29, 2006, previously noted Middle East correspondent Robert Fisk, residing in Beirut, wrote in an article for *The Independent* how 'unknown Americans' were provoking civil war in Iraq. He cites the story of "a young Iraqi man who was trained by the Americans as a policeman in Baghdad who spent 70 percent of his time learning to drive and 30 percent in weapons training. They said to him: 'Come back in a week.' When he went back, they gave him a mobile phone and told him to drive into a crowded area near a mosque and phone them. He waited in the car but couldn't get the right mobile signal. So he got out of the car to where he received a better signal. Then his car blew up."

What struck Fisk is that he had heard Iraqis tell similar stories when he reported from Baghdad. In fact, some pilgrims to holy places outside the country, he writes, talked rather freely of American tactics in Iraq.

To make the point, he notes one more example. "There was another man, trained by the Americans for the police. He too was given a mobile and told to drive to an area where there was a crowd – maybe a protest – and to call them and tell them what was happening. Again, his new mobile was not working. So he went to a landline phone and called the Americans and told them: 'Here I am, in the place you sent me and I can tell you what's happening here.' And at that moment there was a big explosion in his car."

"Just who these "Americans" might be," Fisk continues, "my source did not say." But he underlines that "in the anarchic and panic-stricken world of Iraq" many US groups are active, including "countless outfits supposedly working for the American military and the new Western-backed Iraqi Interior Ministry – who operate outside any laws or rules."

To underline how impossible it is to see through the murky machinations taking place, Fisk mentions one more factor for which he says there is no explanation: the murder of 191 university teachers and professors since the 2003 invasion and the penning of his article in 2006, that is, during a period of a mere three years.

Tragically, this would not be the end of the killings.

Charges of endangerment

Soon after the release of the incriminating documents, charges of endangering US and NATO soldiers, of "having blood on his hands", were leveled against Julian Assange and WikiLeaks by the Pentagon and pundits alike. Assange spoke about those accusations on *Democracy Now!* with Amy Goodman, August 3, 2010.

He acknowledged that his group realizes that it has the responsibility "to be careful" about publishing the names of informers, even as he stressed that, according to the Defense Department, there had been no reported incident of anyone getting hurt, much less killed, because of the publications.

"So it is a speculative charge," Assange continued, adding, "Of course, we are treating any possible revelation of the names of innocents seriously. That is why we held back 15,000 of these documents, to review that. We always use code names. … And the US has simply shown contempt for these Afghans. They never really cared about them at all – and that's why it didn't help us to try to go through this enormous quantity of material to find these names. [They] never engaged in correct security procedures to protect [their] sources in the first place, because they didn't give a damn about them."

He also insisted that it is important to understand that "many of these informers are using special forces and other parts of the military to conduct vendettas against their political or business opponents. Others are taking bribes and framing people by coming up with outlandish allegations."

The Diplomatic Cables

On its website, *The New York Times* described the release of a huge cache of diplomatic cables as serving "an important public interest, illuminating the goals, successes, compromises and frustrations of American diplomacy in a way that other accounts cannot match."

The classified documents cover correspondence between US diplomatic missions abroad and the State Department in Washington. They highlight negative perceptions of various world leaders and reveal unflattering American views about close EU allies and countries like Russia and Turkey. The thousands of cables furthermore show a sinister side to the Middle East and its rulers. There are several explosive revelations in the diplomatic notes detailing repeated calls by Arab leaders to attack "evil" Iran.

They also document the advice given by the State Department to US diplomats on how to gather intelligence and pass information on to the country's spy agencies. According to media reports, senior UN figures were the target of intelligence gathering by US diplomats.

Based on White House sources cited by a correspondent with the US website Politico, none of the documents is classified as 'Top Secret', 6% are listed as "secret" and 40% as "confidential". This indicates that the revelations are the experiences, impressions and views of a lower tier of diplomats.

One can only surmise the scope of the secrecy and intrigue that exists among the highest echelons of assorted governments.

In a statement accompanying the newest releases on Sunday, November 28, 2010, WikiLeaks' Julian Assange said, "The cables show the US spying on its allies and the UN; turning a blind eye to corruption and human rights abuse in 'client states'; backroom deals with supposedly neutral countries and lobbying for US corporations."

He further commented that by their release – the first in a series of planned steps over the next few months – "the contradictions between the US's public persona and what it says behind closed doors" will be brought to light.

However, it is not only the deception and discrepancies existing in US political circles, but the hypocrisy and duplicity of Arab leaders. Besides the Saudis' advice to the US "to cut off the head of the snake" in reference to Iran, Lebanon's Defense Minister Elias Murr offered Israel strategic military advice on how Israel could defeat Hezbollah if a new war erupted on Israel's northern border, a classified US cable shows. He suggested to the United States embassy in Beirut that in a future replay of the 2006 invasion of southern Lebanon, Israel should take care not to antagonize local Christian communities. "The Christians were supporting Israel in 2006 until they started bombing their bridges," Murr observes.

The defense minister also said he had told the army's commander at the time, Michel Suleiman – currently Lebanon's president – to keep out of the fighting "when Israel comes", adding, "I do not want thousands of our soldiers to die for no reason." In another cable he is quoted as saying, "If Israel has to bomb all of these places in the Shi'a areas as a matter of operational concern, that is Hezbollah's problem."

To place this matter in context, it is important to know that Lebanon's defense minister is charged with defending *all* of Lebanon's civilians, both Christian and Muslim. Hence, in light of the disclosures, for Mr. Murr to be inviting a foreign army to bomb civilian infrastructure in Muslim areas is an act most observers would call treason and most certainly heartless.

Perhaps not surprisingly, Elias Murr was not the only

politician to express contempt for Hezbollah or invite its destruction. Leaked documents reveal that in May 2008 Saudi Arabia proposed deploying an Arab military force supported by US and NATO naval and air power to destroy the Shi'a group led by its charismatic leader Hassan Nasrallah. This attack was necessitated, so the argument went, to prevent Hezbollah – and by extension Iran – from taking power in Beirut. The cable sent by US diplomat David Satterfield after a meeting with Saudi Foreign Minister Saud al-Faisal, indicates that then Prime Minister Fuad Siniora "strongly" supported the idea. Members of the Arab League, including Egypt and Jordan and the head of the League, were also aware of the plan.

To have such a scheme come to light reveals that some Arab politicians were inviting invasion and bombing, thus conspiring against their own citizens. Words are inadequate to describe the depth of such a betrayal.

When viewing the released documents as a whole, it becomes obvious that in today's world of diplomacy and international relations, war, security and terrorism are the most discussed items. In addition, cables dealing with Middle East governments are not only saturated with talk of terrorists, but seem to be obsessed with Iranian influence and its alleged nuclear weapons program, Hamas' staying power, and Hezbollah's popularity. Such are the addictions of leaders who rule by edict and security forces, not by the consent of their people.

There is, however, one positive revelation with respect to Iran and Australia. On December 14, 2010, *Democracy Now!* mentioned a US cable indicating that the Australian government has broken with the assessment of the US and its allies on Iran's nuclear program. It shows Australian intelligence agencies as seeing Iran's nuclear program as a "deterrent" in the face of threatened military attacks by Israel and the United States. The cable also discloses that Australian officials have raised concerns about the likelihood of a unilateral military strike on Iran and have rejected labeling Iran a "rogue state".

If this remains the official position of the Australian government, then it must be seen as one of the most encouraging developments regarding Iran and the safety of its people.

Assange the villain; Assange the hero

The outcry against WikiLeaks and its founder, Julian Assange, in the American media has been loud, harsh and unrelenting. On October 30, 2010, syndicated columnist Jonah Goldberg had a particularly offensive op-ed piece in the *Arizona Daily Star*. He disgorged his vile words under the audacious title, *Why is WikiLeaks mogul Assange still vertical?* He called aggressively for Assange's assassination, while never once addressing the real issue, namely the contents of the WikiLeaks disclosures.

Those revelations show a pattern of such cruelty and disregard for principles and values that they could, if fully disseminated and freely discussed, shake the citizens of this country out of their collective stupor. Instead, the corporate media decided en masse to ignore the message and malign the messenger. And regrettably, most Americans seem to have fallen rather quickly back into lockstep with the proverbial see no evil, hear no evil, let's get back to having fun.

Meanwhile, Assange is risking his life to publish truths passed on to him by American sources. For that, some Washington politicians want him to be tried for potential treason. How ironic! For it is WikiLeaks that has revealed to the world the intrigue and *actual* treason committed by political leaders both in this country and around the world.

While such disclosures may not be appreciated by a secretive Pentagon or evasive State Department, unmasking what is happening behind the scenes provides a vital service for the functioning of a democracy. In fact, there is no way we can ever reclaim America's initial promises without such truths. One can only hope that Assange will at some point be honored for the service he is rendering along those lines – entering dark, hazardous chambers and shining a penetrating light on grim governmental machinations, secrets and lies. Instead of engaging in spin and vilification in reaction to his courage, we ought to match his daring by pronouncing him the hero he is.

As for Goldberg's thirst for blood, two shameful wars are raw and searing enough without adding the incendiary speech of a belligerent writer.

Hacktivists to the defense

In a subsequent development, WikiLeaks supporters launched attacks against the websites of a number of companies, such as MasterCard, PayPal, Symantec and Switzerland's Postfinance, which had succumbed to US government pressure by closing WikiLeaks' accounts. This, of course, made it impossible for supporters to make contributions online.

A group of "hacktivists" operating under the label "Operation Payback" claimed responsibility for causing disruptions to the various providers. They described their efforts in a simple statement on the WikiLeaks website: "We want transparency and we counter censorship. ... This is why we intend to utilize our resources to raise awareness ... and support those who are helping lead our world to freedom and democracy."

It is encouraging to see similar views expressed by a number of other writers and voices, among them Mark LeVine, professor of history at UC Irvine and senior visiting researcher at the Center for Middle Eastern Studies at Lund University in Sweden. He maintains in an article published December 9, 2010, by Al Jazeera English online how the WikiLeaks revelations have "made it harder for Western governments to dupe their citizens into accepting potential future wars." (One can only hope that he is right, despite the fact that presently all indications are that Americans especially are as shockingly gullible and malleable as ever.)

He further argues that "No one outside of the Washington establishment and the myriad foreign leaders shamed by revelations of their penchant for hatred, hubris and pedestrian peccadilloes can seriously argue that the release of these classified documents has done anything but good for the cause of peace and political transparency. Not only have all these leaked cables shed light on the significant issues of our times, but in the future they will make it much harder for Western and Middle Eastern governments to lie to their citizens when it comes to engaging in the various 'wars on/of terror.'"

Prof. LeVine concludes with the heartfelt suggestion that the person deserving to receive the next Nobel Peace Prize is none other than the courageous Bradley Manning.

I agree, but would add Julian Assange and WikiLeaks to the list of possible recipients of that distinction, for without him and his team providing the final channel to carry the messages across the broad expanses of the Internet, the information would have remained on a CD labeled "Lady Gaga".

Playing with numbers, messing with minds

Official US military documents released by WikiLeaks show that many more Iraqis were killed than previously reported; in other words, the truth was kept hidden. This encourages a comment on an issue that has grown in significance for me the more research I do on the topic. I am referring to the tendency by the ruling powers of this world to use numbers for self-serving purposes.

In other words, in the great struggle between truth and falsehood, the proponents of falsehood have discovered the malleability of numbers as one of the more potent tools in the arsenal of their propaganda chest. We are all familiar with the aphorism that it is the victors who write the history after a war – and of whatever else they may choose. And part of that history is numbers. Yet, as we have seen, numbers can be manipulated. For those dedicated to seeking truth, it is therefore of utmost importance to ask themselves who benefits from certain "official" numbers.

If in doubt about their validity, if you suspect fraud, take these steps: If the number is very large, divide it in half. If it is rather small, double it. If nothing else, this exercise will start a new groove in your brain so that you don't have to interact with the same old figures by which people and whole nations are brainwashed. Be prepared for flashes of insight that point you in a new direction. Trust your intuition more than what "formal" documents tell you and you might just discover how many of them have been tampered with for one gain or another.

Again, if you treasure truth and your freedom, be wary of numbers! It's part of the us/them syndrome – "us" is good, "them" is always bad. We exaggerate the good *we* do and minimize the shameful. Conversely, we exaggerate the bad *they* do, and minimize their suffering.

Take, for example, the firebombing by Allied forces of Dresden just before the end of WWII, in February 1945. The "official" number of the perished, revised by a former East German "historian" after the reunification, stands presently at 25,000. Commemorating the anniversary of the catastrophe, the German version of *Deutsche Welle* broadcasting from Berlin, put the casualties at precisely that number. The English version that same evening spoke of 50,000!

Compare this to the Red Cross, which, after the firebombing, reported approximately 250,000 dead because of the enormous influx of refugees fleeing advancing Soviet troops from the far eastern parts of Germany, now Poland. The figure of 250,000 was also cited by German chancellor Konrad Adenauer (1949–1963) in an official West German government publication, *Deutschland Heute* (page 154, at footnote 2). That figure remained the accepted number for decades after the war.

There were other estimates over the years. The British author, Labor politician, one-time Cabinet Minister, and editor of the *New Statesmen,* R.H.S. Crossman, estimates upwards of 150,000 perished. His article in *Esquire Magazine*, November 1963, under the subtitle: "The long suppressed story of the worst massacre in the history of the world" gives a comprehensive account of the events from someone active in the British government at the time.

Author Kurt Vonnegut, who was a prisoner of war during the attacks, witnessed the devastation first-hand and was able to convey a sense of those 14 hours of terror in his novel *Slaughterhouse 5*. He notes, "More people died there in the firestorm, in that … single column of flame … than died in Hiroshima and Nagasaki combined." Saturation bombing using more than 700,000 incendiary bombs created the mammoth blaze, sometimes depicted as a tornado of fire.

Now, none of those who so cruelly perished in two nights of terror will be brought back to life by the correct size of the casualty figures. Yet, for us, the living, the truth matters, for without it humanity can never find genuine liberation. This is why the present estimate of 25,000 is an inexcusable fabrication. (On a personal note, I went to school with a boy who, with his 25-year-old mother, survived the inferno. However, when they emerged from the shelter, her dark hair had literally turned white overnight from the shock and terror they experienced.)

Dresden in 1939 had approximately 660,000 inhabitants. By 1945 the city's population had swelled to almost double its size due to the already noted influx of refugees fleeing advancing Soviet troops. Thus, in February 1945, Dresden was so overcrowded that all indoor places and all makeshift shelters outdoors were filled to capacity. Consequently, new arrivals were told by city officials to find a place for the night in outlying areas. One boy and his mother were among those unable to enter the city, and as he would later reflect, that strange twist of fate spared their lives.

How many perished in that beautiful city known as the "Florence of the North" will never be known, but the claim of 25,000 is an outrage. Humanity and truth deserve better.

Similarly, the Allied firestorm of Tokyo is estimated to have claimed the lives of 100,000 people. Yet, according to alternative sources, the number may have been as high as 150,000 or even more.

There is furthermore the Soviet Union and its claim of how many of its citizens were killed in WWII. I have seen in amazement the numbers climb from around 10 to 17 to 20 million. Then, some years ago, it suddenly jumped to a mind-boggling 27 million!

Yet, in the early 1960s, when I lived in the Philadelphia area, an elderly Russian gentleman who had fled the country after the Bolsheviks seized power, showed me a copy of *Pravda*, the Soviets' official newspaper. On the front page was a huge headline proclaiming that, according to Stalin himself, the number of Soviet citizens who lost their lives in the war was 7.5 million. The date of the publication was, I believe, 1947, and one can only surmise that Stalin had his own enigmatic political reasons for the stated number of war dead.

Still, any serious student of history must ask how the

much later grotesquely inflated number had come about. Might it be that the 27 million figure actually contains the approximately 20 million who perished in Stalin's death camps known as gulags? That possibility takes on even greater significance when considering that, after the demise of the Soviet Union, a powerful group from the old regime successfully blocked any attempt to have Stalin's collaborators and executioners brought to trial for their heinous crimes. A country was thus deprived of the kind of catharsis only truth and justice make possible.

Whatever the reason, in this case and all others, it is important to remember that numbers can be fabricated. Therefore, let the wise be aware. Statistics can be exploited for various gains – for creating collective guilt, for garnering sympathy, for extorting money, for keeping hatred alive, for stoking the fires of fear. There is an entire numbers industry at work in our world, distorting truth for the sake of control and exploitation. Hence, when numbers come before your eyes, pause and ask questions: For whose benefit or detriment is this large/small number? Who gains, who loses because of it?

In addition, remember: what applies in general also has validity when it comes to numbers: The Big Lie is most savagely at work every time people are not allowed to ask questions, but are forced to accept the authorized version of things. Worse, each time someone gets too close to the truth, he or she will be attacked and vilified. That threatening possibility is what makes manipulating numbers so easy – and presents such a hindrance to arriving at the truth.

Magic and reality

This leads me to what, in my view, is a related subject, the topic of magic – yes, as in hocus-pocus. In a study at Durham University in 2008, experts confirmed what many of us have known: magicians are very adept at understanding human nature. Co-authored by Dr. Gustav Kuhn, from the university's Psychology Department, who is also a practicing magician, the results explain: "Magic is one of the oldest art forms in the world and relies on people's ignorance of its methods."

He draws attention to three key techniques magicians use to manipulate perception. The first is known as *misdirection*, whereby seeing that certain things are happening is prevented by distracting people's attention. Which means unless you specifically attend to an event, you just don't see it.

The second is known as *illusions:* what we see is what we believe the situation to be. Reality is based on our expectations, rather than what is really out there. Because of this subjective perception, magicians can manipulate expectations so that individuals perceive things that haven't actually happened.

The third element is called *forcing*. It contains techniques that can influence our choice, our free will, without our being aware of what is occurring.

If you wonder why I am including this information, let the answer be straightforward: Post 9/11, the American public was manipulated by political magicians of the shrewdest kind. Recall the intense maneuvering of the Bush/Cheney administration with its claims of "yellow-cake" and WMDs in the lead-up to the illegal invasion of Iraq.

Moreover, because of entrenched power, the show continues. A little less obviously, perhaps, but no less effectively.

As for those interested in coming closer to the truth, for those yearning for liberation from lies and deceptions, WikiLeaks is a kind of miracle, an unexpected rescuer, to help humanity find its way back from the dark side. We ignore its revelations at our own peril.

Chapter 7

SEPTEMBER 11ᵀᴴ REVISITED

Then the lie passed into history and became truth.
>~*George Orwell, "1984"*

Those who can make people believe in absurdities can make them commit atrocities.
>~*Voltaire (attributed)*

Dissent is the highest form of patriotism.
>~*Thomas Jefferson*

We must neglect nothing that could give the truth a chance of reaching us.
>~*John Stuart Mills*

Before completing arguments and reflections on the specifics of 9/11, I shall once again return to the topic, but this time from a totally different perspective and thanks to information and insights garnered from other than governmental sources, or from what has turned out to be a largely controlled media. I feel compelled to include these (a) for the sake of serving truth, and (b) because, without them, a major part of my own awakening would not be included in this series of books on personal and societal renewal.

Explosive exposés

Like most Americans, I accepted in general the US government's explanation, confirmed by the 9/11 Commission, of what took place on September 11, 2001. As pointed out in previous chapters, what I differed on were the motives for the attacks.

As it turned out, however, my initial acceptance was

purely provisional. During the years that followed, a shift took place in my comprehension, thanks to an article or a book here, a conversation there, an interview caught, a DVD watched. Something did not make sense, was incongruent, implausible, feeding doubt and raising questions. It felt at times like I was indeed encountering Joseph Goebbels' "A lie too big to be disbelieved".

Then came the final confirmation, a DVD modestly titled, *September 11ᵗʰ Revisited.*

A concerned citizen had asked me to reconsider 9/11 once more by receptively watching and listening to news reports, the "Breaking News" of that incredible morning, with broadcasts from New York City by all the commercial stations: ABC, CBS, NBC, CNN, Fox.

The footage was literally a bombshell: Exploding, collapsing buildings, references by news anchors to "controlled demolitions", screaming, traumatized people, massive clouds of smoke and pulverized concrete across lower Manhattan and beyond, symbolically shrinking the proud Statue of Liberty to an insignificant miniature version.

It was staggering. *This is it,* a voice in me sobbed! Indeed, as I witnessed the destruction, saw the utter chaos and confusion, heard the desperate cries, sensed again the stupefying shock and pain, I realized with a start that the truth had been with us from day one. It was the government that had twisted it into the biggest lie ever told.

But I am leaping prematurely to a conclusion.

First I would recommend that all Americans, if not all citizens of the world, see this retrospective documentary of 9/11 and watch for themselves the news footage from those early hours of the catastrophe, as they fill the screen with scenes seemingly straight from Dante's *Inferno.* Visually overwhelming, they are transmitted interspersed with incredulous voices and the stunned reaction of news anchors and reporters at the scene.

What powerfully stands out from all those comments following the first hours of bewilderment and horror, are, as noted, the many references to "controlled demolitions". At the same time, firemen, rescue workers and survivors, many caked in dust and blood, emphasize words like "a huge explosion" and "a very loud explosion" as they speak of various sections of the buildings before collapse. Some explosions, they report, occurred in the basement even before the structures fell!

Eyewitnesses and First Responders

When I began to grasp the significance of what was being revealed by revisiting the initial images of the 2001 trauma, I feverishly started to take notes, all the while telling myself: Listen to what these eyewitnesses are saying, recognize what your own eyes are seeing! This is the real thing, the unadulterated story of 9/11 captured on film by the leading television news channels of the United States the moment it occurred.

The following mosaic was created by specific responses to the event, which, even while taking place, was described by Peter Jennings of ABC News as "defying belief".

Eyewitness 1: "The lobby looked as though a bomb had exploded; ten by ten marble panels had blown out…the chandelier shook…"

Eyewitness 2: "There was a loud explosion coming from the lower basement/boiler room, and then a man emerged dazed and bloody, with skin torn from his arms and face…."

Survivor 1: "There was a heavy-duty explosion, then everything went black…"

Survivor 2: "We were working our way down, got to 8th floor – there was a big explosion…"

Female reporter: "The Fire Marshall told us if there was a 3rd explosion, this building might not last."

Fox News: "It sounded like an explosion…it sounded like gunfire—bang, bang, bang—three big explosions … a huge explosion…"

Firefighters: "Like they had detonated, floor by floor, boom boom boom all the way down."

Commentator: "Cars were turned over by the force of the explosion …"

TV reporter: "Huge explosion, raining debris on all of us... knocked everybody over... "

CNN: "There has just been a huge explosion ... almost like a mushroom cloud..."

ABC's Peter Jennings: "The Tower ... just collapsing on itself; we have no idea what caused this ... anybody who's ever watched a building being demolished on purpose...You have to get at the under-infrastructure of the building to bring it down."

Jennings, continuing: "We can all remember watching an old building being demolished – very careful operation to make sure a building comes down safely – stunning to see these things come down..."

Dan Rather, CBS: "It looks like one of those scenes of an old building being purposely dynamited and blown up."

ABC: "The 2nd building just collapsed as if a demolition team set it off; it just came down on itself and it is not there any more."

Peter Jennings to reporter at the scene when the second tower collapses: "The whole building has collapsed? Then, still incredulous: "The whole building has collapsed??"

"This defies belief..." he finally mutters.

Female Reporter: "I spoke to the Chief of Safety for the NY Fire Department ... and city officials think there were devices planted in the buildings."

Frantic voice of a woman: "It sounded like the 4th of July ... you heard a big explosion before the building fell; sounded like the finale to the fireworks on the 4th of July."

Fox News: "There was another big explosion and the 2nd tower just collapsed."

Rescuer: "All of a sudden, out of nowhere, you hear a clap like thunder, see windows blast out, shock waves ... there was black smoke..."

Don Rather commenting once again on the collapse: "It's reminiscent of those pictures we've all seen too much on TV before of buildings deliberately destroyed by well placed dynamite."

Ten days later, Governor Pataki, being interviewed by a

reporter: "The entire concrete was *pulverized*. The dust was two to three inches thick and it covered huge areas. It looked like a foreign planet…"

Finally, there remains the biggest mystery of them all: WTC Building 7. Owner Larry Silverstein: "The fire chief said he couldn't contain the fire, so we made the decision to pull."

To pull is slang for controlled demolition, and it obviously is not something that can be decided on the spur of the moment. Moreover, there were only two relatively small fires burning, visible on two floors out of forty-seven, and the structure had not been hit by an airplane.

Clearly, the disappearance of WTC-7 at near free-fall speed is a "mystery", a hot item, in other words. In fact, maybe *too* hot, because, incredibly, it was not even mentioned by the 9/11 Commission!

I reiterate: one does not have to be a conspiracy theorist to be struck by what one sees and hears dating back to that fateful morning. "It looks like one of those controlled demolitions"… "There was another big explosion."

Now you hear it, again and again ---- and then it is gone. And with it the old world, the world of laws and rules and human decency…

Unanswered Questions

Although huge amounts of dust and debris descended when the Twin Towers and Building 7 fell, symbolically obscuring sight and clarity, not everyone stayed permanently blinded, especially with respect to what is paramount: moral vision. Those who regained their inner balance, such as Architects and Engineers for 9/11 Truth, Professor David Ray Griffin (a Process Theologian), Professor Michel Chossudovsky (Professor of Economics), and an impressive number of others, have since lectured and written about the event and the implausibility of some of the official explanations. Their final conclusion? The *real* conspiracy theory is the official story given by the United States government and rubberstamped by the 9/11 Commission.

For individuals inclined to cast doubt, if not derision,

on those who question the official version of events, let us remember that when the Freedom of Information Act was signed into law, it retroactively confirmed what investigative minds had long known: the US government lies.

Let us further be aware that after 9/11, the government can deny certain requested information relevant to "national security" as once it could protect secrets in "the interest of national defense or foreign policy." Needless to say, those exemptions do create problems, as they shield certain governmental records from scrutiny, thus interfering with the public's "right to know".

As to 9/11, here are some questions we should all ponder, and demand answers to:

1. Why was the airspace over the United States of America left without defenses that day, allowing for the supposed hijackers of four airplanes to commit their atrocities?

2. Who prevented the greatest military power in history from protecting its citizens from a mind-boggling catastrophe?

3. Why was the Pentagon, the most protected office complex in the world, left without defenses even after the attacks on the Twin Towers had become known?

4. How could the massive amount of concrete contained in the tallest buildings in the world have become *pulverized*, reduced to fine dust two to three inches deep and scattered all over the city and beyond?

5. How could relatively small fires from the kerosene of two airplanes, giving off black smoke (a sign of an oxygen-starved burn), have melted the great steel structures and caused their collapse at near free-fall speed?

6. What did all those very loud explosions signify, especially those in the basement of the buildings? Might those sounds have been extremely powerful explosives planted in advance to facilitate the collapse?

7. Why was there still molten metal at the bottom of the pit six weeks (!) after the fall of the towers?

These are only a few of the most obvious inquiries that should be made. Read any of Professor David Ray Griffin's books (see below) and you will quickly come up with a hundred others. Above all, make the effort to watch the DVD: *September 11th Revisited* (available from Amazon.com) and let yourself be riveted … and possibly galvanized.

Urgent: a new investigation

Because there are so many unanswered or inadequately answered questions, at a minimum, the American people and, indeed, the citizens of the world, need a new and impartial investigation. Anyone who calls the previous one "impartial" has done no independent thinking or heard anyone else but government-vetted experts/witnesses, all of whom were approved by the White House's permanent director of the investigation, Mr. Philip Zelikow.

A new investigation would have to be conducted openly and broadcast nationally. Every American citizen, every member of the human race, should have access to these proceedings per radio or television, as well as the print media.

During all proceedings, architects, engineers, investigators and authors who have declared the official story as "implausible" and have risked everything to serve the truth as they see it, should be invited to express their views.

Above all, Mr. Bush, Mr. Cheney and Mr. Rumsfeld and all the men and women supposedly in charge of protecting this country and its citizens must be subpoenaed to appear in court to testify. (Recall, the 9/11 Commission sought to have the President of the United States do just that but he declined unless his Vice President would be there with him! It can only be assumed that Mr. Bush's handlers must have been quite nervous about what a rather unsophisticated president might divulge. Before long, of course, the request was quietly dropped.)

The judges presiding over such an in-depth look cannot be retired politicians, but must be non-political experts from the great centers of learning in this country – men and women of impeccable reputation and high moral standards. Present also should be observers from every nation, especially those that lost citizens on that fateful day, reported to be 372 casualties from 90 countries. Openness, honesty and accountability will have to be the guiding lights of such a commission.

An idealist's dream? Possibly, even probably. In fact, I rather suspect both the political Right and Left would fiercely oppose such a deal, the former because even to just imply the Bush administration is responsible for such an awesome crime would be considered "sacrilegious", and the latter because of the apprehension of what it might reveal and whom it could end up indicting. In short, too many sacred cows are at stake for either wing's level of comfort.

At the same time, if an inquiry were to reveal that the official story is true, would that not be a relief? After all, it would proclaim that the government of the United States was honest, that it can be trusted, and that every doubt could forever be put to rest.

If, on the other hand, the investigation would confirm that the official story of 9/11 was a cover-up, indicating complicity at the highest echelons of the US government, how would the American people and the people of the world react? Would they allow that truth to set them free? Or would all hell break loose? Yet, would not that hell be preferable to the hell of a nuclear holocaust, which hangs over us as a constant threat due to a prevailing cult of deceit, death and destruction – all made possible by the atrocities of 9/11?

I believe what happened on that day is the most reality-shattering event in human history. People react differently to such devastating moments – some are forever silenced and compliant; others continue to be highly critical in their quest for truth. For the latter, Wendell Berry, tiller of the soil and wise man of letters, has recommendations worth contemplating: "Protest that endures is moved by a hope far more modest than that of public success. Namely the hope of preserving qualities in one's heart and spirit that would be destroyed by acquiescence."

Clearly, at risk in all this is not only the collective destiny of humanity, but the fate of every individual soul.

There is a final, undeniable fact: 9/11 took place under the Bush administration's watch. That such a crime could be committed against the people of the United States shows clear dereliction of duty on the part of those who have sworn to protect this country against all enemies, domestic or foreign. Regardless of who the terrorists were that day, why has no one in the government been held accountable? This especially in light of the various reports that substantial forewarnings were ignored, and employees who sought to draw attention to them were routinely dismissed.

Of equal importance are the latest developments in the saga of September 11. On its 10th anniversary, Former Senator Bob Graham of Florida called for a reopening of the 9/11 Commission to investigate new evidence pointing to a possible Saudi connection with some of the hijackers. This is because telephone records show that a wealthy young Saudi couple had ties to Mohamed Atta and at least ten other al-Qaeda suspects. Just a week before 9/11, they fled their home in a gated community in Sarasota, Florida, leaving behind three cars and nearly all of their possessions. Although the FBI was tipped off about them, the information was never passed on to the 9/11 Commission.

Beyond that, a former FBI agent, in a newly published book, has accused the CIA of deliberately withholding photographs and information about two al-Qaeda members living in the United States before the Sept. 11 attacks. The agent, Ali Soufan, writes that the CIA rejected repeated FBI requests for information before 9/11 about possible al-Qaeda operatives. (*Democracy Now!* 9.12.2011) Those of us who recognized some time ago that the government was not telling the truth about 9/11, see in these latest developments more signs of secrecy and cover-ups.

As to the individuals who have had their suspicions, none has ever claimed to know exactly what happened and why on that day or during the years it must have taken to plan for such a monumental assault. This is why a new and true investigation is essential. Even if it did not reveal the full truth, it would at least create serious doubt in the minds of enough people to begin to break the spell of the Big Lie. Leo Tolstoy has written, "You need only free yourself from falsehood and your situation will inevitably change of itself." We are in desperate need of a changed situation.

Un-American behavior

In the summer of 2010, a new and unexpected twist was added to the trauma of 9/11 – the planned construction of an Islamic community center with mosque in a decrepit, vacated building that has stood empty for over ten years. The structure is located two city blocks from ground zero.

The opposition was stirred into a frenzy by a New York City right-wing agitator named Pamela Geller and her *Atlas Shrugs* blog. On May 6, she posted an essay with the warped headline: *Monster Mosque Pushes Ahead in Shadow of World Trade Center Islamic Death and Destruction.*

The ensuing vehemence of primarily right-wing demagogues (with a few self-serving Democrats tossed into the mix) led to outlandish historical comparisons designed to generate fear and hatred in gullible citizens.

That a number of Democratic leaders also unmasked themselves in this case as purely expedient politicians does not bode well for our country. Even the President, after making an unequivocal statement in defense of the Constitution and Freedom of Religion, seemed to backtrack enough the next day to elicit concerns from those who yearn for a leader unafraid of conflict, and willing to courageously stand for what is right.

In the end, the traction this case and its intense fear mongering found in the mainstream media has revealed that despite the initial denials by the Bush administration, 9/11 is seen by many American citizens as intrinsically connected with the religion of Islam. And nothing confirms that more than a piece of T-shirt propaganda, haughtily proclaiming: "All I need to know about Islam I learned on 9/11." Sounds like 9/11 was the needed "catastrophic event" to demonize and declare war on Islam, doesn't it?

This was underlined in particular by the appearance of one of Europe's most racist politicians, a man who rejects all things Islam and loathes all Muslims – Dutch Parliamentarian Geert Wilders. He was invited to rile up the crowd at the Four Seasons in New York City – and that is just what he did.

When Daisy Khan, the wife of Feisal Abdul Rauf, a Sufi and imam of the proposed Islamic Center, was asked by Amy Goodman what her fears were, she replied that she had no fear for herself, then added, "I fear for my country."

So do I. So do millions of other Americans.

Ironically, at the time the controversy broke, Imam Rauf was on a US government-sponsored goodwill trip to the Middle East, in which his assignment was to convince Muslims that the US is not anti-Islam!

Outcomes of 9/11 to date

As I have elaborated before, the colossal crime has given the seen and unseen rulers in Washington carte blanche to generate an endless war on/of terror, while allowing for the worldwide invasion of privacy, global tracking of money and information, total surveillance, "extraordinary rendition" and torture. Every nation which does not want to experience the wrath of the United States has to comply with its dictates. Total Spectrum Dominance has become, by all measures, a stunning display of raw power across every corner of the globe.

The progenitor of this and other aberrations is 9/11, an event which, in the lexicon of independent thinkers, has already been registered as the most heinous crime ever, a betrayal by a government of its own people that has no equal in human history.

Now, how is all this perceived in the Muslim and particularly the Arab world, where more than anywhere else, the people have had to bear the consequences of that cataclysmic occurrence?

In a "Memo from Cairo" in *The New York Times*, dated September 2009, Michael Slackman reported on the general view in the Arab world as to who is responsible for 9/11. He noted, not without frustration, that most people persist in not believing the official US government story. Aiming to show how "bizarre" such "conspiracy theories" are, he writes:

(1) Again and again, people said they simply did not believe that a group of Arabs – like themselves – could possibly have waged such a successful operation against a superpower like the US. But they also said that Washington's post 9/11 foreign policies proved that the United States and Israel were behind the attacks, especially with the invasion of Iraq.

(2) The broad view here is that even before Sept. 11, the United States was not a fair broker in the Arab-Israeli conflict, and that it then capitalized on the attacks to buttress Israel and undermine the Muslim Arab world.

(3) "They went against Arabs and against Islam to serve Israel, that's why," is the opinion of Zein al-Abdin, 42, an electrician. Similarly, Hisham Abbas, 22, [who] studies tourism at Cairo University argues, "And look at what happened after this – the Americans invaded two Muslim countries. They used 9/11 as an excuse and went to Iraq. They killed Saddam, tortured people. How can you trust them?"

Slackman responds, saying, "That such ideas persist represents the first failure in the fight against terrorism – the inability to convince people here that the United States is, indeed, waging a campaign against terrorism, not a crusade against Muslims." (I would interject here that if it is the aim to convince people in the Muslim world of our good will, this effort experienced a real setback with the already mentioned venomous attacks perpetrated by individuals and groups, including the Jewish Anti-Defamation League, against the proposed Islamic Center.)

Finally, what explanation does Mr. Slackman give for those views, offered with "casual certainty – and no embarrassment" as he characterizes the response? "It is a reflection of how they view government leaders, not just in Washington, but here in Egypt and throughout the Middle East. They do not believe them. The state-owned media are also distrusted," he concludes.

Is Mr. Slackman implying that, by contrast, all of us believe our government leaders, and everyone trusts the media? Surely, he can't be serious – not in view of the fact that his own paper, *The New York Times*, had to issue an apology for spreading lies concerning Iraq's nonexistent WMDs prior to the invasion of 2003. But, of course, not until the paper first zealously advocated for preemptive war, and continued to support it until it had been declared "Mission Accomplished".

What Mr. Slackman needs to know is that since George W. Bush and his NeoCons came to power, many of us think about government and the corporate media in much the same way as citizens of Cairo, Egypt, do of theirs. And that suspicion persists even with a new administration, because Mr. Obama himself seems constrained by forces beyond his control from fulfilling his "Yes we can" promise of fundamental change.

To remain silent is to acquiesce

As I stated at the beginning of this chapter, it was architects, engineers, and professors whose impressive knowledge and startling explanations for what occurred on 9/11 first spun my consciousness into a dramatically new direction. Any remaining hesitation was then put to rest by watching the DVD *September 11th Revisited,* referred to in detail above.

At this time, I can only add that the triumph of those who manufactured 9/11 has been their ability to convince the American people this is a free and independent nation. In reality, usurpation on all levels of influence was fully set in motion with the 9/11 attacks and their aftermath. This fact is considerably blurred by the illusion of what are in essence empty rights: the right to make money, to go shopping, to travel, to have fun, to experience instant gratification; in brief, to indulge in all things desired.

This invitation to pander to every pleasure of the senses, from drink to drugs to sex to gambling, is indeed deceiving many into thinking they still possess all the liberties granted by the Constitution. Read any newsletter issued by the American Civil Liberties Union, however, and you will soon find your trust misplaced. Freedom of speech, freedom of the press, freedom of assembly? Think again – or better yet, test it for yourself. You may be shocked to discover, just as investigative reporter Jane Mayer did, that the war on terror actually turned into a war on American ideals.

But let me return to my statement about the primary "freedoms" so enticingly highlighted these days – the freedom to make money and the freedom to spend it. Even as they are offered, and with them all the excesses of consumerism in seductive television ads, citizens are also relentlessly indoctrinated to believe that they are perpetually under threat from another attack by terrorists.

At the same time, of course, government officials inform the public that no military expenditure, including the sacrifice of young soldiers, is too large a price to pay to combat those "terrorists" anywhere in the world, but especially in Muslim countries, so that "we don't have to fight them in the streets of our cities."

Controlled and pacified at home, and eagerly willing to fight an endless war abroad – that is the triumph of those who executed September 11, 2001.

I recently gave *September 11th Revisited* to a new acquaintance. When she returned the DVD, she spoke of her instant realization that we had all been duped. "I just cried," she confessed. "And then I realized I had to share this with everyone on my email list," she somberly added. Naturally, the response of most was quite negative, even hostile. Truth inevitably gets that kind of treatment whenever and wherever people are not ready for it.

Those who committed the hideous crime of 9/11 shocked and traumatized the American people so thoroughly that they were able to achieve much of their most desired goal: worldwide war on terrorism. Moreover, by succeeding in branding Islam "a violent religion" in the eyes of many, militarists have indeed been able to wage a barely disguised war on Islam. And from what we are learning, fundamentalist US chaplains are doing their best to indoctrinate vulnerable soldiers that this is indeed a modern-day crusade.

Today the destruction of two Muslim countries is by all measures complete. But there remains one more nation the dominance-addicted have in their crosshairs: Iran.

We can't undo the horrors inflicted on millions of innocent people over the last decade, but perhaps by knowing the *real* mastermind behind 9/11, we can avoid that looming catastrophe, the one with the greatest potential for escalating into World War III.

Being enlightened and becoming galvanized will allow us to demand of our present government not only a new direction, but equally, nothing less than justice for the horrendous crimes committed.

The future lies in our hands and in those of all humanity. Yet, none of us can choose wisely unless our feet are firmly planted on the sacred ground of truth. And that ground was devastated on 9/11, to be replaced by the synthetic turf of lies. Should it come as a surprise then that today our country stands divided against itself? Truth alone is the rock on which all people of goodwill can stand together, strong and united.

Here is one more item that might lead us closer to the truth. It concerns the supposed mastermind of 9/11. Theologian David Ray Griffin writes in *Christian Faith and the Truth Behind 9/11*, published by Westminster John Knox Press, that Osama bin Laden denied having anything to do with the attacks, and the Taliban (who actually had fairly good relations with Washington, being in conversation about a possible natural gas pipeline across the region) even informed the Bush administration that it would hand bin Laden over – if proof of his guilt could be provided! The administration chose not to respond but attacked the Taliban and with it the entire country of Afghanistan instead.

Finally, here is a factoid that should make us think … and wonder. On January 8, 2010, Rudy Giuliani, mayor of New York City on 9/11, defended former President George Bush's record on terrorism, saying the country was not subjected to domestic terror attacks when he was in office. "We had no domestic attacks under Bush…" he insisted on ABC's Good Morning America.

Giuliani's comments are similar to those of former White House Press Secretary Dana Perino, who told Fox News in November of 2009, "We did not have a terrorist attack on our country during President Bush's term." Was this amnesia or a Freudian slip?

A litany of consequences

On March 30, 2011, Al Jazeera English Online carried a report that highlighted the growing discrimination in daily life faced by Muslim citizens of the United States. This manifests itself in violence, vandalism and arson, a US Congressional panel was told.

Earlier that month, Republican congressman Peter King of New York held hearings on the "radicalization in the US Muslim community". Amnesty International, alongside a coalition of 50 other organizations, described the proceedings as resembling Senator Joe McCarthy's campaign against those suspected of having communist sympathies in the 1950s. Speakers said that evidence of anti-Muslim bigotry included inflammatory remarks made by elected public officials.

Republican Senator Lindsey Graham, on the other hand, told the Congressional panel he supported "Muslim rights" – but called on Muslims to do more "to protect the United States from attack". "Get in this fight," he said. "The front lines of this war are in our own back door and our own neighborhoods."

Muhammed Malik, a Muslim-American community advocate in Florida, commented that these are signs of "wild manifestations of an increasingly rabid Islamophobia which aims to cause division and mobilize the fear vote in 2012."

Endless warfare, endless questions

Hardly a day goes by when I do not think of the immensity of what occurred on 9/11 and how it changed our world. In the Preface to these writings, I deliberately contrast 9/11 with another history-altering event of 2000 years ago in order to show that there is nothing insignificant, much less inconsequential, about that day in September 2001 and how it impinges every moment on the life of the whole of humankind.

Meanwhile, the more I contemplate the story told by the US government, the more I see the entire scenario as preposterous, a play written for the Theater of the Absurd. And yet, nearly everyone bought a ticket to it, hoping to gain some understanding – distraught and bewildered as most of our citizens were, this writer included.

While I recommend for details on the subject the meticulous work of Prof. Griffin, I would here simply invite the reader to consider once again these simple basics: four supposedly hijacked airliners are crossing American airspace undetected by the most sophisticated defense system in human history, exposing hapless passengers, the tallest towers in the world and the mighty Pentagon, to a wretched fate. All this while the impenetrable NORAD (North American Aerospace Defense Command) could not be relied upon to fulfill the purpose for which it was created and funded because it was nowhere to be found! Maneuvers, far from the scene, were supposedly being conducted that morning, with not a single plane able to respond. Who is accountable for that colossal failure, if indeed it was one?

Then there is the Pentagon, the most fortified and protected edifice on the planet. It too, astonishingly, was left unprotected that day so that a deliberately crashed airplane, not from above but from a near ground position, was able to set part of it on fire. And after it was already well known that the Twin Towers had been targeted.

Truly, it takes an extraordinary naiveté, excessive gullibility, or better yet, a traumatized mind, to accept such a fabrication. And yet, we all did, even those brilliant architects, engineers, and professors who are now proving to an ever-increasing number of us that we were deceived.

Such is the power of a lie too big to be disbelieved. Yet, there is another, counteracting belief, which says, once Americans know the truth, they do the right thing. This chapter is written in the hope of increasing the required knowledge in order to facilitate just such a deed.

"Extra, extra!"

On May 1st, 2011, the news flashed across the globe that Osama bin Laden had been eliminated by American Special Forces in Pakistan. A wide variety of comments from various "experts" have since incessantly crowded the airwaves.

All of them came in response to the President of the United States, Barack Obama, as he faced the cameras and the nation, saying, "Justice has been done."

Mr. President, since when is extrajudicial killing considered justice, especially after it was revealed that the suspect was unarmed?

In any case, now that bin Laden has been assassinated instead of captured, no court, and none of us, will ever hear the man's own testimony about 9/11. How convenient for those who honor neither truth nor justice!

Imagine, on the other hand, if there would have been a public trial, compelling all to "speak the truth, the whole truth, and nothing but the truth". While such proceedings might not have brought to light the whole truth, we would certainly be far better informed than we are now.

Knowing this, we have to ask: Why did the government of the United States choose to slay the most notorious figure so far of the 21st century and then hurriedly dump his body into the sea?

September 11, 2011

Ten years ago the news flashed across the airwaves of attacks on the World Trade Center, the Pentagon, and later the crash of United flight 93 near Shanksville, Pennsylvania.

Once again the great propaganda machine is heard operating at high decibels, once again emotional exploitation is intense. This includes news of a possible, but "unconfirmed" terrorist plot. The memory and the fear must not be allowed to fade lest Americans become complacent. After all, US soldiers are still fighting the "terrorists" abroad and are dying in Afghanistan and Iraq.

On September 9, in advance of the commemorative events, *The Washington Post* published an article that caught my attention. It deals with an incident kept secret for an entire decade by its central character, Lt. Heather Penney, now Major Penney. The story takes us to Andrews Air Force Base, just outside of Washington, D.C. on September 11, 2001.

What struck me after reading and contemplating the article is how easy it would be to miss statements within the report that are simply incredible. Why? Because most individuals would probably read the information in the light of its ominous headline, "Her suicide mission: Take down flight 93 with an unarmed F-16."

It's quite an emotional hook which makes objectivity that much harder, not the least because there is also a good-sized photo of a rather attractive woman with several fighter planes in the background.

Nonetheless, here is what I noticed. (Keep in mind this is Andrews Air Force Base, one of the key places on which the defense of our country, and definitely Washington, DC itself, depends.)

Quote 1: "Because the surprise attacks were unfolding in that innocent age…" (Since when can a world of nuclear weapons ever be designated as an "innocent age"?)

Quote 2: "The first counterpunch the U.S. military prepared to throw at the attackers was effectively a suicide mission." (A suicide mission leading to the gruesome deaths of innocent airline passengers? Why were no fighter jets from the next nearest Air Force Base called upon in order to force the supposed hijackers to land?)

Quote 3, a lengthy one: "On that Tuesday, they had just finished two weeks of air combat training in Nevada. They were sitting around a briefing table when someone looked in to say a plane had hit the World Trade Center in New York. When it happened once, they assumed it was some yahoo in a Cessna. When it happened again they knew it was war." (Not two missiles, not two bombs, but two civilian airplanes – and they knew it was war?! Yet, Air Force personnel, as it turned out, were clueless as to what to do.)

Quote 4: "But the surprise was complete. In the monumental confusion of those first hours, it was impossible to get clear orders. Nothing was ready. The jets were still equipped with dummy bullets from the training mission." (Did Major Penney really mean to say "monumental confusion" lasting for hours?! Are we talking here about the US Air Force?

Moreover, does that mean *every* aircraft designated to defend our country had been on maneuvers for two weeks, leaving the nation unprotected?)

Quote 5: "As remarkable as it seems now, there were no armed aircraft standing by and no system in place to scramble them over Washington."

"Remarkable"? It defies belief! But so it shall always be with fairytales.

part two

A different world is possible

Chapter 8

CROSSROADS REFLECTIONS

There comes a time
(perhaps this is one of them)
when we have to take ourselves more seriously
   or die...
        ~Adrienne Rich

We seek not rest but transformation.

        ~Marge Piercy

The starting point for a better world is the belief that it is possible.
Civilization begins in the imagination.

   ~Norman Cousins

After experiencing being lost in a wilderness which introduced us to humanity's terrifying capacity for being inhuman; after visiting dungeons of despair and chambers of depravity, and after hearing the drums of war and the screams of the tortured, it's time to concentrate on the other side of what is humanly possible: goodwill, kindness, generosity – the path of the heart, the way of love, justice and peace.

No doubt, this is a considerable leap, but after spending seemingly never-ending hours in oppressing darkness, it's time to step into the light, and to inhale the clean air of genuine life with its boundless opportunities to love and be free.

I am juxtaposing these two portrayals of human potentials because I believe being human does not have to be such a disgraceful affair. Being human can be noble and praiseworthy, beautiful and inspiring – and the best of spiritual teachings point to those latent capacities within each one of us. Which means we have all the ingredients to metamorphose from a human caterpillar into a human butterfly.

As Rumi tells us, "Wherever there is a ruin, there is hope for a treasure." Based on Rumi's insight, we can therefore say: The NeoCons may have created turmoil, torture and death in the physical arena, but spiritually – and quite unwittingly – they started to shake millions out of their sleep. In fact, they were the nightmare that rather rudely wakened a number of us.

Ten years of shame

On the 10th anniversary of the 9/11 attacks, Princeton professor and Nobel Prize laureate, Paul Krugman, who is also a *New York Times* columnist, posted a blog called "The Years of Shame," in which he charged that "what happened after 9/11 was deeply shameful."

He castigated Rudy Giuliani and President Bush as "fake heroes" who exploited the attacks for their own personal, political or military gain, and said that many in the media had "[lent] their support to the hijacking of the atrocity." He concluded, "The memory of 9/11 has been irrevocably poisoned; it has become an occasion for shame. And, in its heart, the nation knows it."

Not surprisingly, condemnation from the Hard Right was swift and fierce.

Now, while it is obvious that Prof. Krugman did not watch the video "September 11th Revisited", his post-9/11 analysis is correct and his writing about it courageous. With more individuals like him, America could begin the long road home to its original purpose and true destiny: to be a model of democracy and a friend to humanity.

Meanwhile, however, the masterminds responsible for 9/11 have shown that they would have no hesitation to increase humanity's suffering a million-fold if it were to serve their objective. Because of that appetite for creating chaos in order to ensure dominance, we have presently stumbled upon a crossroads never before experienced. The two roads before us lead in very different directions and carry totally different outcomes. Accordingly, the one will take us to an abyss and certain death, and the other to the mountaintop and new life.

To avoid heading blindly toward a catastrophe, we must

grow large in mind and heart, for the newness that awaits us is inclusive of all of humankind and life on Earth. Only by refashioning ourselves in the most humane image can we hope to build an entirely different tomorrow. In other words, putting behind us the misery of centuries, the immense tragedy of the last decade, and the potential for an unspeakable calamity, will not happen without a deep commitment and enduring effort on our part. And that means inner work, the kind most of us usually avoid – until something harrowing, a truly staggering event, gives us no other choice but to turn our gaze from the outer to the inner.

Few would doubt that we have reached such a point, for the trauma of 9/11 was so profound and the consequences so devastating that humanity finds itself stranded in exceedingly treacherous terrain. One false step and we could plunge over the precipice, carrying with us our world and dreams, immense destruction virtually guaranteed.

Thus, for better or for worse, a crossroads has appeared before us, compelling us to choose or lose.

Born in times of shock and awe

The 20th and beginning of the 21st century, with their atrocities and betrayals, are an enormous indictment of humankind. Yet, this stretch of time has also seen some of the greatest changes in human history, amazing breakthroughs on all levels of life, including awareness of universal human rights and responsibilities.

Yet, it appears, the new paradigm has shown success mostly in those places where world wars swept across countries, killing and maiming millions, causing damage so severe that in certain places physical scars and psychological disfigurements remain three generations after the end of hostilities. It literally forced survivors to begin a new way of relating.

When it comes to the United States, however, as the previous chapters reveal, just the opposite is the case. Here the old consciousness can still be buttressed by propaganda, fueled by fear, and whipped into frenzy by patriotic slogans and the blind nationalism reminiscent of earlier times.

For here we find the individuals responsible for a new kind of barbarism in the shape of permanent war, with its support systems of Abu Ghraib and Guantanamo, extrajudicial killings via drone attacks, and only a few years back, extraordinary rendition and black sites. Here are the ruthless ones with their coldly calculating intellects, their stony hearts and unbending wills, who have pulled us toward this crisis in a relentless drive to dominate. Such men, and a sprinkling of women, once again clamor for war as they spew misinformation and train their guns on the country that is the sharpest thorn in their side, the Islamic Republic of Iran. Not even the potential of setting in motion a calamity beyond human imagination seems to give them pause.

Such alarming developments have propelled us toward a turning point, a juncture where a vital decision must be made. Such a choice will be by all accounts the most consequential in history: Shall individuals driven by arrogance of power, and capable of destroying everything, be allowed to have their way – or will the majority of humans choose to move in the opposite direction: collective life shared in a spirit of oneness and love?

To the degree that we yearn for a life of wholeness, harmony and peace, to that degree will it be necessary to see through the lies and deceptions, hypocrisies and manipulations in order for us to realize with Voltaire that "those who can make people believe in absurdities can make them commit atrocities."

However, unmasking the falsehoods that keep humans subservient to anti-spiritual forces would be a hollow victory if we were not simultaneously committed to developing lives based on clear ethical principles and solid universal values. These include caring for self and others, as well as for this precious, now deeply injured planet. Clearly, it is not enough, to deactivate the outer influences of those who would make of us puppets and pawns; rather, we must evolve from submissiveness to self-empowerment and from separateness to a sense of solidarity with and support for others.

The making of a brighter tomorrow will depend not only on significantly increasing our responsibility in order to prevent future damage, but also being able to transmute past wrongs by consciously acknowledging them rather than letting them unconsciously shackle us. (For suggestions on how to proceed with the task, see *Envisioning a New World,* specifically the chapter, "You and Your Shadow".)

Again, this means inner work. Inner, spiritual, work is sustained work, because it involves traversing not only the sunny side but also the dark side of our being, the shadow within, in order to integrate both aspects. Yet, such work is also enormously gratifying, for, if done well, it will reward us with an exhilarating sense of inner freedom. This is when we can truly begin to blossom, nourished by the light within.

Currently, the call to pause and contemplate what is and what might be has gone out to all in order to develop the clarity and courage to proclaim what we do and don't want.

Seeing

Let me see the world
with the clarity
of a June day

Let me look reality
in the eye
without flinching
or judging

Let me conquer
fears and demons
within
so that I may
see beyond prejudice
and illusions
perceiving all that is
through the lens
of the open heart
able to respond
to the light and darkness
beauty and disfiguration
pleasure and pain

185

of this world
like a doctor
a teacher
centered on adding
what is needed
instead of bemoaning
what is absent or empty
ignorant or ill.

Let me see the world
with the clarity
of a June day
while offering thanks
for human freedom.

RC

Perils and promises

In our generation, messages of liberty, universal human rights and empowerment are being transmitted to every hamlet and hut, exposing people to ideas that stir a resonance and hunger in the hearts of millions. This prompted Martin Luther King to say that "these are revolutionary times [when people everywhere] are revolting against old systems of exploitation and oppression." Based on that, he was able to foresee that "out of the wounds of a frail world, new systems of justice and equality are being born."

This transformative potential is highlighted in a poem by Theodore Roethke in which he states, "In a dark time, the eye begins to see." Which is to say that the very lack of light can stimulate the eye to become more penetrating, to develop a vision that perceives beyond appearances a deeper truth.

Knowledge of that latent gift is reflected in the story of a young boy who seeks to understand the phrase "to keep one's eyes peeled." A wise old woman finally reveals to him its meaning, saying, "To keep one's eyes peeled is to see the clown before he appears on stage." In short, to be able to recognize someone's true character prior to the makeup or the mask.

Applied to today's national and international political

state of affairs, this means identifying beyond the lies and propaganda the true nature of what is occurring in our world; in short, having the capacity to see behind façades and through pretenses.

Not surprising, then, that an ever-increasing number of voices are calling and campaigning for social and political restructuring based on all people's inalienable right to life, liberty and self-governance so eloquently articulated by the wise Founders of our nation. We have witnessed this, for example, with respect to the women of Africa and indigenous people in many parts of the world. We have been able to hear it in the cries for freedom and self-determination from Tibet to Chechnya, from Egypt to Yemen, from Bahrain to Burma. And we have seen it for decades in the valiant struggle of the Palestinian people for justice and statehood.

All these are indications that humankind has graduated from one grade in the school of life – the one where dominance and submission played its role – and is eager to advance to the next level, the next grade, where true freedom and self-mastery will be taught.

I believe this is possible because the human family has earned the right to a more humane way of life, having suffered indignities, ill treatment and humiliation for too long. Still, it will take great courage to say no to those who would keep us yoked to an invalid, out of date paradigm.

In addition, we can be sure there will be a considerable opposition to attempts at renewal. But there are also ways to increase our resolve. We can work to free ourselves from self-defeating behaviors by recognizing the most vital and sustaining element needed to create a fairer world: the inherent worth and dignity of every person, starting with our own. Here is the ideal platform for building a life flexible enough to accommodate growth and change. We shall explore this topic at length in the next chapter.

I must, however, point out that there remains one massive obstacle, which has the potential to derail our most valiant efforts. The sinister forces ruling the world, in particular since 9/11, have successfully deceived and brainwashed many, especially in the country with the greatest potential for either good or evil, the United States of America. This is because they have disguised themselves so thoroughly as "good". Moreover, they audaciously demand to be acknowledged and treated as such! And a gullible public obliges, unable to connect the dots, angrily lashing out at those who seek to open eyes and hearts to a greater truth.

Therefore, whether we recognize it or not, the fate of our world lies largely in the hands of the citizens of our country. This must not be seen as making us more important, but rather as making us more accountable, than any other people. Why? Because, as we have seen, the decisions we make, and the direction this nation takes affect decisively the destiny of the entire global community. Thus, to avoid the unspeakable depends largely on the degree of awareness shown by our citizens. We have, after all, at our disposal the biggest arsenal of weapons in all of history – and have shown in stunning ways that our government does not hesitate to use them, even atomic ones. In a word, unawakened, we are the gravest danger to the world; becoming conscious, we can make the greatest difference in fostering harmony and peace.

All this points to the fact that in our time, a titanic struggle is being waged between the forces of truth and falsehood. This accounts for the heightened intensity palpable at the present time as everything is magnified, multiplied and accelerated to impel us to awaken. Divisiveness, polarization and enmity are telling us that the situation is extraordinarily dense and dangerous. Crossroads usually are. They are the great markers, the prophetic warnings throughout humanity's perilous journey. They are, for example, the historic stone tablets erected by the ancestors along Japan's coastline that admonish, "Do not build beyond this spot; it is not safe from tsunamis." Over the years, some obeyed, and others perished.

And what is the message for us at this crucial turning point in history? If we are to live, and live with dignity and in freedom, the old must die – the old guard mentality, the old formulas, the lies, the injustices, the cruel machinations of fear mongers and militarists. For they are the symbolic, the human-made tsunamis, which are equally capable of destroying everything in their path.

Now, when speaking of the significance of crossroads, we must emphasize no less their inherent potential for growth and renewal. Moreover, while the perils surrounding them are outside of us, their promises are all within, i.e., accessible.

Awareness of those potentials and promises is a resounding reason to embark on a voyage into the last frontier, the interior of Self. For to believe that we can find ultimate answers any other place than here, at the core and depth of our own being, is illusory.

Additionally, this inner journey has become crucial because, despite the progress we believe we are making, we still find ourselves facing this awesome abyss, which will not go away – unless we do. That is, unless we turn in the opposite direction, turn toward Self – the source of light and power, and the gateway to actualizing life's Oneness.

To reach that point, there are concepts and behaviors that must be eliminated if humankind is to live and advance. Outdated, for instance, are a number of long-held, but now anachronistic notions:

- The idea of "enemy" with its aura of threat, paranoia and hatred.
- Its demonic twin, war of aggression.
- Ultra-nationalism (My country, right or wrong).
- Terrorism, in particular the State-sponsored type.

We need a new model of equality and partnership, human rights and pluralism, instead of "might makes right." In addition, primary allegiance must shift from tribe or nation to humanity as a whole, knowing that once the heart is anchored there, we cannot but be humane toward people everywhere.

The good news is, ever more people are realizing that the old ways are no longer sufficient for what we desire to become, what we believe ourselves ready and capable of being.

This is why today, from all directions, winds of change are stirring. There are those who greet the movement joyously as a sign of a new season, a new life upon the Earth and in the heart of humanity. And there are others who respond to the burgeoning newness with deep anxiety, seeing only the crumbling of the old, the loss of familiar ways of life.

It has always been thus: when change comes, it is welcomed by some and resisted by many. In the end, however, who would want to be blinded by the last desperate snows of winter when spring crocuses are already blooming?

Now, any metaphor used from the natural world for accentuating the state of the human condition is soon exhausted. This is due to the fact that, for either their benefit or detriment, humans have managed to step outside the seasons, thanks to the gift of self-directing.

While such a privilege can be invaluable indeed, it is also a sword that cuts both ways. It cuts the restrictions that bind us, and it cuts *us* when we lose our balance and go to extremes, when self-restraint is not part of the equation. This is how free will can quickly disturb and even destroy the natural order of things in and around us.

In our time, we have seen more than ever the steely determination of the "willful ones" of the human race, of those who want to preserve absolute control. Such attempts can be as harsh and painful as the notorious winter storms just prior to the breaking of spring. Yet, those tempests contain a silver lining: they often tear off and sweep away the last traces of things parched and outworn, all stubborn hindrances to new growth. Moreover, while such wintry remnants may be reluctant to concede victory to spring by wrecking havoc on early blooms, in the end, the flowers always triumph.

There is additional good news when it comes to the life of humans: almost any season can be made into a conducive time to shed old skins, old habits, old fears, and adorn ourselves with newness.

Thus, as in nature, so among people, periodic renewal is inescapable. The way I read the signs of our time is that we are presently moving toward such a renewal point in history – a Kairos moment, a supreme moment – if we are wise enough to choose life and a path with heart.

In addition, like the yearning for spring after a hard and

icy winter, the longing for something warmer and more befitting the human soul has drawn us into the midst of change, with all the turbulence and uncertainty that mark such occasions. And there is no going back. For I believe, as others have said, that the only way out is through.

A final point: spring can be an external or internal season. Either one holds promises none of us should miss. Best of all, while the outer spring arrives and departs, the inner is not subject to clock time. Once in bloom inwardly, the state of beauty and joy can last indefinitely. And, indeed, there are many signs that a new awareness wants to be born, and we can be sure that its urge to manifest will not disappear.

Coming of Age

For thousands of years the people
have bowed and curtsied
and prostrated themselves
before idols and tyrants and dwarfs.
For thousands of years they have
trembled at the threat of the bully
shrinking themselves to escape being seen
but ending up sheep for exploits and slaughter.

For thousands of years the human race
has been ruled by the power-obsessed
the ruthless, the cunning
desiring to fashion the world
into a playground for their
wills and their whims.

For thousands of years the people
sleepwalking
have obeyed and followed
have lied and spied
and died for the despots –
groveling slaves
walled in by fear.

And while intermittently

191

some rose and revolted in wild
outbursts of despair and disgust
in the end the hapless masses
merely exchanged
one dictator for another
for their gaze remained fixed on
the external, on a rescuer to loosen
their insufferable chains.

Thus the people continued to trudge on
driven like cattle by herders and hunger.
But now, behold, a new spirit has risen
calling souls out of their trance!
And suddenly individuals
with their eyes newly opened
are seeing the fetters constricting
their motions and minds.
And the sounds
we are hearing
across this great globe
are the breaking of shackles
and the shouts of defiance
by which humans reclaim
one by one
their power and place in the sun.

RC

Yearning for change

It appears more individuals in all parts of the world align with movements that promise a saner way of life, that envision a new type of humanity emerging – a humanity that has, indeed, come of age.

Take, for instance, the ongoing resistance to wars that conquer other people and colonize their land. Today peace activism has advanced far beyond that goal; today the military-industrial complex with its mindset of conquest and its culture of death has itself become the target.

Of course, slowing down, much less disabling, such a

massive machine is a formidable task, yet activists have, as previously highlighted, an illustrious name on their side: In 1960, President Eisenhower singled out that particular confluence as a grave threat to this nation and the welfare of all others.

Regrettably, Americans are not given the unvarnished truth or implications of this, which would have to include many of the alien values that today undermine our political structures and the spiritual well-being of our people. If these were fully revealed, most of our citizens would, in all probability, angrily refuse to let themselves be used and abused any longer.

Instead, participatory democracy has been undermined and even made irrelevant with little objection and even less resistance. Still, it is of vital importance to reclaim those stolen principles, and with a deep sense of moral obligation, begin to rebuild brick by brick the edifice of our broken system.

For are we not the nation that proudly displays the Statue of Liberty and gives freedom and civil rights a place of high honor? We have, after all, the Declaration of Independence that speaks of inalienable rights. We have the Constitution, the greatest ever conceived. And to deepen its meaning as well as avoid misinterpretations, we have the Bill of Rights.

The inspired revolutionaries who gave us those precious gifts while declaring a New Order of the Ages, knew what is most appealing to human beings everywhere: civil rights and liberty. They made us guardians of that legacy.

Over the generations, we have more than once failed to live up to that high calling; however, after 9/11 there was a callous and concerted effort by some to undercut the efficacy of the documents that are foundational to our democracy.

Now, as I have stressed repeatedly, while civil rights and liberties are absolutely essential, their polar opposites, justice and responsibility, are no less vital. Simply put, emphasis on liberty leads to political rights; emphasis on justice ensures economic rights, equality. This clearly tells us where America shines and where it limps and falters, i.e., where much sociopolitical work remains to be done.

Beyond the specific and enormous challenges affecting our country, there is a related heroic struggle taking place for the soul of humanity and the future of the world, and one of its defining questions is this: Will it be Big Brother/Sister who determines our destiny or shall it be the idea that we are all brothers and sisters? Needless to say, the former will keep us enslaved; the latter is our path to freedom.

Recent surveys across the larger world tell us that a yearning for freedom, human rights, equality, justice – in a word, for democratic ideals – is not unique to any one group, but is common to all people. The West, with its pronounced focus on such principles – if at times only in word, rather than deed – has, nonetheless, been quite successful in reminding others of their own inalienable rights, in the process stirring a longing in the heart of millions.

Like the air itself, the eloquence of such treasured words as freedom, truth and justice has encircled the globe and been eagerly inhaled and absorbed, encouraging efforts toward their attainment by citizens of numerous and disparate nations.

Sadly, the resulting revolts against oppressive regimes, especially in the Arab world, have continued in certain places to be rather bloody because those in power will not relinquish control and would rather kill than allow governance of the people, by the people, for the people.

Still, despite live bullets from so-called security forces, many humans would rather die than continue to live like sheep, like slaves. This very fact is an immense source of hope, telling us that no matter how long it may take, there is a spirit of freedom living in human hearts that cannot forever be repressed.

Revolts are explosive events, rising like volcanoes out of mountains of oppression. They occur despite huge obstacles and their proponents know that history is on their side. This is why an old Quaker hymn can exultantly proclaim, "When tyrants tremble as they hear the bells of freedom ringing."

Since the start of 2011, bells of liberty have been tolling in many places in the Middle East, and it is hoped that they will not cease until the true tyrants and terrorists of this world are unmasked and brought to justice – or the fertile ground for their presence is no longer available to them because people have refused to be obedient servants to the ones who appoint themselves masters over others and use them for selfish ends.

This is precisely the consciousness that must be gained by our citizens, who live under the illusion that they inhabit "the freest country on Earth", and are thus blinded to the fact that we are an occupied nation. Granted, there are no foreign tanks and military checkpoints. Rather, this is a far more subtle occupation: a take-over of the mind that prevents clear-seeing, clear-thinking and clear-acting. Nothing like it has ever been imposed on a citizenry before. This is why it is so difficult to detect. It takes big lies, big liars, and big money to accomplish such a feat. Yet, it was done in an instant to a people shaken to the core and made acquiescent by 9/11, that most vile and despicable crime.

What will have to occur to give us back our country and its true, but still unfulfilled, purpose? As I watch the great drama that is present-day America, my first reaction is that it will take a miracle. Yes, a miracle! A natural disaster, perhaps, of such magnitude that it will tear the very fabric of our society and compel us to return to the values of a simpler life – or a revelation so potent it will rattle us out of our stupor and make us glad to return to the values of a more caring existence.

Either scenario, I realize, entails much suffering. This is why I am so intensely focused on offering alternatives, on suggesting less violent ways of change. Change *chosen* by us, not *forced* on us.

Regardless of what our attitude may be, Kierkegaard knew what is needed: "Human beings are asleep," he lamented, "and the deeper they are asleep, the stronger must be the means of their awakening." This is how an entire house may fall in on us because we didn't hear the knock at our door, our window, our conscience. Change chosen and implemented by us would be a lot less painful.

Learning a new language

Autocrats and manipulators have played grim games with human beings since time immemorial; have molded political and societal milieus in their own heartless image. Over the centuries, they have become ever more clever at doing this, with technology providing the tools to sharpen their ability to engineer complete control.

Hence, while their numbers on this planet may not have increased proportionally compared to the growth of the entire population, their capacity to dominate lives and inflict pain on those who will not submit to their scheming certainly has. Simultaneously, however, something else in our world has grown stronger: many people no longer want to be controlled, no longer are willing to be used as lackeys.

The idea of egalitarianism has taken root in the heart of millions of people. Hence, while hubristic rulers are doing everything to seduce, cajole, deceive, and repress, resistance to those efforts has also increased, indicating the lords of lies and masters of manipulation can no longer so shrewdly hide their intentions. Human sensitivity to their plotting has intensified, thanks to worldwide communications, political education and deeper inner knowing.

Not surprisingly, when awareness expands, patterns are noticed and deception becomes more difficult to hide. It is like learning a new terminology or language. What once seemed like gibberish, suddenly tells a story, offers insight. In the same manner, the craftiness of the deceiver becomes incrementally more transparent.

When blatant lies and audacious maneuvers, like termites, undermine civil society and eat away at the foundations of moral values, it is time to learn a new language in order to flush out the invaders, the usurpers of the edifice of state.

Autumnal surprises

As usual, just when the night is darkest, a sliver of silver in the east tells us that dawn is approaching.

This, at least, is how some of us have perceived the unexpected genesis of Occupy Wall Street in the fall of 2011: as a crescent of hope, and a most favorable move in the right direction. No matter how dark the situation, dedicated participants are shining an indicting light on the institutions responsible for the financial meltdown of 2008 and the continuing devastating effect on people in our country and abroad. In addition, there has emerged a far greater awareness of how the raw power of money (or as someone said, "money as a weapon") determines the political climate in Washington, with high-paid lobbyists ensuring that special interests and corporations remain in charge of policies and politicians.

Through Occupy Wall Street, protesters are drawing attention to one of the major culprits responsible for the loss of democracy in America. A mere 1% of the population, by their greed, wealth and power, are depriving the other 99% not only of their fair share, but most offensively, have robbed America of its democratic principles by controlling Congress and the White House, foreign affairs and, above all, corporate media.

Restoring democracy, regaining and healing our country, must begin somewhere. Wall Street is an appropriate place to let the people's anger and demands be heard. It would have been a decisive victory, not only for Americans but for humanity, if "Change we can believe in" had been delivered by Barack Obama during his presidency. That he so far has not succeeded in delivering what he promised is a sign of the overarching control of those behind the scenes who are the real power players in Washington. Now the only ones remaining to press for change appear to be "we the people".

Indispensable: self-understanding

As highlighted in great detail in my previous works, human beings cannot participate in life consciously unless we follow the ancient dictum: *Know Thyself.* Unfortunately, too many persons still are illiterate in the deepest sense of the word: they have not yet learned how to "read" who they are, thus lacking both self-awareness and self-understanding. It is a very expensive liability, for by being ignorant of our own being, we can be controlled and taken advantage of. No one knows that better than those waiting in the wings to exploit ignorance and naiveté for self-serving purposes.

And never is that weakness more effectively manipulated than during a time of war, when masses of citizens with no feelings of personal animosity toward another people are ordered to murder them at the directive of their rulers. Like zombies, citizens become killing machines; like obedient animals, they willingly face death and dreadful injuries to serve the grand schemes of those addicted to carnage and chaos.

Additionally, without knowing ourselves, how can we truly *be* ourselves, much less be *self-empowered?* Not being empowered is perhaps humankind's greatest individual and collective handicap. I can't think of a single destructive deed that has not been caused by disempowerment's disruptive, even violent, energy, even as acts of love and compassion are made possible by its opposite: empowerment.

Self-aware, empowered individuals do not shirk responsibility or blame others; they are open to new ideas and do not resist positive change. Toward that end, they stop intensifying human problems and instead become contributors to solutions. Moreover, they recognize that societal reforms with a lasting impact cannot be achieved without a consistent commitment to self-reform. Thus they take ownership of their lives.

In other words, if we do not want to remain in bondage to the powers of this world, but seek to reduce the hazards under which we presently exist, we must not only endeavor to change the outer contours of our world, but learn to equally cultivate the inner landscape, the ground of being, the hidden roots of all things visible. We will then know that only healthy roots can bring forth wholesome fruits.

To connect with our inner center of power, and conduct our lives while firmly rooted in it, is thus a most valuable gift – to ourselves and the larger society.

We function in a world of duality: inner and outer, personal and public. When these two interrelated, interdependent aspects are aligned, that is, when the roots and branches of the tree of our life receive equal attention, we can evolve to new heights and bear spiritually nourishing fruits.

Potentials

Humanity stands not only at the brink of a precipice, but, if seen from the opposite perspective, at the cusp of something fundamentally great and new. However, the ensconced rulers with their tenacious grip will not relinquish the reins without a fierce counteroffensive before their self-serving influence is vanquished. This can only happen if we gain spiritual and moral maturity, in order to stand tall against everything that would dismiss and diminish us.

Open the newspapers, turn on the radio or the TV, surf the Internet, and the picture that emerges is unmistakable: humankind is in bondage; materialistic values and militaristic worldviews dominate. Moreover, we are shown daily what happens when a world of oneness is divided and sliced into fragments for the sake of narrow gains. And we are witnessing the degree of depravity human beings can sink to when deprived of a moral compass.

This state of affairs will continue until our citizens in particular start to recognize how they have been used as pawns and cannon fodder for manipulative, misanthropic forces. As elaborated before, this was made possible by the fact that Americans are in general strangers to the ways of dominance and dictators. It has left them vulnerable to the assaults of lies and deceit in the aftermath of 9/11.

For while a new and freer consciousness is eager to manifest in our world, unless the citizens of the United States of America convert to it, an ever-present threat will continue to churn storm clouds over humanity and its future.

I do not wish to create with these words the impression that I am singling out our country for excessive criticism. On the contrary, I believe even today that, on the whole, the American people are the most decent, generous, open and tolerant in the world. In fact, they are the very opposite of the suspicious kind. Which means they are *too* trusting, especially of their government.

Ironically, as we are witnessing, this can be a serious psychological liability in a world full of deception and shrewd operators. For it increases naiveté and gullibility, qualities that can be fatal under certain conditions. What is fatal to us is equally lethal to the rest of the world. The reason for this is simple. We are the most powerful country in the world, with the military means to bring life on Earth to a halt. And the temptation to settle quarrels through military means will always remain for those afflicted with a hubristic sense of entitlement, especially when equipped with the weapons to match it.

At the same time, America has the potential to offer the world a totally new, greatly enhanced future. To explain why this is our only real option is the purpose of these reflections.

So to reiterate: Without awareness of the interrelatedness of life, we can't reach tomorrow unscathed, or perhaps not at all. Without reconnecting with Spirit, with the natural life, the wholeness/holiness of our being, we cannot generate the qualities of love and compassion essential for ascending to newness.

A world in transition

As one who has been intrigued by the story of humankind since first I was exposed in 5th grade to the chronicles of ancient Mesopotamia, I rarely miss an opportunity to deepen my understanding of the great epochs in history and what they can teach us about human nature. This is the reason I recently completed a cycle of 24 taped lectures on the Byzantine Empire by *The Teaching Company*.

It was all very fascinating and characteristically gory and treacherous, but what mattered most was the excellent summary of the presenter. He spoke eloquently about the great civilizations that had developed during those 1,000 years of faith and bravery, struggle, warfare and disease – from Western Europe to Byzantium to the Ottoman Empire.

I almost felt relieved, saying to myself: perhaps things *are* unfolding as they should, and I can, therefore, let go of this pronounced sense of urgency that tends to color my days.

The temptation lasted only moments. For I quickly also realized that yes, things may be unfolding as they should, but does that mean our consciousness must forever be stuck in the same old groove? And that groove, as we know from both history and current affairs, involves far too much deceit, belligerence and bloodshed, not to speak of homelessness, hunger and disease. Deep down, we know we can do better.

Thus the pressure to birth something new, something more worthy and reflective of the state of consciousness of an increasing number of people. Simply stated, we deserve better than to continue to cater to the animalistic tendencies of tribe and territory. Let's find a new groove and let things unfold as they should based on that improved position, and when it begins to sound like a broken record, move "onward and upward" until we settle on a track that allows us to be more inclusive and decidedly more humane.

In the meantime, many people are already gathered at a threshold which they are eager to cross. But look around and you can see the keepers of the will to power single-mindedly attempting to block it.

It seems, the forces of frigidity and callousness are inexhaustibly clever in their effort at preventing the new from entering our world: they will use every method conceivable to remain entrenched in their position of dominance. They will lie, coerce, force, torture and kill to choke off newness.

Still, if one listens carefully to the cacophony of those rather seductive voices, one might detect now and then an unexpectedly different note, such as the one sounded by Defense Secretary Robert Gates on July 15, 2008, when he warned about the militarization of US foreign policy, saying, "We cannot kill or capture our way to victory." Imagine a voice of reason and recognition coming out of Washington at a time such as this!

While this reality check had been long overdue, how many innocent citizens of Muslim countries were killed, captured and tortured before the civilian supposedly in charge of the Pentagon came to the conclusion he did? It is doubtful, of course, that the rest of the military brass even shared Mr. Gates' view. However, just the fact that his blunt statement became public knowledge is encouraging.

As I have mentioned, there are numerous false gods we are pledging allegiance to – gods which place us no less in bondage and servitude than our ancestors were to their gods, false or otherwise.

We can be certain that false gods are always capricious gods. Having made military prowess our false god, we are reaping everywhere the bitter fruit of insecurity. We are easily made fearful and compliant. For the sake of feeling "safe", we discard our most precious civil rights; for the sake of things and success, we sell our soul; for the sake of "getting even", we relinquish our moral compass. Like automatons, we grovel and do the bidding of those who deceive and dominate. Naiveté and angst continue to feed merchants of greed and makers of war.

Conditions like these have led to a state of hopelessness in more than a few. Yet, this can be minimized if we are astute enough to perceive that what is happening in our world is not just about domination and death, but also about liberation and renewal. And as has been repeatedly shown, in the end, the forces of light are stronger than those of darkness. However, in order to overcome the darkness, many more of us must bring forth the light *within*. That source of illumination is ultimately the only guarantee for a brighter life and future for the human race and all the Earth.

When we increase our inner light, when we are more enlightened, it follows that we shall make self-restraint and discipline a virtue in our life and land. With that emphasis, we can begin to reduce the excesses and dismantle the prisons within, all of them terrible indictments of the misuse of liberty and the flourishing of a culture of self-indulgence.

Though daunting, these imbalances are within our power to correct. And here we must indeed be willing to make a 180-degree turn and start conducting ourselves contrary to habitual patterns of behavior. This will prepare the way to birth a life of greater self-awareness, truth and compassion.

The time has come to transit from the winter mode of our lives and align with the promises of spring.

Expansions and contractions

The expansion of Western awareness began to seriously gather momentum in the late 1960s when pressure from several sources compelled our country to rethink its purpose and direction. Prominent among the influences at work were, on the positive side, exposure to Eastern spiritual thought, and the remarkable discoveries of modern science, in particular the new physics. Contributing through negatives were the hollowness of materialism, the depravity of totalitarian regimes, and an angry discontent with the ways of war and militarism.

Whereas, up to that point, focus had been heavily on the external world, with its success mentality and accompanying supremacy of "things", a serious consideration of the inner life and its spiritual values began to emerge.

Further contributing to a shift in consciousness were the shocking and cunningly executed assassinations of a roster of exceptional progressive leaders, all individuals in their prime, from the Kennedy brothers to Martin Luther King Jr. to Malcolm X. Meanwhile, the war in Vietnam was turning ever more vicious and bloody. Young people, in particular, through their music and marches, stridently advocated for peace abroad and political changes at home.

Gradually, the West opened to greater spiritual awareness, centering on the idea of the interconnectedness of life and the corresponding interdependence of people and nations. The trend culminated in the excitement and worldwide ceremonies welcoming the 3rd millennium. Humanity was riding a powerful wave of hope toward a dawn of once-only-dreamed-of possibilities. Personally and publicly, progress promised to be the hallmark of the future.

Less than two years later, however, the human race was put to the test to see whether those joyful sounds and words of planetary unity were actually an expression of what we had become, or only an image we preferred to have of ourselves. Lamentably, the blinding eruptions of September 11, 2001, and their severe consequences shattered the budding millennium consciousness. This loss was made complete by Washington's arrogant declaration of war on all who are "not with us". Clearly, the collective consciousness of the human race, and that of America in particular, was not yet stabilized enough to allow for a different line of response, as almost everyone fell into lockstep with the Bush administration's course of action. This brought to mind a brilliant insight by British author Christopher Fry, "Strange how we trust the powers that ruin, and not the powers that bless."

In many ways, this was not surprising. For on that bright September day, a group of sinister subjugators – behind the scenes and unbeknownst to nearly everyone – executed the greatest coup d'état of all times. Their singular power play and take-over blinded the overwhelming majority of American citizens, while creating lasting reverberations around the world.

Agents of death, not guardians of life, gave notice of their self-appointed reign. The immensity of what occurred, and the psychic shock across the globe, was enormous. America was shaken to its foundation, reduced to a state of helplessness, which allowed those in control to generate a groundswell of fear. When hopelessness and fear turned to rage, it permitted the declaration of a terrifying worldwide War on Terror, which soon turned into a War *of* Terror, now in its 12th year.

These extreme reactions underscored what had been missing from the American way of life: genuine spirituality that can ensure clarity of vision and inspire a strong commitment to moral principles.

As I have stressed in previous writings, there is a lot of religiosity in our country; there are many "worshippers" who attend services each week, yet at the moment the American psyche was confronted with its greatest challenge and gravest temptation, the people could not rise above the basest of survival instincts and thirst for retribution. All the noble teachings of Christ, all the great moral precepts of other religions active in our country, even the highest principles of secular humanism, collapsed and went into free-fall like those mighty towers of New York City.

Stunned by the fast-moving events, few voices called for self-searching and restraint, much less for a thorough investigation of what really occurred and who were the ultimate perpetrators of those atrocities.

Thus, if anything was able to show just how shallow our faith and life had become, it was that momentous event of 2001 and America's tragic, morally self-destructive response.

Disconnected from the depth of our being, we gave fear the first, and Mr. Bush and his handlers the last word in deciding the direction of our national destiny.

Moreover, while the economy wobbled for a while, crass materialism continued to offer all the goods money can buy, and shrewdly promoted, as ever, cravings and addictions, thus keeping consumption and profits high. Who needs change, much less God, when life is *that* "good"!

But it really isn't. It is all based on illusions, or what Scott McClellan, after his resignation as former White House press secretary, characterized as "a culture of deception". This is what he called the political and psychological climate under the Bush administration. And, of course, like the weather itself, which cannot be limited to a single locale, such a climate soon found its way into the entire body politic, destroying what remained of a governance "of the people, by the people, for the people."

Unfortunately, seeing through the disguise or noticing the pitfalls was, and is still today, made even more difficult because those who expose fraudulent behavior are immediately labeled and ostracized. Observing what happens to persons who stand up or speak out quickly persuades the many to withdraw to their prison cell of silence rather than risk stepping out into the open and ending up hurt or even destroyed.

Opting for what is real

Several of my works contain references to the financial meltdown of 2008 and the addictions that lie at the core of the problem. With the European Union presently struggling to find its equilibrium, a few more comments about the origin and scope of the predicament are in order.

First of all, none of what is taking place in Europe would have occurred without the breakdown of the global financial markets, largely perpetrated by an orgy of greed and deceit in the US. With insufficient federal regulations, bankers had free rein in the marketplace. The result was a horrific crash toward the end of the Bush presidency. It led to the largest bankruptcies in world history, pushing tens of millions into unemployment, millions into home foreclosures, and a number of countries to the edge of bankruptcy.

Several years prior, the dishonesty of the Greek government, which, with the help of Wall Street's Goldman Sachs, hid its debt-ridden financial status before adopting the euro, set the stage for a disaster to come. Goldman Sachs was, of course, the same firm which soon thereafter would sell its toxic "bundled securities" to unsuspecting banks and investors in Europe and in fact, all over the globe.

Last, but not least, humans, subject to temptations no matter who they are, were, in large numbers, infected by the virus of "easy money" and the desire to spend beyond their means. When those tendencies are not curbed by governmental regulations and oversight, the results are what we witnessed in Ireland, Iceland, Spain, Italy, Portugal, but above all, in Greece.

Now, those who learned through their own previous difficulties to live with foresight and fiscal discipline are expected to bail out the rest. And the chancellor of Germany, Angela Merkel, earns, on one hand, criticism for advocating reduced government spending while insisting on international financial regulations, and, on the other hand, praise for remaining faithful to her vision and conviction.

Obviously, without sufficient domestic and international rules and regulations, and a healthy dose of self-restraint in fiscal policy on the part of governments, the crisis cannot be permanently resolved. Meanwhile, in the aftermath of financial institutions lacking such a framework, we have an alarming example of what happens when human beings test the limits by playing recklessly with fire.

Of course, what went wrong in the financial market is not very different from what has been taking place with regard to the environment and global climate changes. Here again, it is the United States that stubbornly refuses to acknowledge reality and responsibility. This is essentially a self-defeating attitude whereby Congress in particular has disdainfully resisted joining international treaties designed to protect the planet by implementing, at the very least, significant alternatives to fossil fuel consumption.

One might have thought that the devastating 2005 hurricane Katrina would have shaken the conscience of this nation; but alas, little changed. Seven years later, will the ferocity and immense destruction of superstorm Sandy, offering a taste of things to come, finally bring us to our senses? If not, then we can be certain that ruinous events associated with global climate chaos – largely the result of Western anthropocentrism, now with the added weight of China's amplified industrialization – will await us.

The impact of this is already being felt in various ways and places around the world, not least our own country, as mentioned above. Because we dismissed all the warnings and discarded the signs pointing to a disaster, we may be in for a long stretch of losses and suffering. In the end, for a second time this century, life may never be the same.

Yet, because there is more than one side to any event, major alterations affecting our lifestyle could produce one of those proverbial silver linings. This might mean, for example, moving from excessive consumption, hyperactivity and general escapism to an, albeit forced, less hectic, more quiet way of living. Under such circumstances, we might actually grow in consciousness and find solace in humility and thankfulness.

There are transient values and there are lasting ones, and it is the lasting ones, the tested ones, to which all humans must ultimately turn when those of a transient nature reveal their hollowness and insufficiency, their inability to sustain us in time of crisis.

Human beings have been tempted and challenged during the last decade as never before. If we can keep in mind that these are tests that come at the end of a long and difficult period of training, and that they are about core values, inner strength, and clarity of mind and heart, we might more easily accept their severity.

In summary, we are being tested to determine whether we are ready for something great and beautiful and rare: Peace on Earth and goodwill among her people.

Chapter 9

PRINCIPLES TO LIVE BY: WORTH AND DIGNITY

If I could give you one key only to more abundant life, I would give you a sense of your own worth, an unshakable sense of your own dignity as one grounded in the source.

~Greta Crosby

What lies behind us and what lies before us are tiny matters, compared to what lies within.

~Ralph Waldo Emerson

"Namaste" – I greet the Light within you.

~Traditional Hindu greeting

There is an inmost center in us all,
Where truth abides in fullness...

~Robert Browning

Each spiritual movement, each religion, has its guiding principles, and while they may be expressed in different words, they all spring forth from the same deep inner knowing. They are the bright stars that guide human beings in the search for wholeness and meaning, even as they articulate how to covenant with life and one another.

Embracing them cannot but strengthen our sense of self and our relationships. Such principles are not so much about theology or beliefs as they are an invitation and a framework for living consciously in an interconnected world. Serious commitment to them will allow anyone to become spiritually grounded and socially aware and active.

Speaking personally, my own worldview rests on the twin premises that none of us exists apart *from* humanity and that no one is devoid *of* humanity, even those condemned as "the worst of the worst". There simply is no outside to the non-hierarchical Web of Life and thus no exception to the spiritual equality of all people. Additionally, no individual is all good or all bad. In fact, the best and worst always live side by side in each one of us.

Accepting this as a credo impels me to distinguish between deed and doer, between acts committed out of ignorance, and the actor's innate humanity. None of this, however, holds me back from working for justice – nor does it mean that implementing the concept is easy. Some crimes are indeed so gruesome it is difficult to still classify the perpetrator as human.

Inherent worth and dignity – truth or fiction?

Oneness, interconnectedness, inclusion, are the realities of natural life and creation. They are the unifying elements in whose embrace all are held. Here is the great circle, the heart of the universe which births all and excludes none. When we awaken to it, we intuitively realize that, besides the universe we perceive with our eyes, there is a spiritual/mystical version within us, which we do not see but which is incumbent upon us to discover. For those who have done so, it is easy to recognize what for others remains a hidden reality: the inherent worth and dignity of *every* person. For how can something that arises out of Oneness and Wholeness be anything but whole and, indeed, holy? Moreover, self-worth it is not something we earn, nor can we be deprived of; rather it is innate, life's gift to us, true life in us.

Still, there are those who protest unapologetically: "The principle [of the inherent worth and dignity of every person] is a fiction. People are...not equal; worth is not a biological characteristic. Worth and dignity are standards described by human beings; they are not inherent." You can read this in a letter by Darwin R. of Colorado to the editor of the Unitarian Universalist publication UU World, May/June 2002.

Darwin, I would argue, is correct in saying that a person's worth is not a *biological* characteristic, because what the principle highlights is a *spiritual* truth, something beyond the mere capacity of the intellect or eye to discern. But it is possible to discover. Love and compassion – these are the lenses that can see beyond the personality of the individual to the inner core of being – the holy ground of worth and dignity.

If that is true, you might ask, why do numerous individuals not live up to that potential?

The reasons are many, but, upon further reflection, they can all be traced back to a lack of self-esteem and self-love. And such a lack is caused by various experiences, particularly in childhood, which lead to the warping of a person's self image.

Yet, even those who have had fairly supportive parenting, display, like all humans, a persona. The word is derived from the practice of the ancient Greeks to wear masks during theater performances, and implies that we indeed wear masks, play roles. And until we embark on a journey of self-discovery, we consistently tend to confuse the roles we play with who we are. Is it any wonder, then, that we have difficulties not only vis-à-vis knowing ourselves but in our relationship to others?

However, let us return to Mr. R's objections. No doubt, to affirm the inherent worth and dignity of *every* person is a lofty ideal, a bold commitment, a noble goal. Should such a declaration, we might ask, be more selective, more "realistic", instead of being all-inclusive? Were we perhaps a bit naïve? How can, for instance, in our time, Stalin, Hitler, Idi Amin, Mao Ze-dung, Pol Pot, Kim Jong Il, Castro, Milosevic, Mubarak, Gadhafi and thousands of others, especially war makers and torturers, be endowed with such high qualities of being, such pure essence? How can we speak seriously of inherent worth and dignity in light of such individuals' despicable crimes against humanity?

The question is definitely one that challenges humanitarians, and a topic deserving of ongoing discussion. And it is not only the well-known tyrants but also the violators and abusers in our midst who test our beliefs about human nature along those lines.

While it is certainly not my intention to diminish horrible acts, I would like to contribute to this necessary conversation a number of considerations. Most important, when speaking of "the inherent worth and dignity", the emphasis is on *inherent;* that is to say, on a potential, a seed, not a full-grown plant or tree. Now, you might ask, where does such a seed originate and who placed it within every person?

For the religiously inclined, the idea that all human beings have worth and are endowed with dignity is self-evidenced by the fact that they are (a) "created in the image of God" (Judaism, Christianity), or by God (Islam); (b) that "Atman is Brahman" (Hinduism); (c) that the core reality of all sentient beings is their "Buddha nature" (Buddhism); or (d) that "All are created equal" (Deism, the Declaration of Independence). Finally, (e) Humanism and Secularism also pay homage to the essential worth and equality of all people by proclaiming, "If human rights are not universal and don't apply to everyone and every culture, then they are meaningless." (Dr. William Schulz, former director of Amnesty International, USA)

What has been said about the gift of liberty, namely, that it is not genuine unless we allow even for its abuse, applies equally to the principle of inherent worth: unless we incorporate that some will act in ways that shed grave doubts on the very idea, it is only a decorative notion. Besides, what is "inherent" may lie fallow deep within a human being without ever taking root and growing into visibility. But that is no reason to see such an individual as less endowed, less worthy. In fact, the more someone is unaware or in denial of such an in-depth reality, the more he or she is in need of empathy and compassion. Self-denigration is the worst form of punishment.

Finally, if all of those arguments in favor of the idea of the inherent worth and dignity sound too idealistic or far-fetched, here is one closer to what we humans are familiar with: falling in love, that most inexplicable of all phenomena in the repertoire of personal experiences. "The heart has reasons that reason does not understand." This is how Blaise Pascal and the French in general assess the condition of those touched by love's "divine madness".

Who can argue with them, since we have all been there? Yet, what is it that we fall in love with, especially in view of statements such as, "I don't know what she sees in him – or he in her." Of course, in an age of gay rights and civil unions, we definitely need to expand this to say, "I don't know what he sees in him – or she in her."

I would suggest what all of them see in the other is precisely that invisible part of self that "houses" inherent worth and dignity – the light that is our true self, our divine spark – the core component which a heart touched by love alone can perceive. Logic, as we know, inevitably loses when it comes to recognizing such essentials.

The eyes, the intellect, can reveal much to us, but they cannot uncover the whole story. In fact, they easily mislead us. That's where the phrase made famous by Quantum physicists takes on yet another meaning: "Things are not what they appear to be."

Those who are not misled, however, recognize that life is one, and all beings are created equal, as a fundamental spiritual reality. This does not mean that all share the same gifts and talents, or make the same contributions to the world. It simply means that each of us is "a child of the universe", a being of noble birth and intrinsic worth, independent of what we do, the position we hold, the money we make, the neighborhood we live in.

Thus, the more we operate out of the Oneness and align with the Wholeness of creation, the more we include. And the more inclusive we are, the more we can reach out to the entire human family. "Nothing human is foreign to me," confessed Goethe, cosmopolitan par excellence. This is precisely why individuals who are equally inclined to include much, take such pleasure in being with one another without having to argue about various "fine points" as they stroll together through the garden of life.

Human worth and transnational connections

With words like terror and terrorists, war crimes and torture, continually in the news, it seems appropriate to add a historical note concerning the age-old struggle to promote the inherent worth and dignity of all people.

As we have seen, the principle proclaims a spiritual reality that recognizes every member of the human family as deserving of love and respect. It affirms freedom and equality as each person's birthright and stresses radical inclusion.

Valued especially by progressive Christian denominations whose dedicated members would become known as the Social Gospel movement, the principle became the impetus for all manner of 19th century social reforms: abolishment of slavery, equal rights for women, public education, the humane treatment of children and animals, and dedication to the common good.

Of particular concern were the atrocious conditions of mental hospitals and prisons. Energized by the realization that humans may be wicked, but they are not worthless, activists advocated for various reforms, including the end of capital punishment, and rehabilitation rather than retribution for those imprisoned for a crime.

One of the ramifications of a morality that recognized the innate worth of every person culminated in opposition to anything violent or degrading, especially the ultimate violence and debasement that is war.

The denomination of Universalists in particular came to be known and appreciated, but also ridiculed and scorned, for their passionate belief that no wrong is so great that it can exceed God's love, which is to say that a human being is worth more than the worst he or she has done. Because of that, they put forth that no one is permanently exiled from the Circle of Life, no one condemned for eternity.

These revolutionary assertions were made at a time when most other theological teachings emphasized depravity and sinfulness, and preached hell and eternal damnation.

There is a story about the Universalist preacher Hosea Ballou and a Baptist minister meeting by chance while riding their circuits on horseback. The two begin to debate theology, with the Baptist preacher at last saying, "Brother Ballou, if I were a Universalist and feared not the fires of Hell, I'd hit you over the head and steal your horse and saddle." To which Ballou replied, "My brother, if you were a Universalist, such an idea would never have entered your mind!"

An astonishing gap, indeed, between two who both call themselves Christians, but whose view of life and how to live it is as different as ice from steam.

Yet, while that story is both amusing and instructive, soon another Universalist preacher, Adin, a distant cousin of Hosea, gave the name Ballou a more weighty and even transnational significance with the 1846 publication of his acclaimed work, *Christian Non-Resistance, in all its important bearings, illustrated and defended.*

In April 2002, friends of Adin Ballou, during a conference on "Non-Violence in the Contemporary World: Society, Politics and Religion", paid tribute to his work and those in other parts of the world who were equally devoted to the idea. Some of the information below is gleaned from that event.

"Christian Non-Resistance," Ballou wrote at the beginning of his work, "is that original peculiar kind of non-resistance, which was enjoined and exemplified by Jesus Christ and his teaching in the Sermon on the Mount (Matthew 5) in which he exhorts, 'resist not evil'".

With that, the stage was set for an idea whose time seemed finally to have come 1,800 years after it had first been articulated.

Soon the news spread that the concept had touched not only certain groups in America, but was also being promulgated in Russia with the publication of a radical new interpretation of Christ's teachings by the illustrious Leo Tolstoy. His comprehensive non-traditional beliefs were ultimately made available in a lengthy book titled, *The Kingdom of God is Within You: Christianity not as a mystical doctrine but as a new understanding of life.* Translated into a number of other languages, its fame soon spread beyond the author's homeland to other parts of the world.

The major theme of the book addressed the failure of Christians to acknowledge "the law of non-resistance to evil by violence," not only with regard to war and the legalized violence of governments, but through the hypocrisy of justifying war and injustice in the name of Christ.

Shortly before his death in 1890, Ballou began a correspondence with Tolstoy. Although he judged Tolstoy's pacifism as "too passive", the latter, upon receiving Ballou's writings, observed, "I have seldom experienced so much gratification as I had in reading Mr. Ballou's treatise and tracts."

However, the idea whose time had come would not stop there. In 1894, when Mohandas Gandhi was studying law in London, he was introduced to Tolstoy's *The Kingdom of God is Within You,* a work which, he confessed, "overwhelmed" him. He explained why. "Its reading cured me of my skepticism and made me a firm believer in ahimsa (nonviolence)."

Gandhi started to correspond with the great Russian writer, which led to an exchange of several important letters between them. Tolstoy's last communication to Gandhi was prophetic: "Your activity is the most essential work, the most important of all the work now being done in the world."

Though their praise for one another was high, it must be noted that their methods were quite distinct. While Tolstoy taught pure and absolute nonviolence, Gandhi was far more dynamic in his approach. Inspired by the thoughts and deeds of another American, Transcendentalist Henry David Thoreau and his *Civil Disobedience,* he saw nonviolent action not just as a refusal to participate in governmental violence, but also as a means to compel the state to change its policies. He chose a political route, seeking to transform society through nonviolent means and social reform, in the process demonstrating that his focus was not *non-resistance,* but rather *nonviolent resistance.*

To accomplish this feat required the moral power of what came to be known as Satyagraha, or truth-force. After Gandhi's approach led to the successful liberation of his country, the idea of truth-force and nonviolent resistance would, decades later, find its way back to America, where it was brilliantly and courageously reflected in the life and work of a young African American from the state of Alabama. Martin Luther King, Jr. engaged in a nonviolent spiritual-political revolution for the dignity, inherent worth, and civil rights of his people, and in the process, transformed and enriched the life of Blacks and Whites alike.

The dedicated men and women – from the Social Gospel to the Civil Rights movements – who tirelessly worked for the creation of a more dignified way of life, left a remarkable legacy for Americans and indeed the people of the world, to build upon.

All are created equal, entitled to life, liberty, and the pursuit of happiness. That is the timeless message written on the heart of every human. Being inherent, inborn – an inalienable right – guarantees that once an individual awakens to it, the yearning for attaining it cannot permanently be suppressed.

Seeing beyond the obvious

Knowing of the human capacity for abhorrent conduct, is it gullibility, or perhaps wishful thinking, to believe that such high standards as inherent worth and dignity apply to *every* person? After all, when scanning the vast archives of human behavior, what worth and dignity are we referring to?

In fact, when one considers all the dark and diabolical deeds human beings have done and are committing, it is not surprising that some would conclude that the religious concept of original sin lies at the root of our problems.

I suppose an argument could be made for such an interpretation, in accordance with Dostoevsky's, "Human beings were given paradise; they wanted freedom," but I would prefer staying closer to home. In brief, I think there is something more immediate that explains human behavior and that is the concept of "original wound". It starts in childhood and has much to do with the fact that we are raised by flawed human beings. The effects of those flaws, those many shortcomings, some rather severe, prevent us from being wholly ourselves and fully loving. Why? Because to the degree that we have been injured, to that degree we have become disempowered.

With disempowerment comes fear, and often pent-up anger at the mistreatment we had to endure. And when serious disempowerment, fear and outrage combine, the explosive hatred they generate becomes the root of all violence, of everything that makes us appear as less than worthy – and human.

At moments like these, it is vital to recall that while we are quite capable of committing unworthy acts, we can never taint the worthiness that is our core component. It never forsakes us, though we often ignore and not infrequently desert it.

Knowing this, we can describe Homo sapiens in these words: unpredictable behavior on the surface, essential being and peace at the center. Or, to apply another metaphor, ever changing waves on top, vast stillness below as in the dual reality of an ocean.

This is why wise teachers all have the same objective: to lead seekers to their depth dimension, the source of every person's true nature, yet far too often hidden from the involved individual.

There is a jewel of a story, an ancient legend, taken from the archives of India's great spiritual tradition, which brilliantly describes the human predicament when we don't make a special effort to become aware of a deeper reality.

According to the parable, there was a time when all human beings were gods, but they so abused their divinity that Brahma, the chief god, decided to take it away from them and hide it where they would never again find it.

Where to hide it became the big question.

When the lesser gods were called to consider the problem, they said, "We will bury their divinity deep in the earth."

But Brahma said, "No, that will not do, for human beings will dig deep down into the earth and find it."

Then they said, "We will sink their divinity into the deepest ocean."

But again Brahma replied, "No, not there, for human beings will learn to dive into the deepest waters, will search out the ocean bed, and will find it."

Then the lesser gods said, "We will take it to the top of the highest mountain and there hide it."

But again, Brahma replied, "No, for humans will eventually climb every high mountain on earth. They will be sure some day to find it and take it up again for themselves."

Then the lesser gods gave up, admitting, "We do not know where to hide it, for it seems there is no place on earth or in the sea that human beings will not eventually reach."

After a lengthy silence, Brahma decreed, "Here is what

we will do with the divinity of human beings. We will hide it deep down in themselves, for they will never look for it there."

Ever since then, the legend concludes, human beings have been going up and down the earth, climbing, digging, diving, exploring, searching for something that is already within.

Here, in a short tale of hide and seek, lost and found, lies the frustration and glory of being human. Books have been written, this book has been written, to bring this intriguing story to people's attention, that we may be led home to who we really are, to become aware of our true nature. For as different as our journeys may be, we are all searching for the same: love, wholeness, harmony, a reassuring sense of belonging. And each one awaits our discovery – within.

Until that hour, we engage in every kind of acrobatics and maneuvering to get what we believe we do not have. And this is why it often takes years, sometimes a lifetime, before we realize that, contrary to the snail, which carries its house on its back, humans always carry their home and true belongings inside themselves. Until we perceive that reality, we search for shelter and protection in the most unlikely, and sometimes perilous, of places.

Conversely, once we are fully established in the only home we ever really own, then everywhere we go becomes home because we are settled and at peace with our self.

We have for too long emphasized the outer, visible, over the inner, invisible, and the rational over the relational. The price we have paid for that peculiar exclusion in terms of damaged and wasted lives is both enormous and unnecessary.

Unfortunately, especially in America, few of us are familiar with the inner landscape of our lives. We are simply not very well educated about the interior realm (remember, this is primarily an extroverted society), and that lack of knowledge can be a significant hindrance to exploring what is unseen and intangible. It does not, of course, have to remain that way.

Let none be excluded

Since most of us are prone to self-forgetting, to not being consciously anchored in ourselves, we tend to drift or get lost in a spiritual wilderness where we are exposed to all kinds of dangers and temptations. In fact, we can say that whenever primary elements of our being are hidden from us, the consequences are costly indeed, as Part I so thoroughly and shockingly sought to illustrate. This is why, as we learned, teachers, by story and/or example, seek to lead us back to the riches of our own undiscovered Selves. They know that the deeper we dive to touch the great currents of our humanity, the more we meet our own divinity. In that embrace lies the freedom that empowers us to envision a different world.

Equipped with that freedom and vision, we can assist others in their struggle for liberation, becoming activists against injustices. Like Martin Luther King, we are able to recognize the need for a radical alteration of values, in order to conquer "racism, extreme materialism, and militarism".

Racism, materialism and militarism are the outcome when human dignity is ignored and the hollowness of things and arrogance of power are substituted for human worth.

Now, while considerable progress has been made since King's time with respect to the first component of the triplet, racism, the two others, materialism and militarism, have never held more sway over human life than they do today. And the great irony is that they are being generated and stoked in our own country with its obscenely bloated military budget, perpetual war mentality, and "shop 'til you drop" attitude.

We are no longer sleepwalking but running toward a cliff – unless we wake up and become conscious in time to avoid plunging over the edge.

Clearly, there can be no justice, no peace and harmony, and possibly no life, without the recognition of every person's worth and value. Otherwise we erect a wall of separation hazardous to the flow of life, starting with our own. Consequently, those who seriously doubt the veracity of inherent worth and dignity, and act accordingly, do create a long list of grievances, from the ill treatment of humans to the exploitation of animals.

The whole of us, by its very name and nature, is all-inclusive. The extraordinary Helen Keller paid tribute to this when she said, "The welfare of each is bound up in the welfare of all." Leaving anything out of that circle of concern, including elements we consider marred and undeserving, would negate the very definition of wholeness. And it is through the whole, through wholeness, that our life and very being are given worth and dignity. Yet, should this reality be limited to humans?

Having watched for many years with a sense of wonder the character of animals, whether wild or domesticated, I, for one, admit that animals never cease to amaze me. Additionally, having had the privilege of a 14-year companionship with a magnificent dog, I can speak from direct experience of the purity, honesty, and certainly the devotion, of an animal.

This is why I believe inherent worth and dignity should not only be ascribed to humans, but to all members of the community of sentient beings. Whether highly developed or only at some rudimentary stage, I am convinced that everything contains a divine spark or a touch of the Holy. It would indeed be strange if "in God we live and move and have our being" only applied to humans, and the rest of creation would be excluded from that blessed state, as though there were an "inside" and "outside" to the contours of the universe, not to speak of the great circle of love!

Although having held such a view for many years, I am, nonetheless, always delighted to add another validating incident. The latest was offered in a most vivid and touching manner when I came across the story of a black-necked stilt, a waterfowl, looking at a mural on the wall of its enclosure (AP wire services, January 2011). As it turned out, what he was seeing was an enlarged painting of a bird looking much like him.

With my curiosity aroused, I read on, soon to be enveloped by a sense of wonder. Titled, "The heart mends", the photograph introduced us to Skippy, a twenty-three-year-old stilt, who felt so bereaved by the demise of his mate several years ago that he barely ate, stopped grooming himself and appeared depressed.

At the beginning of 2011, his enclosure at the National Aviary in Pittsburgh was enhanced by a mural depicting his deceased companion. Immediately upon noticing the image, the report stated, he began vocalizing. Realizing that something extraordinary was occurring, alert keepers offered him food in front of the painting. As though transformed, the bird began to eat heartily. His long spell of grieving had been broken by the depiction of his mate.

And we have behaved toward animals as though they have no feelings, treat them inhumanely, use and abuse them. As I experienced with our Weimaraner, there is often more dignity and incorruptibility in an animal than can be found among humans.

Darkness: A chance to grow our light

How shall we respond to those who demonstrate the worst of characteristics, who disappoint, frustrate, enrage, appall and disgust by their behavior – how deal with the many transgressions against all that we treasure in and around us?

My experiences under the totalitarian regime of East German communism have given me antennas for recognizing deception, hypocrisy and the hubris of ideologues and fanatics wherever they attempt to stamp their mark on collective life. It is not hard, then, for me to be incensed by such behavior. However, commitment to my own humanity and spiritual vision sternly reminds me that, while I am permitted and even encouraged to oppose injustice and cruelty, I have an obligation to separate the deed from the doer, or else I could end up inflicting on another the very element or act I despise.

Which means when we recognize the inherent worth and dignity of a person, we neither condone, nor permanently condemn. The focus must therefore be on justice, not revenge, and beyond that, on rehabilitation.

Our legal code makes that quite clear: no cruel and unusual punishment, not even for a convicted criminal. It has been designed in this manner not just because of the accused but because we know that when we do cruel and inhumane things to others, we simultaneously injure our own humanity. Moreover, how a society treats those who have committed a transgression is a measure of how evolved and civilized we are.

Again, by focusing criticism and a healthy anger on perturbing acts, we deflect ire from the wrongdoer and can thus more easily preserve respect for innate worth and value – that of the perpetrator as well as our own.

Because emotions always run high in cases where conflict takes place, it requires discipline and strength to embody the ideal of valuing the person while denouncing the deed.

On the other hand, none of us would even be sensitive to, much less outraged by, wrongdoings if we ourselves did not have within, the gift of innate worth and dignity against which to measure such acts. When others are treated unfairly, harshly, something inside of us responds to the pain of the wronged. Depending on the degree of our courage, we will speak out in protest or act in ways that assuage the injury.

Those doubtful or cynical about such innate gifts might ask themselves how it is that despite egotism, greed, apathy, and arrogance, humans are capable of deeds of great love, generosity, forgiveness, fortitude and heroic sacrifice. And if those latter qualities had not been practiced over the generations far more than the former, humanity would never have grown to seven billion, but would long ago have become extinct.

The human spirit is clearly capable of poignant and self-transcending acts. Who would insist that such abilities are native to some but not to all? Granted, if we look only at the tip of the iceberg, it is easy to get dispirited. Yet, when exploring beneath the surface, a far more reassuring reality awaits our discovery. This is when we can see firsthand that everyone is endowed with a precious core of great value, though its potentials may never be actualized. However, even when "in hiding", the energy for its manifestation is perpetually present, and ready to be ignited under the right conditions.

We see this especially in a time of crisis, with its consequent stories of heroic actions. This was demonstrated once again in February of 2013 after the cruise ship Carnival Triumph lost power due to an engine fire and perilously drifted for a "cruel" week at sea. With 4,200 people aboard, life soon was made miserable by the stench of raw sewage due to unusable toilets and rotting food due to lack of refrigeration.

Passengers could have been selfish and looked out only for themselves and their loved ones. Instead, "they became comrades in a long, exhausting struggle" as they themselves testified. They shared and traded precious supplies and helped each other as much as possible, even making room for strangers in private cabins. As one passenger put it, "I really think we've made some lifelong friends going through this ordeal."

Such incidents, such times of testing, tell us much about human nature; tell us that when the heart is called into play, our species has a future, and a bright one at that.

As to the other side of the coin, the appalling stories we learn about in the media, anyone who investigates the root causes of such behavior will soon discover that people don't do dark and hideous things unless they live in darkness, that is, in ignorance of their own true nature, their inner light. The dimming of that light frequently occurs when individuals are too young to resist the harsh and heartless behavior of those upon whom they depend for their very existence. But as modern therapy and spiritual counseling have shown, with the right tools and goodwill, much that seemed lost can be regained, transformed. The garbage of our lives can be turned into compost for growth.

I believe that none of us has been given life simply to accommodate old patterns, but to add something new to the world. For instance, in view of the darkness of our age, it is critical for each of us to share a stronger inner light in the context of our living and relating. With that revolutionary act, we can add our very being as something fresh and powerful to the life of humankind.

Wanting for others what we treasure for ourselves

No king or queen of old, no people before us experienced the privileges we enjoy today, as evidenced by our liberties, copious choices, conveniences, comforts and leisure time. Due to lack of awareness, we may misuse or abuse these options, or simply take them for granted, but ours has become a life of almost limitless possibilities. From that perspective, we are indeed a fortunate people.

Fortunate people are generally grateful people, and grateful people are inclined to be generous. People who are grateful and generous usually want for others what they treasure for themselves. Which means we cannot allow our principal values of freedom, equality, and human rights to be tainted by exclusion or haughty rejection of anyone. In addition, if we have difficulty affirming the inherent worth of others, it may be time for an honest self-examination to see whether we have actually accepted such a reality in *ourselves*. Because only when we have fully embraced our own self-worth, can we realize that such worth is equally present in all others.

Therefore, the individuals we need to be concerned about are those who are not only unable to see the worth of others, but, more importantly, their own. Out of touch with the core self, they pose various risks. For there is no limit to the harm that springs from ignorance of self. The archives of history are stacked with endless reports of such damages.

By contrast, every individual who aligns with what is genuine and enlightened within is able to manifest magnificent attributes: love, compassion, fairness, forgiveness, dependability, courage, service, sacrifice.

We are standing today at the threshold of a new consciousness, and for those who have crossed it, the clock cannot be turned back. The most tangible aspect of that newness is the sense of preciousness and equality of every life. Out of that deep knowing have been born the great movements of our times: human rights, self-determination, the partnership model in all areas of human endeavor, environmental protection, and the emerging global family and village.

To participate in the liberation of the human spirit, and the shaping of a saner future, it is of utmost importance that we inquire: Do I adequately love and respect myself? Do I recognize my own worth? Do I act with integrity, walk in dignity? Do I have the courage to speak my truth, speak my yes, speak my no? In a word, am I able to be true to my Self?

How we answer these questions will allow us to see the quality of two relationships – to self and to others. To the degree that we love and respect ourselves, to that degree will we love and respect others. It is literally as simple as that.

There is a holy ground that sustains our inner, spiritual

tree of life. And while a lot of trash gets dumped on the front steps of our dwelling, that holy ground, that magnificent garden, can never be polluted by anything we do or by what is done to us. The inherent worth and dignity remains untouched, undefiled, regardless of what happens on the outskirts of our being and life.

Yes, we can be so badly injured that we turn scruffy and ugly. Think of the variations of the age-old story of Beauty and the Beast. In the end, each version unfolds in the same way: we come to recognize the repulsiveness, the mean-spirited behavior, as a mask and a shield around the heart. As such, it is meant to protect the wearer from further hurt, a hurt that was so deep originally that it led to the closing of the door to the inner being, turning a vulnerable human into a menacing "beast".

The terrible spell can be reversed by only one element: love. Love is the miracle, the miracle worker. Love is the transforming, healing power. Love can bring forth what has been there all along. It may be deep in hiding, but it never went away, never *can* go away. And thus love allows the true being to (re)emerge – that which is beautiful and loving, even in the ugly ogre. In fact, being touched by love, all that is hideous now turns beautiful as though by magic.

And love is the element in us that wants for others what we cherish for ourselves.

So the next time you encounter a nasty, mean-spirited individual, remember that beneath the ugly surface hides someone estranged from love, someone disconnected from the core of his or her own being. What such a person needs most is to be loved. Please don't misunderstand; I do not suggest you take abuse. Rather, I recommend you do not allow any person to control the flow of your love or steal from you your humanity.

Self-alienation versus self-love

I would like to further deepen our understanding of the principle that speaks of inherent worth and dignity by offering a brief reflection on the tragic end of one of the 20th century's most remarkable men.

On August 16, 2005, Brother Roger, founder after WWII of the ecumenical community of Taizé in France and a man of peace and reconciliation, was murdered by a mentally ill woman. How to interpret the gruesome killing of such a saintly individual in front of a stunned gathering of worshippers from around the world?

Seen through a spiritual lens, we must start with the fact that the woman was mentally ill, mad, insane. In other words, she was removed from reality, and thus from her own true self. She did not know what she was doing. She then murdered someone the very opposite of herself, someone fully at home with himself and all of creation.

In contemplating this, I asked myself, is not every murder based on the same disconnect from reality, on dissociation from who we are at our core? Can we not, therefore, take this a step further and say that all acts of criminality arise from the fact that we are not ourselves; that we live estranged from our being – our inherent worth and dignity? And is this not a form of illness?

I would argue that it is, and that we, consequently, need another category of illness, one which also explains massacres, genocide, wars of aggression, and other forms of cruelty delivering death to thousands. The woman who killed Brother Roger was mentally ill; those who order killing for political or any other reason suffer an even more serious sickness: spiritual illness, a disease of the soul.

What does this mean for humankind as a whole? It means that the healthier we are spiritually, the more we will see through the intrigues of those who feed on the spiritually ill. Having gained clarity, we will then no longer submit or become unwitting tools. We will break the debasing spell.

None of us can possibly change unless the power and potential for that change is inherent. All religions, whatever their aim – salvation, liberation, surrender, awakening, transformation, enlightenment, self-realization – are based on what is naturally, inherently, within. And none of it is greater than the love that sustains us, the love which essentially *is* us.

Those who know it and freely share it speak of it as the

healing power for the most serious and devastating soul illness there is. Explains Martin Luther King, "Hatred and bitterness can never cure the disease of fear; only love can do that."

During a capacity crowd address at New Mexico State University in Las Cruces in the spring of 1996, Alice Walker, too, reminded us no less of the truth of that love when she counseled, "It's really all about your ability to love...There is one thing you can do when it seems there is nothing left to do: improve your own compassion. You can make a difference."

Intentionally harming another is self-damaging because it reduces our humanity. Yet, we do it because we have neglected to deepen our own compassion, cultivate our love. And all love must begin with self-love, must first be directed toward our self before flowing outward, toward others.

To actualize spirituality is humanity's most valuable endeavor and challenging goal. Yet, spiritual growth is a slow process because none of us inherits the gains of our parents. Rather, everyone must engage in their own unique journey. While that guarantees our freedom of choice, it also means that each individual has to learn basic lessons all over again. At the same time, however, there is good news, for when enough people are starting to wake up and impact the human environment with greater awareness and compassion, everyone's learning is fostered rather than continually frustrated.

What has become clear in our time is that we have the tools to break the chains of the past. By accepting that the eyes of history are on us, we can seize the opportunity to dispense with the no longer useful and strengthen that which enhances and assists. We can start to free ourselves from the shackles of erroneous beliefs by recognizing the most fundamental and sustaining elements of what it means to be human: the inherent worth and dignity of every person.

And because inherent worth is about a life, not a lifestyle, everyone deserves basic rights, love, respect; everyone deserves to have his or her dignity protected and preserved.

Chapter 10

A DIFFERENT WORLD
IS POSSIBLE

Wherever a human being comes, there comes revolution.
The old is for slaves.

~Ralph Waldo Emerson

Hope has two beautiful daughters, anger and courage – anger
at the way things are and the courage to change them.

~St. Augustine

Whatever you can do or dream you can, begin it. Boldness has genius,
power and magic in it.

~Johann Wolfgang von Goethe

You can best serve civilization by being against what usually passes
for it.

~Wendell Berry

Change. In its rhythm lie the splendor of the seasons, solace for the afflicted, and hope for those in waiting. As early as the 5th century BC, Heraclitus noted that "Nothing endures but change." It is a truth that has passed the test of time, and today is active deep in the human heart like a seed ready to sprout, to bring forth something new and promising.

Indications are that desire for genuine change is gaining momentum. In fact, the word change has become so ubiquitous and popular it is being usurped by opportunistic politicians who have not the slightest intention of bringing it about! There is, however, a significant reason why it has become fashionable to proclaim it: humanity yearns for it. And what humanity whole-heartedly longs for cannot for long be denied.

Indeed, cynics notwithstanding, humanity is even now

in the process of demonstrating that a different world is possible. A critical mass is building for a more aware and empowered citizenry, proving once again that there is, as always, an unintended gift to the machinations of dark forces: the emergence of new light in the heart of humankind.

Consequently, now is the time to place everything in perspective in order to arrive at a new understanding of what matters most at this crucial point in our evolution. Those in particular who agree with Socrates' aphorism that the examined life alone is worth living are invited to open minds and hearts to a broader spectrum of ideas, especially ones that are at a considerable distance from an individual's comfort zone.

Disenchantment on the rise

As variously pointed out, since the 19th century, the direction of Western societies has been heavily determined by science and its technological applications. As a result, many aspects of our existence have become mechanized, fragmented and made impersonal. Think of the phone calls to providers that are supposed to serve clients, and rather than being able to speak to a real person, what we get is a long menu of options for pushing buttons.

Thus, while technology has greatly expanded our lives – and our life spans! – it has also depersonalized what used to be human interactions that offered a sense of relating and even belonging to a larger world. Instead, the value of a human being has shrunk to the degree that he or she is replaceable by a machine or electronic innovation.

Thus, what was once lauded as progress has shown itself to be a double-edged sword. While it has brought many conveniences and previously unheard-of opportunities, it has equally compelled us to realize that things in and of themselves can never meet the deeper needs of human beings; in fact, they leave us precariously undernourished and depleted. We are hungry for connections, the human touch, in the midst of plenty. Not knowing what it is we are lacking, we often end up accumulating even more possessions in an attempt to fill the inner vacuum. This is how we have become in numerous ways an addictive society, especially when it comes to the ubiquitous need to have "fun".

Imagine if someone or a group had been plotting to destroy the moral fiber of a nation; they would certainly have plenty of reasons to congratulate themselves on a sinister deed "well done".

Moreover, this decline has not only affected personal and social values, but has had a disastrous impact on politics. Its theater of operations has been contaminated, besides other pollutants, by obscene amounts of money, making every politician dependent on enormous financial contributions. This is reflected especially by those newly minted hybrid corporations/political action committees made possible by the Supreme Court of the United States, thanks to the idea of "corporate personhood". Their ruthless and relentless attack ads certainly changed the climate of American politics in 2012.

Developments like these, with their emphasis on riches and special interests, uncaringly override people and their needs, while adding assorted temptations to the lives of individuals in public positions. It seems billionaires and Wall Street tycoons, with their bulging wallets and overseas bank accounts, decide more and more the direction of our country, and a no less affluent entertainment industry sees to it that we have enough diversions not to notice our impotent status as citizens.

Of course, such harmful currents create their own counter pressure. As mentioned previously, the Occupy Wall Street gatherings and camps a la Tahrir Square were encouraging indicators that something was shifting in the consciousness of at least some Americans. Activists and their supporters insisted that those who greedily accumulated wealth in this country should be held responsible for the crimes that led to the financial crisis of 2008 with its ongoing repercussions here and abroad. Those voicing grievances recognized themselves as representing the great majority of citizens in this country.

This was a sudden, unexpected movement, much like the surprise uprisings in the Arab world, with demands for ultimately the same objective: participatory democracy. For that is what has been lost in America, even as it had been denied the people of the countries of the Middle East for a long time.

The activists committed to Occupy Wall Street clearly took to heart a truth once voiced by Supreme Court Justice Louis Brandeis, who recognized, "We can have a democracy in this country or we can have great wealth concentrated in the hands of the few. We cannot have both."

It is a hopeful development that more citizens are beginning to realize that there simply are too many riches in the hands of a few who use them to influence the fate of our country for self-serving purposes. If that iron chain could be broken or at least weakened, the spirit of America could begin to be revitalized.

And not only in America, but anywhere in the world where money and Mammon are king. For example, England, too, birthed an Occupy movement, a fact which did not escape the newly appointed Archbishop of Canterbury, Justin Welby. He realized that the movement "reflects a deep-seated sense that something is wrong," even as he famously denounced multimillion-pound executive pay packages in big British companies as "obscene". He is a man who knows whereof he speaks, having been for more than a decade an oil executive before he was called to the priesthood.

Few would want to convert from the status of an executive to the rank of a priest; however, disenchantment with ways that are superficial, divisive and unjust is leading an increasing number of individuals to dedicate themselves to an alternative worth striving for: a rebirth of soul and spirit. They are realizing that this is the only way to bring humankind home to itself and the great riches of the inner world.

As someone who looks at life primarily through a spiritual lens, I could not be more fully in agreement. In fact, from my perspective, it is not only the disillusionment caused by the selfishness and consumerism of modern life, but the militancy of philosophical materialism with its life-as-accident assertions and pronounced antagonism toward spirituality, that have contributed to the present malaise. In short, human beings have multiple reasons to feel disenchanted.

In the meantime, the assumption that change could

come to an "occupied" country like the US without fierce opposition from those in control has shown itself to be illusory. That's why none should have been surprised to see TV screens light up with the "Breaking News" that the Occupy Wall Street camp in Zuccotti Park, New York City, was raided and dismantled by police and SWAT teams one cold midnight in November 2011. Yet, a spokesperson for the demolished camp did not permit hope to vanish. "You can't evict an idea whose time has come," announced Hans Shan calmly and encouragingly.

Only the ignorant build on sand

Why do so many aspects of our world feel insecure and unstable? The answer is rather simple: because the ground on which we have built is not solid, but sandy – the shifting sands of our willfulness and excesses.

This is why, faster than anticipated, the Earth is warming, the Arctic ice is melting, ecological disasters are looming. Unfettered growth has left a precious planet pockmarked and weakened; has even placed life in the oceans at risk. As a result, all aspects of nature are suffering because of the degradation which greed and carelessness have wrought.

Process theologian John Cobb maintains that when humans are placed at the center of all significant concerns, it gives us permission to manipulate nature for our ends and satisfaction exclusively. Ethical systems (if we can call them that!) are then shaped accordingly.

An anthropocentric perspective is one in which all that matters are the needs, wants, and desires of Homo sapiens. Such an attitude estranges us from all that really matters: the Divine, the Earth, our own spiritual being and one another. This kind of thinking, Cobb concludes, "can make us environmentally suicidal and spiritually and ethically impotent."

Not a reassuring prospect, although not all is lost. On the other hand, nothing will change until we do. We need to muster the courage to stand for our rights, while insisting on rights, respect and protection for the Earth and her creatures. We have acted like spoiled children and narcissistic adolescents. Which means we need to grow up, and grow up rather quickly if we hope to change the direction in which we are headed.

As events indicate, this can only happen if we make preserving the life on and of this planet our primary commitment. There are no longer any legitimate excuses for negligence; interconnectedness and interdependence – and the effect of ignoring them – have long been made visible to us. This is why decades ago we needed to move from hubris and self-indulgence to protection and prevention. It may be too late to reverse much of the harm caused by having failed to do so, but it is never too late to learn the lesson – and urgently apply it whatever the challenge.

Factoring in different stages

It would be easy to become irate and remain that way when contemplating the damage done to the quality of life by the unawakened. In the long run, this would not, however, serve our effort at fashioning a new and different world. Why not reacquaint ourselves instead with the work of a pioneering thinker of the 20th century and perhaps gain a different perspective and deeper understanding?

In the 1950s, psychologist Lawrence Kohlberg initiated a philosophical discussion about the fact that humans, on their journey toward maturity, are at different points along the way. Kohlberg highlighted this fact in his research and subsequent theory of the stages of moral development. He names and describes various levels of morality, designating them as pre-conventional, conventional and post-conventional.

For instance, there are those who act in accordance with a morality of reward and punishment, with proper behavior driven by such questions as "How can I avoid punishment?" on one hand, and "How can I gain approval and reward?" on the other. It is a stage where concerns are shaped by self-interests and the possible consequences certain actions might bring. This combines with a deep-seated deference to those who are in power. Such attitudes and behaviors are the mark of pre-conventional morality.

The next phase, conventional morality, is characterized by a person's acceptance of society's conventions concerning right and wrong. Such persons tend to conform to social norms and obey laws, rules and edicts because they consider them as necessary for a well-functioning society. Here we find the law and order mentality, with morality predominantly dictated from the outside, by experts and institutions, as it is in the previous pre-conventional category.

Kohlberg estimates that these two groups constitute the large majority of the Earth's population.

Existing side by side with that majority is another group defined as post-conventional. Here men and women embrace universal ethical principles, which include such basic human rights as life, liberty, and justice. For them, the rights of each human being are as important as the rights of the collective. Such individuals treasure a principled conscience and act because it is right to do so, not because it is expected or prescribed. They furthermore elect to abide by the spirit if not the letter of the law because post-conventional morality is rooted in a sense of inner authority. As one might expect, people thus constituted feel comfortable in the midst of change.

Their numbers comprise a much smaller percentage of the whole of humanity. One can only hope that the number of those belonging to the third category of inclusiveness and conscience has grown over the last half century, thus shrinking the size of the membership within the pre-conventional and conventional categories.

But whatever might be the present distribution across the spectrum of Kohlberg's model, it seems to me that this non-judgmental way of pointing to different developmental stages is a rather useful and quite compassionate reminder that not all inhabitants of this planet speak the same language, nor do they abide by the same moral code. There is, however, no question in my mind that in time *all* Homo sapiens will graduate from this school of life with its extraordinary challenges. Every person will then receive a post-conventional certificate.

Meanwhile, there is plenty of work to do, and plenty of tests to prepare for.

One final and rather crucial point: regardless of what his or her "conventions" might be, the idea of responsibility (although for different reasons) is stressed in all three stages of Kohlberg's moral development. Considering how far apart they otherwise are in emphasizing what is important, I think this is quite striking. Responsibility, it appears, is a virtue and a value that cannot be separated from what it means to be human.

With that in mind, an invitation goes out to anyone ready to take the next step, to be part of something new and revolutionary and deserving of our humanity. And in any case, if the wing beat of a butterfly in Africa can ultimately climax in a hurricane pounding Florida, then there simply isn't anything humans do without an enormous ripple effect, for good or ill.

From that point of view, we can examine some of the issues that have haunted human beings throughout history and which today, like never before, cry out for radical change.

To study war no more

The list of wrongs associated with the human race is long and the work before us formidable. However, topping them all is the scourge of war that reduces humans to callous killers responsible for the mass graves of soldiers and civilians alike, while leaving broken spirits in returning fighters, and desperate survivors in bombed-out cities and scorched environs struggling to stave off starvation.

Evolved men and women in every age have known about the diminution of humanity's essence in the rawness of war. This is why, as we learned in Part I, the prominent 19th century Unitarian minister, William Ellery Channing, charged the people of this country to be extra diligent guardians of the Constitution when it comes to war. He implored those in government not to support engagement in war unless "it be palpably necessary and just". Turning to the citizens, he pleaded, "In war, then, as in peace, assert the freedom of speech and of the press. Cling to this as the bulwark of all your rights and privileges."

Imagine if the majority of our representatives in Congress had stood firmly on that hallowed ground of moral clarity instead of giving George W. Bush and his ilk unchallenged authority to invade Iraq – to start an illegal and immoral war, which dragged on for nearly nine years of carnage and destruction, not to speak of dividing a people and religion.

Imagine further if we still had a free press in the United States of America to allow for the expression of true political diversity on the part of citizens; if we still had participatory democracy, or representatives in Washington doing "the people's business"!

It will be important to keep in mind that humans and war have been entwined to the point of synonymity since nomads became settlers and owners. Which means, regardless of how unbecoming it may be of humankind, realizing that war is not the answer will probably take longer than any other learning before it is finally accepted as a liberating truth.

How to deal with that delayed learning? With both passion and patience. We must advocate for the abolishment of war with commitment and fervor, yet, at the same time, not expect overnight results. Rather, we begin by addressing the underlying issues, which all too often become the causes of war. Martin Luther King named them at Riverside Church, New York, in 1967, and challenged us to dedicate ourselves to attaining them: to convert from a thing-oriented to a person-oriented society, from being profit-driven to being people-focused.

Imagine the constructive changes that could arise from such a radical transformation, both domestically and in our international relations. Instead of being the world's largest exporter of weapons, we would export goodwill and offer assistance to humankind everywhere. Instead of building military bases abroad, we would encourage genuine democratic movements around the globe. Instead of declaring, "You are either with us, or against us," we would broadcast the truth of life's oneness and humanity's kinship.

These changes are imperative, for as former President Carter has said, "We cannot be both the world's leading champion of peace and the world's leading supplier of weapons."

Finally, in an interconnected world, no country can thrive without acknowledging its bond with and responsibility to all others. That is the great lesson gleaned from the arrogance and folly of the Bush/Cheney/NeoCon administration.

Best times/worst times

A socially conscious Charles Dickens famously mused, "It was the best of times, it was the worst of times." Today's conditions appear to be a continuation of his appraisal.

The best of times, the worst of times -- unless we choose to live consciously and conscientiously, and in the process add wisdom and balance to the unfolding of our lives. If we do, we can demonstrate that another world is possible, that diversity and pluralism, unity and cooperation, equality and justice need not remain vacant words. Yes, the task is immense; yes, the obstacles are many and intransigent, but it has been given to us to turn stumbling blocks into steppingstones, barriers into building material for a stronger, loftier future.

There are transient values and there are lasting ones, and it is to the lasting ones, the tested ones, that all humans must eventually turn when those of a transitory nature reveal their insufficiency and their inability to sustain. The difference between the two has, in our time, become starkly apparent, as our Western lifestyle of ever-increasing consumption, busyness and diversions has shown its hollowness and unsustainability.

Conversely, dynamic self-expression, interdependence, the union of opposites, truth, universality, a consciousness transcending separateness – these are but some of the promising alternatives, some of the enduring values, set before us with which to color the canvas of the future. Simultaneously, there is a new and potent energy active in our world that is breaking down established patterns and conditions. It will assist us in creating something entirely different in the life of our species.

New England's acclaimed poet, Robert Frost, put it thus, "Two paths diverged in a wood, and I – I took the one less traveled by, and that has made all the difference." May we, like Frost, have the courage to do likewise.

Demands for freedom from unexpected quarters

There are unmistakable signs of something exhilarating occurring on our planet, a groundswell that proclaims enough is enough. A whole new line of thinking is preparing to manifest because a sufficient number of people are tired of "business as usual", or perhaps more to the point, they have learned the lessons of business as usual and now yearn for something more appropriate for their expanding awareness.

To mind come especially the political changes in the Arab world. The intense cry for freedom and self-governance, even at the price of precious lives, tells us that change cannot forever be postponed. That such manifestations took place in a part of the world which has not been in the forefront of political revolutions, is even more significant. Much of that delay, of course, has been due to governmental support for entrenched dictatorships by the West, primarily the US and Israel.

The surprise revolts of 2011 were electrifying and very encouraging, for humankind cannot move on without the participation of our brothers and sisters in that region of the world. Having been held back, oppressed and exploited for generations, the citizens of those newly unshackled countries could in time play a vital role in turning the tide through political and spiritual liberation. Their challenging religious practices have prepared them well for the task. And because the Middle East has been for several generations at the center of the struggle for tomorrow, to see its circumstances altered by a 180-degree turn in direction is inspiring and humbling indeed.

History shows that constructive societal changes begin with a shift in people's awareness, with an awakening within. When a critical mass is reached, consciousness widens and kindles a grassroots movement, gathering the people-power necessary for fundamental change. However, as recent developments reveal, genuine change is a slow process because elements bent on divide and conquer never miss an opportunity to sabotage progress. Nonetheless, the story of the Arab Spring remains exciting and hopeful, despite interferences from ill-willed groups of actors.

Therefore, in view of all that is occurring, and various obstacles notwithstanding, it remains a great privilege to be alive at a time when transformation is emerging as humanity's primary agenda, setting the stage for people of goodwill to journey together toward a new dawn.

Choosing life, living responsibly

With the rapid advance of technology, the human race has not only developed amazing opportunities for uncounted millions, but capacities which have led to two disastrous results: the creation of horrendous weapons of mass destruction and the destruction of the environment through ravenous appetites and mammoth pollution. Anthropocentric indulgences and addiction have thus created a terrible crisis, a perfect storm, whereby the human race shall either have to birth a new way of life or experience its end in a common, planetary grave.

In light of this reality, let us contemplate the admonition of the prophet Jeremiah: "I have set before you life and death ... Choose life that you and your descendants may live."

If we are to choose life, then something must significantly change. It starts with becoming aware of the blind spots that have led us to the present perilous crossroads. And it must lead to the question: What beyond the obvious erroneous attitudes and misbegotten policies is holding us hostage?

Answering, we could easily place the blame on utterly self-interested political and exorbitantly high-paid corporate leaders who care little about the welfare of humankind, much less the well-being of the planet. But would that solve the problem? As I have suggested recurrently, liability for the reality we have created lies in the thoughts, feelings and actions of every one of us. We are all accountable because we are part of a collective consciousness and share an entwined destiny, which means what we do or don't do affects the whole of humanity. Besides, by not accepting responsibility, we merely increase our sense of disempowerment and hopelessness.

What Albert Einstein so clearly perceived about living in the nuclear age, namely, that we shall not survive it unless we change our old ways of thinking, applies equally to all other emergencies we are experiencing. We must change our thinking as prerequisite for changing our lives and most importantly, for saving life on Earth.

To arrive at such a point could be made easier if we kept in mind that this life was not designed to make things easy for us, but to teach us lessons, to wake us up, to make us grow.

Since humans tend to be rather dense and generally quite stubborn, the way unseen agents of change get our attention is via the intensification of whatever problems demand resolution.

We have all experienced the phenomenon: First, all that needs changing begins to manifest in a more extreme manner to get our attention. For example: if we want more order in our lives, we can count initially on an exaggerated amount of disorder to get us moving; if we want to be a more empowered person, then incidents of severe disempowerment are sure to be encountered. If we yearn for peace, increased conflict will rattle our complacency. The proverbial need to be "hit over the head" seems to be applicable to individuals and societies alike. It appears that only then are we are finally willing to retrace our steps back to the center and sanity.

Take, for instance, scientific discoveries and the resultant technological advances affecting the material elements of our existence. Thanks to them, we presently enjoy lifestyles previously beyond imagination. But there is also a dark and disturbing aspect to this momentum, from severe damage to the environment, to the anaesthetizing impact of excessive consumerism, to the continuing depersonalization of life. By themselves, however, scientific developments are not responsible for the destructive side effects of various technological inventions.

Therefore, to blame external players alone for those imbalances will not solve the problems of modern life. On the contrary, it will ensure that we remain trapped. The uncomfortable truth is, we can overthrow all the oppressors and exploiters within sight and reach, but if we are out of harmony with the laws of life, if we cannot subdue excess or conquer ignorance and fear *within* ourselves, we will experience endless outer conditions whereby we either end up being controlled by others – or controlling them.

Fear, in particular, feeds and keeps alive the despots of this world. Which means if we are to emerge out of the hiding places of our lives into the sunlight of freedom, we must begin by overcoming fear. Fear is the prison. When fear rules us, the best of us gets incarcerated, opening the way for the worst to rule over us.

The wise know circumstances are not beyond our influence, and at no time is life "out to get us". Rather, life (a) reflects back to us where we stand spiritually, and (b) seeks to awaken us so that we can move from believing that things are happening to us, to knowing that we contribute greatly to making them happen. Such a fundamental shift in beliefs will take moral clarity, honesty and courage.

There is a way home to a sense of balance and strength and it opens up when we choose life and engage in living mindfully. And there is the continuation of the old pattern with its inevitable trek toward a precipice. Considering such polar opposites lets us see what a fateful parting of the ways we have reached. Like no other generation in recorded history, we are, at this time, given the opportunity to drastically and permanently alter the destiny of humankind.

It is hoped that, despite continual attempts at brainwashing, more and more of us will realize that we can, indeed, end the reign of fear, conformity and silence by claiming our own inner power, by being conscientious and unwaveringly committed to the gifts of life, love, truth and justice. Empowered, we can then say *no* to the militarists and profiteers of war, and *yes* to the makers of peace and renewal. In fact, we ourselves can become the peacemakers and menders of what is broken and in need of repair.

Now, learning the art of conscious living is a course in which we get enrolled the moment we declare with that singular piercing cry our arrival on this planet. Many would rather ignore the assignment, yet being a requirement, it is like a computer program continuously running in the background, ready to surprise us with yet another challenging lesson.

The beauty of taking such a never-completed course is that it takes place solely in the laboratory of our own lives. This provides us at all times with concrete, testable facts, and hence with the most valuable tool we could ever want: the power of direct knowing. Under such conditions, every experience can turn into a teachable moment. And every teachable moment can be the sparkplug that ignites change. I believe we are presently poised at the cusp of precisely such an opportunity.

Balance and the need to "stand under"

Direct knowing will eventually bring us face to face with a fundamental reality: the law of cause and effect. It is a law which says that, in the larger scheme of things, we are destined to reap what we have sown. (I am sufficiently influenced here by Eastern and Native American spirituality to think in a circular rather than a mere linear fashion.)

This same law also teaches that all misapplications of energy must in the end be balanced. Not punished, for that is a product of our limited human view, but balanced. Balanced in the sense that we must "stand under" in order to "understand". For is not most of what we fear, reject, exclude and even harm, something not yet understood?

If we accept the premise, can there be a fairer compensation for a wrong committed than the correcting of imbalances, the righting of the scales of justice? This is astutely symbolized in worldly settings by a female figure, blindfolded so as not to be prejudiced against one or the other of the parties.

Of course, in the case of a higher, universal justice, all of this unfolds on a psychic/spiritual level and does not necessarily enter the awareness of the average observer, including the one who must reap what has been sown. To know that this is a universe of absolute justice should give us solace. For what the concept tells us is that, contrary to the proverbial saying, no one ever really gets away with murder – nor is anyone ever condemned eternally. We simply have to become what we have not yet comprehended so that we never cease growing.

This is as good a time as any to remind ourselves that we humans are not known for achieving balance easily. Free will, self-will, has the tendency to quickly interfere with such delicate matters. We either lean too far to the left or too far to the right, tend to stretch too much toward others, or remain too tightly wrapped in ourselves.

Yet, regardless of the direction of our "leaning", each time we are out of balance, we compromise part of our genuine self, and depending on pre-disposition, end up as weak and compliant or tough and domineering. In the process, we reap ironic mirror images, for both the weak and the tough are afflicted with the same spiritual malady: disempowerment.

In addition, we are constantly disconnected from our depths by a demanding ego, which operates on the surface of our being and acts embarrassingly immature unless disciplined. It frequently and defiantly tends to slide into the driver's seat to take charge. Should we be surprised, then, by the many wrong turns, crashes and even wild rides over cliffs that mark our personal and collective lives?

All these are indications of how devoid of equilibrium our lives really are and how essential it is to generate the self-discipline to work on correcting such shortcomings. For all those unruly and unchecked disturbances by egocentric humans must surely be frowned upon by a universe magnificently interconnected and adroitly balanced.

Incidentally, I was reminded of that interlaced element a year ago when a friend of mine had a car accident. Nothing major, except for the fact that it caused a ripple effect in her activities and relationships that was simply astounding! I suppose if we could ever see how intrinsically all elements of life are entwined, including our acts, or omission thereof, we would either be traumatized or transformed.

New shoes and new truths

Who could deny that the systems in charge of our lives, be they political, economic or financial, are badly out of alignment with the deeper yearnings of a large segment of today's humanity? And what sensitive person is not distressed about the injustices that arise from such a situation?

Yet, as I have suggested in earlier writings, if we were to set aside all the weighty predicaments of our time, and all the judgments we attach to them, we might be able to perceive the human condition through the lens of a softer focus: the metaphor of a simple pair of shoes. We could then say that shoes which served us well, for example, at age six, lose their usefulness and become increasingly painful to wear when we turn seven. In fact, if those once comfortable shoes are not replaced by larger ones, they will permanently damage our feet.

Of course, this metaphor is not primarily about the soles of growing feet and their need for new walking gear, but the expanding awareness of our souls, which need the framework of a new, more properly fitting way of life, having outgrown the present one. That's what makes the dispensing of the old necessary, and to judge by the rising tide of voices calling for change, inevitable.

This, also, is the reason why the proponents of the outgrown show themselves so doggedly tenacious. They know that change is in the air – and they resist it fiercely.

No matter how we walk upon this remarkable planet, which over the millennia has patiently borne a tremendous amount of human traffic, we are at all times supported by universal principles active beyond our inadequacies. One of them is truth – truth affecting both the inner and outer planes of life. Truth not as an abstraction or a belief, but as a tangible reality that can be tested and applied in acts of living and relating.

Yet, despite being buttressed by the power of truth, the depth of the challenge we face today is immense. It is a battle of titans. For the energy that is opposed to truth, the demon of duplicity, is extraordinarily potent today. Operating in the shadows and in secret, its malignant influence vastly increased in the 20th century, and at the start of the 21st, reached a pinnacle of destructive manifestation. Today, scratch the surface of any so-called interminable issue, and you'll soon discover that truth is the repressed, and deceit the domineering, feature.

Not to be conscious of truth in contrast to falsehood is a terrible deprivation. For truth is the element that makes the bread of life rise and become digestible. Should we, then, be surprised that our lives have been flat and listless, having rarely invited truth to lift us up and nourish us? Additionally, truths, especially those which are uncomfortable, even painful, are the alarm bells that admonish us to climb out of the hazardous traps we are in. Otherwise, unawareness will simply keep us "blissfully" asleep and imprisoned.

When at first we don't succeed

Clearly, more and more people are recognizing that

there is something alarmingly wrong with the systems that run our world. In fact, the consensus is that we have simply outgrown them. That is why, in 2008, so many individuals responded with enthusiasm to then Senator Barack Obama's call for change and his confident "Yes we can!" Deep in our hearts, we knew that together we could shape a new and saner world.

In the end, the effort was not enough, especially since the new president appeared to be making too many compromises with regard to his exceptionally tenacious, even mean-spirited, adversaries. This can largely be traced to his personality traits, which strongly endow him with the potential of being moderate and a peacemaker. However, because such individuals tend to feel uneasy about conflict and confrontations, they often cannot rise above being an appeaser. The tendency to appease, which the president has displayed more than once, has served neither him nor the country well. Nor anyone in the world, for that matter, who had yearned for genuine change in America's foreign policy, most prominently among them the marginalized and long suffering Palestinians.

I should, of course, add here that while any individual's personality carries weight, in the final analysis, the causes for the president's inability to fulfill his promises lies not so much with him but those who are the ultimate decision makers in our capital, and beyond. Having been elected for a second term, we can only hope, audaciously, I might say, that over the next four years some of his great potentials will finally materialize.

Meanwhile, let it be said that while the craving of diabolical forces for nothing less than global control is intense, the desire of unifying forces is no less inclusive: the coming together of the people of the Earth in a spirit of oneness and equality. And even if Mr. Obama should not succeed in bringing us closer to that goal, the opportunity will surely come again when other voices will remind human beings of their "yes, we can" – and at that time, perhaps, more will be ready, and none will stumble.

Will Durant, historian and philosopher who gave us the voluminous *The Story of Civilization*, is an acclaimed expert on such matters. His words are encouraging. "There is value in painting a picture of our desires," he said. "Our power of imagination allows us to envision a better world ... Many a dream has grown wings and flown, like the dream of Icarus that human beings might fly."

Despite setbacks, the collective dream of a kinder and fairer world is a dream that will never die.

And indeed, those who see beneath the surface know that the arrival of the new millennium was not only a turning of the clock but also a turning deep inside the human psyche, in spite of the horrors and deaths that marked its beginning. This turning within is the real achievement, and a solid reason for staying rooted in hope, for not letting despair derail commitment to building a more humane tomorrow.

We are standing at the threshold of a new age and a new page in human history, although the birthing of it will not be as swift or easy as some of us had envisioned. The forces that rule the world have successfully duped too many, making it necessary to redouble our efforts – and perseverance.

As we commit to the great work, let us remember that, although we do horrible things to one another, we cannot, despite great ignorance and harshness, destroy the all-embracing Oneness and all-redeeming Love of creation. When we try to split the world in two – friend and foe – or when we diabolically erect walls, fencing people off into opposing camps, we engage in a futile effort: the interrelatedness of life and that of all people cannot be torn apart by words, barriers or bombs.

Moreover, since the end of WWII, but especially since the fall of communism, the yearning of the Earth's people has indeed been for "reunification". We speak of a global village; we have a European Union, the United Nations, and dozens of other organizations seeking to widen the circle of inclusion. None of them perfect, but all of them arising from the desire to mend what has been broken, to unify what has been severed, to make whole what has been fragmented.

Science and religion: Moving beyond either/or

In our time, an intense struggle has developed for supremacy between religious and scientific worldviews, especially in the United States. This is a battle which ultimately serves no one, and is, in fact, detrimental to everyone. Such a divisive issue is urgently in need of addressing if we want to create a more compassionate way of life. Let me explain.

Life on Earth is a school; it is not Heaven. However, these terrestrial classrooms have been and still are, for many, more like a prison, a penitentiary. Clearly, there must be a better way for human beings to learn life's required lessons.

For centuries, religion was seen as a pathway of bringing Heaven, "the Kingdom of God", to Earth. Yet, as with all such endeavors, fallible humans have a tendency to fail. Moreover, leaders everywhere show a particular vulnerability: they are susceptible to the temptation of power, power not as empowerment, but as power over others, i.e., control. And that is what meets the eye when surveying the panorama of history: addiction to power and the abuses associated with it.

With the rise of science, a worldview opposed to religion and dismissive of the idea of working toward the creation of Heaven on Earth, made its appearance. It would not only grow over the next centuries as a rival to religious influence, but decisively surpass it. Soon, science and its application, technology, were confidently touted as the promise of a brighter future. With its implementation, secularism became the dominant feature of the socio-political arena.

However, that rise to power, being no less exercised by fallible humans, revealed itself to be as corrupt as anything which had occurred previously. Even worse, the new paradigm has at its disposal not only progressive ideas but ever more destructive, even monstrous, weapons by which to exert control.

In addition, erasing God from any formula of existence, including the very creation of life itself, allowed for the systematic removal of ethical barriers, making room for materialistic and hedonistic lifestyles. With that, "anything goes" became the attitude of many. And so did resignation, cynicism and anxiety.

These are the bleak consequences inevitably set in motion when spiritual values are disdained as old-fashioned or cumbersome in the blind pursuit of personal "happiness". Moreover, it is unrestrained egocentricity that has introduced humankind and the natural world to enormous hazards. This includes, above all, the military "advances" of the last century with their potential for initiating the worst catastrophe in human history: a war of all against all.

If ever there was a need for spiritual awakening, it is in our time. While it is unlikely that this will occur en masse, those who are opening their eyes to the greater reality in which we live, even as they perceive the menacing threats to the inhabitants of this planet, need to speak with power and urgency to "king and commoner" alike. Silence could literally kill us.

And what are the values that need to be proclaimed and implemented? Above all, the recognition of life's Oneness and magnificent interrelatedness. From that foundation could then arise solid principles and values with the potential to save humanity from itself: truth and compassion, equality and justice.

For the religious, these are but attributes of God; for the humanist, they are the necessary building blocks of a civilized society. Religion, science and secularism could meet in commitment to these universally recognized values and change the destiny of humankind and the fate of our world.

By contrast, the present unremitting battle waged by "modernity" against religion will not solve humanity's problems. As I have argued, progress can be made only by realizing that religion and science are the two great pillars of human inquiry, knowledge and experience, and as such, they are complementary and necessary. With that awareness, the door can open to a new way of life where humans live in harmony with creation, care for the Earth, and strive to be friends and helpers to one another. (For a fuller discussion of this topic, see *One Light, One Spirit – A Guide to Transformed Living.*)

Small is something to reckon with

I believe what is happening in our time is the greatest test humanity has ever had to undergo. We are in the midst of an examination to determine whether the heart of the world's people is sterling enough to resonate to a higher octave of love. And while this can be an exceedingly difficult test, it is, at the same time, a great compliment, for it indicates that we have reached the point in our development when such a strong trial is not beyond our capacity.

On the other hand, because it is such a powerful test, it is equally laden with perils. This is why such potent challenges can go either way – a great rise, or a horrific fall.

Still, the message at this most perilous and promising time is unequivocal: if we are to live, and live with dignity, the old must die – the old guard mentality, the old formula, the lies, the injustices, the machinations of the domineering, the thirst of the power-intoxicated. For they are all suffocating yokes that dehumanize and compel others to be subservient – the human version of beasts of burden at its most degrading.

As we have pointed out, rebirthing ourselves is a magnificent but also enormously challenging assignment; rebirthing the larger life, the society and world we share, is an even greater task. After all, not every citizen has the time, energy or even inclination to gather in-depth knowledge about the human condition. This hinders recognizing what is most urgently in need of change and what is required to birth a new way of life on Earth.

However, we need not despair. For here is where Margaret Mead's observation can be invaluable: "Never doubt that a small group of thoughtful, committed citizens can change the world; indeed it's the only thing that ever has," she said.

Note that the emphasis is on *small*. As we know, individuals are brainwashed en masse, but awaken only one by one. With her wealth of anthropological studies at home and experiences of humans in their multiplicity abroad, it is reassuring to have Ms. Mead conclude that "small" not only can change the world, but is the only catalyst that ever has. In a word, "critical mass", the key element of change, does not require masses! That is in itself a small miracle – or actually, quite a big one!

In addition, the fact that it takes only a minority of dedicated individuals to bring about major change is the principal reason why dictators of every stripe fanatically persecute anyone who dares to be a voice of opposition, anyone who exposes their schemes.

Ironically, however, that very persecution often originates with a minority. For small most definitely also has a cynical side – when, for instance, a small group usurps power, and with iron determination and Total Spectrum Dominance, aspires to rule nothing less than the whole world!

In other words, not everyone on this globe thinks globally in a constructive way; not everyone on this Earth recognizes his or her kinship with all other co-habitants. In some parts of the world, there exist, in fact, the most callous displays of repression buttressed by a sense of superiority and entitlement. Ruthlessness is exercised with impunity.

For such power-addicted individuals, one voice of dissent represents a million dissidents, ten million threats. That's why they go to such lengths to intimidate, vilify and persecute. Even more to the point, this is why they created in our time desolate chambers of torture like Bagram, Abu Ghraib and Guantanamo. It says to anyone who contemplates resistance: Look, this is what will happen to *you* if you should dare to step over the line!

Of course, for some, knowing of the horror that takes place behind those walls has the opposite effect: it arouses an even greater determination to resist the inhumane forces and thus ensures continual recruitment to fight the oppressor.

We can therefore say that when pressures are intensified to the level of being made unbearable, the effect is the reverse of what was intended. It shakes people out of their trance and they no longer buy into the fear and falsehoods with which those in control sought to seduce them. They want to be free from the tricksters that are holding them captive. For them, the old habits cannot be dissolved quickly enough. For them, the road urgently leads on; the verdict is forward. However, until a tipping point is reached in favor of a new way of life, there will be struggle and turmoil.

What all this comes down to, then, is still the weight of one snowflake, that wonderful allegory for illustrating the difference each one of us can make. The idea behind the parable is that while a single flake is light as a feather, when millions of them have settled on a twig, the one landing next could break it. Translated into our present situation, this means when enough citizens wake up and say no to deceit and wrongdoing, the structures of injustice will start to crack, tremble, and suddenly fall. Think Berlin Wall!

For this, we do indeed need fearless pioneers. Yet, as Mead assures us, to start the process requires not multitudes but a minority with a vision and commitment. In brief, each of us can be the snowflake that tips the scale in favor of change.

Modern developments have clearly shown this principle in action. We recognize it in the acts of defiance of the few, inspiring the many, from women's rights to civil rights to gay rights to environmental protection. Often against fierce opposition, the gigantic iceberg of collective human consciousness suddenly begins to float in a different direction, and the philosopher's idea of how new truths rise to prominence in an entrenched setting receives one more confirmation. (Just to refresh our memory, according to Arthur Schopenhauer, groundbreaking truth passes through three stages: 1st it is ridiculed; 2nd it is violently opposed; 3rd it is accepted as being self-evident.)

There never was nor ever will be safety or security in dividing humanity into those who matter and those who don't. The only elements fostered by such a dualism are fear and conflict – and in the relationship between nations, a never-ending arms race. However, seeing the worth and dignity of all people, being compassionate and just, treating others with respect – that is another matter. Therein lies hope *and* a new future.

Hence, let us not become discouraged if those committed to equality and justice remain small in number. Margaret Mead's words can be relied upon.

The responsibility of hope

Playwright Tony Kushner, in an article in *The Nation*, remembered Arthur Miller at the time of his death as "a grieving pessimist". He then asked rhetorically, "But what truly progressive person isn't?"

I beg to differ with Mr. Kushner's conclusion. In my lexicon, a progressive is an individual strongly convinced that transformation is both necessary *and* achievable. A progressive is one with a powerful vision, a clear goal and inspired agenda for reaching it. He or she is not just an observer bemoaning the state of the human condition, but an activist determined and committed to change the dynamics.

If, on the other hand, we call ourselves pessimists, we should not be surprised if those who believe in the certainty of reactionary causes will shape the future. Progressives, let's be appalled and outraged by what is happening, but let's not be depressed and fatalistic! We have work to do, and we must do it without self-pity.

This is where the energizing quality of hope plays its vital role. Hope is, in fact, so essential to a healthy, productive life that one might best describe it as being akin to oxygen: we take it for granted until deprived of it. It is therefore not surprising that the spiritually aware have seen it as part of a great triad essential for life and meaning: faith, hope and love.

This explains why, after having for so long experienced spiritually vacant lives, we are confronted with such pervasive discontent. When the most vital spaces of our being are not claimed by us, squatters like boredom and cynicism and their unruly offspring will inevitably move in to become disturbers of the peace. It is then that scuffles are provoked by such elements as alcohol, drugs, crimes, pornography, vile movies, and violent computer games; that is to say, all the elements that mock and degrade the human spirit.

Watching a people self-destruct on so many fronts can indeed bring on feelings of despondency. Yet, do we not, once we classify ourselves as caring human beings, have a responsibility to not lose hope? We may momentarily despair, weep, shout, rant and rave, but we are not permitted – if we truly care – to lose hope. If we do, anti-spiritual, and ultimately anti-human, forces will step into the vacuum – and be the victors.

Granted, finding hope at this crucial turning point when a paradigm of truth, equality and justice struggles to emerge against a background of lies, intimidation and ruthlessness is not easy. At such times, more than ever, hope is indispensable for generating the stamina to remain attentive to the task.

Therefore, when moments of despair strike us – as they surely will when odds seem overwhelming – may we remember that communism collapsed, patriarchy dissolved, apartheid was swept away, and in the Arab world, protesters marched despite security forces confronting them with live bullets and no scruples about using them. Still, bold men and women continued to demonstrate having broken the wall of fear.

What inspires such bravery in people is the knowledge that without truth, freedom and justice, humans do not live but merely subsist.

In the meantime, their daring deeds assure us that the rigid ideologies and debilitating divisiveness afflicting our own country can be altered. Which is to say, hope is not a misplaced virtue but one that can carry us into decisive action. As I have proposed in *The Ultimate Choice: Armageddon or Awakening*, this country would benefit greatly from a Second American Revolution. For the present generation is rapidly losing what the original one stood for.

Finally, for those who, nonetheless, can't shake their sense of hopelessness concerning the state of the world, I recommend visualizing a small candle and how it can bring light to a space thousands of times its size. We can choose to be such a flame of hope by refusing to succumb to gloom, thus becoming an alternative to darkness and division.

In addition, no one needs to do this alone. There are today many incredibly bright and caring heart-lights active in our world. They speak eloquently and act fearlessly as they voice their opposition to injustice and oppression. They are the harbingers of a new age, a new life yearning to manifest. They need many more to stand tall against all that would diminish the human spirit and subdue the light of love in and around us.

We *can* reject selfishness and cynicism. We *can* choose to be a candle. We *can* engage in the sacred task of promoting for *all* people life, liberty and the attainment of happiness.

"Emancipation is the demand of civilization," the distinguished pioneer of American spirituality, Ralph Waldo Emerson, proclaimed during a lecture in Washington, D.C., on January 31, 1862. And he was referring not only to the abolishment of slavery as an outer form, but the many ways humans are in chains within.

To free ourselves from those inner impediments is the ultimate emancipation – and the work of a lifetime.

Those who care cannot ignore the call, for we have the great responsibility, and the unique privilege, to help restore the prominence of light and joy to our world by being lighthouses in the dark. History, despite the slow process of ascendancy, needs those who preserve their clarity of vision and are thus able to show others the way.

To usher in the year 2008, Mark Morford, columnist for the *San Francisco Chronicle*, wrote a stirring article about the human condition. He concluded by saying: "Believe you are a part of a groundswell, a resistance, a seemingly small but actually very large impending karmic overhaul, a great shift, the beginning of something important and potent and unstoppable."

Faith and hope are essential for making it happen.

A star to guide us

"The ideal must not touch the real," wrote the revolutionary German playwright Friedrich Schiller. The ideal is something unreachable, yet it can, nevertheless, be the guiding principle determining the course of our lives, much like the stars and constellations which, for thousands of years, assisted sailors in navigating the high seas.

Ideals do not have to be fully realized in order to be valid. Take, for example, the idea of optimal health. It is doubtful that any one of us could achieve it, regardless of how hard we make the attempt. Yet, theoretically, ideally, there is such a state of being, and if we can be guided by its radiance, we will all be better off.

Should we, however, at any time manage to somehow attain and actualize an ideal condition, we would soon have to replace the previous ideal with a new star, or else we would stop moving, and subsequently cease growing.

Today, having gone off course, drifting in dangerous waters, we are at the point where we need just that, a new star, a new vision, to guide us, based on what we can presently perceive as the best we are capable of being and becoming.

This is why an ever-increasing number of people are getting messages from the heart that signal dissatisfaction with the way things are. In response, they find themselves yearning for a tomorrow quite different from today. They are the cutting-edge inhabitants of Earth who are articulating the vision of a more people-friendly, life-protecting future. And not for a moment do they doubt that it is within the human capacity to demonstrate that a more sane and humane world is indeed possible. Clearly, they are guided by a new and brighter star.

As we explore what might be, it is natural to reflect on what has been. One might ask, for instance, whether there has ever existed on Earth in some distant yesterday a golden age of goodwill and sharing, harmony and peace. Or is such an ideal condition merely a yearning in the heart of humanity – and as such a powerful impetus for a more meaningful tomorrow, encouraging us to keep our eyes on the prize?

For me the latter definitely rang true while listening to a presentation on NPR about the circumstances surrounding the Olympic games of ancient Greece. Many of us hold an idealized image of the Greeks and their contribution to Western civilization, much, of course, justified. Yet, from the segment on the radio emerged a different, and rather startling, picture.

The commentator spoke in detail of the primitive setting of the games, lamented the lack of hygiene, the overwhelming stench, the fight to the death, horrible accidents, orgies, misogyny. It all sounded pretty barbaric.

Now, considering that the Greeks gave us the word "barbarian" because of their contempt for what they considered the uncivilized manner of certain foreigners and their inelegant way of speaking – or simply for anyone who was a not a Greek, one can scarcely imagine what those other lives must have been like if the ones who originally coined the word barbarian strike us today as shockingly barbaric themselves!

Of course, we don't even have to go as far back as the ancient Greeks; we only need to read accounts of Europe in the 19th century, England, in particular, or life at the turn of the 20th century in New York City – or the conditions of the marginalized pretty much anywhere on this planet in our own time!

When we do, we will probably come to two conclusions: (a) we have come a long way, especially in the last 50 years, and (b) we have a long way to go to bring reality closer to the ideal. But again – for Schiller is correct – not to the point where the two would merge. For as long as we are in human form, there must always be another "unreachable star". Otherwise we shall sooner or later stagnate on our latest achievement, becoming too tired and exhausted to climb yet another summit, conquer yet another high altitude to gain newer heartfelt "Ahas!" None of this must ever stop if we don't want inner and outer growth to come to a halt.

This, it appears, is the price we pay for freedom: we cannot rest permanently, for to be human is to be perpetual spiritual climbers and explorers.

It takes a clear vision and a great deal of courage to make a commitment to bring change to our world, but these are times conducive to boldness. Moreover, those centered on change are never alone in the great task. Satyagraha, the truth force, the justice-maker of life, always stands ready to assist. And the first aid it offers is to reconnect us with our natural state of being, our authentic self. For it is here that we find empowerment, freedom and strength – essential tools for the task of liberating our world from lies, and the machinations of liars. From that solid foundation we can then reach out into the larger community to inspire others to work for a better world.

Yet, in accepting the assignment, let us also be conscious of Gandhi's words of wisdom, "The victory is in the doing," he said, "not the results."

Such insight is a star worthy of being selected for spiritual assistance, and worthy of guiding us to a freer, fairer, kinder world – one possibly already within our reach.

Chapter 11

SHATTERING THE MYTH OF LIMITATIONS

Life shrinks or expands in proportion to one's courage.

~Anais Nin

If you do not expect the unexpected you will not find it, for it is not to be reached by search or trail.

~Heraclitus

It is our duty to proceed as though the limits of our abilities do not exist.

~Pierre Teilhard de Chardin

The impossible is a human invention.

~Philippe Petit

There are many individuals, who, filled with skepticism, doubt that humankind can ever truly change and become a more caring, cooperative and celebratory presence on Earth. They cite greed and crime and cruelty, and especially the horrors of war, to make their case. And while they grant that there have been miraculous breakthroughs in all areas of life, thanks in large part to science and technology, human nature essentially stays the same: primitive and selfish.

If that is true, must it remain that way?

A day to remember

It had rained heavily at Oxford University on May 6, 1954, and a gusty wind blew across the campus. But medical student Roger Bannister was not to be deterred from the extraordinary goal he had chosen for himself: to break the barrier established as the fastest possible speed for a human to run the mile. The record stood at 4:01.4 minutes set in 1945 by the great Swedish runner Gunder Hägg. Experts were convinced that anything faster than that was beyond human capacity.

But Bannister was determined to prove them wrong. In a race that would gain him worldwide fame, he achieved what had been considered impossible – he broke the world record at 3:59.4 minutes. Euphoria colored the day. He later described his inner state as he leaped across the mental and physical hurdles that had insisted his objective was not humanly achievable. "No longer conscious of my movement, I discovered a new unity with nature. I had found a new source of power and beauty, a source I never dreamt existed."

As it turned out, the epoch-making run was not destined to be a phenomenon for long. On the other side of the globe, Australian John Landy had an equally strong desire to crash barriers. In a race only weeks after Roger Bannister's feat, he shattered the new world record with an astonishing 3:57.9 minutes.

The world of sports held its collective breath and then invited both men to compete against each other in what was billed "The Mile of the Century" in Vancouver, British Columbia, August 7, 1954. Again, both runners broke the once invincible record, with Bannister claiming victory at 3:58.8 minutes and Landy with less than a second behind him at 3:59.6.

The collective belief that 4 minutes was the absolute limit for running the mile had been challenged and broken. First one, then a second individual created the critical mass which gradually reduced the seconds to the point where presently the world record is held by Morocco's "unbeatable" Hicham El Guerrouj at 3:43.13 minutes, established in 1999.

Pioneers and potentials

As we contemplate the making of a better world, it is good to remind ourselves that such a grand goal will take extraordinary commitment and perseverance. As such, it is not unlike other pioneering efforts recorded in history when humans accomplished the seemingly impossible. We can gain encouragement and confidence from those daring undertakings.

Roger Bannister is certainly an outstanding example of a man with a vision and the fortitude to actualize it. And, indeed, there are other similarly inspiring stories of determination and bravery by those attempting to conquer barriers. High on a list of such profiles in courage stand Edmund Hillary, the New Zealand mountaineer, and his skilled Sherpa, Tenzing Norgay, who together accomplished what others had tried but did not achieve: On 29 May 1953, 11:30 a.m., they triumphantly stood atop Mount Everest – at 29,028 feet, the highest point on Earth.

Fortuitously, the feat occurred on the day of the coronation of Queen Elizabeth II, and it was she who would later elevate the great explorer to "Sir Edmund". His companion, Tenzing Norgay, received "only" the highest medal of the British Empire, since rumor had it that Indian Prime Minister Nehru refused permission for Tenzing to be knighted.

Most important, however, was the fact that the two, by scaling the highest summit, shattered a mental block: they conquered what until that hour had been unreachable. Today, the climbing of Mount Everest has become such a crowded affair that any expedition must register a year in advance in order to be included in a very busy schedule. So many, in fact, engage in the strenuous adventure that special expeditions are periodically scheduled by the government of Nepal just to clear away the tons of trash left by the numerous climbers.

Speaking of heights: How could a history of breaking psychological and physical barriers not speak of the most prestigious of pioneers of trans-Atlantic flight, Charles Lindbergh? Until 1927, such attempts had been extremely dangerous, resulting in six skilled and well-known aviators losing their lives in fatal pursuit of the goal.

Then, in the early hours of Friday, May 20, 1927, a dashing and quite daring 25-year-old US Air Mail pilot set off from Roosevelt Field on New York's Long Island for a non-stop flight across the sea. He undertook the harrowing journey in a single-seated monoplane named the *Spirit of St. Louis*. It was a risky adventure, with at times hair-raising challenges. Yet, after nearly thirty-four airborne hours, Charles Lindbergh landed at Le Bourget Field outside of Paris, France. A crowd estimated at 150,000 stormed the field and carried the aviator on their shoulders for nearly thirty minutes.

Overnight, Lindbergh became a star and one who inspired others to repeat the feat. The rest is history, for within less than a generation, the skies across continents and oceans had opened up to nearly anyone – pilots and passengers alike.

A successful crossing of the Atlantic in 1927 changed aviation forever, just as Roger Bannister's race 27 years later would permanently change running the mile. Presumed limits and mental blockages were fractured to free latent possibilities and defuse the spell of long-held imaginary parameters.

The myth of limitations

We encounter them everywhere in our lives and the life of our species: barriers and the potentials they point to. Being alive, being human, is symbolic always of running faster, of climbing higher, of traveling farther, of crossing divides.

Some of us do it quicker, some slower. But while doing it, we all operate under two conditions. One is the strong emphasis on limits generated by the collective consciousness. ("If man was meant to fly, God would have given him wings.") The other is the fact that there would be no progress, no forward motion, without a vision beyond the norm, the established, the status quo. Recall Helen Keller's famous answer when asked what could be worse than being blind. Without hesitation, she replied, "Having no vision."

Suddenly, unexpectedly, after having worked diligently in a particular area of life, someone becomes a trailblazer, setting the stage for a new way of seeing or doing – new architecture, new art forms, new methods of transportation or communication, a medical breakthrough, a rocket that carries humans to walk on the moon, an idea opening up a new way of life. Intriguingly, once the breakthrough has occurred, it becomes possible for others to follow.

After that, it is only a short time before almost everybody accepts the novel forms, the new record, the advanced recipe for living, as the new pattern, the new "normal".

In other words, the once innovative is soon taken for granted. With that, something in the human psyche that abhors stagnation is triggered and the cycle to run faster, climb higher, fly farther, or to know more, starts again. Thus we break through limitations, expand and grow, much like a hatching bird cracks the shell of the egg that has been its home so that it will not become a prison and ultimately a tomb.

The French-Cuban author, Anais Nin, wrote: "It takes courage to push yourself to places that you have never been before, to test your limits, to break through barriers." And then she offers one of her best-known pearls of wisdom. "And the day came when the risk it took to remain tight inside the bud was more painful than the risk it took to blossom."

Taking risks marks the life and character of all the great pioneers and revolutionary spirits that have propelled humanity forward, rattled it out of its slumber, pushed it beyond the bud into blooming. And in each case a new consciousness emerged, now miraculously available to the many. This is how the creative spirit is dynamically at work whenever and wherever barriers are in need of being removed, dissolved, erased.

In the 1970s, research done at Stanford University, and utilized by the *Beyond War* organization in its educational programs, focused on exploring the power of ideas. The study added one of the most significant insights concerning the workings of the human mind with regard to collective change: the idea of a critical mass which, when reached, tilts the balance in favor of something new and renewing.

According to that principle, it does not take 100% of the populace to alter the way a society functions. Instead, when 20% accept a new idea, the energy generated becomes unstoppable, reflecting Victor Hugo's famous adage that nothing is stronger than an idea whose time has come. There is only one catch. In order to gain 20% acceptance, the idea must be brought to the attention of 50% of the people targeted for change. This means but one thing: diligent work and an unwavering belief in the validity of an idea.

Finally, when contemplating barriers, it is important to draw a distinction between a barrier and a boundary. Barriers are believed in or tangibly built because of ignorance and/or fear. They wall us in and always place a limit on movement and growth.

Boundaries, on the other hand, arise because a line must be drawn in order to protect a person or place. Boundaries have to do with what is or is not acceptable in a particular situation. By not allowing encroachment, they do in fact preserve our freedom and dignity. The necessary "no" of boundaries arises not out of fear or rejection, but out of care and protection. Unlike barriers, which divide and diminish, boundaries solidify and strengthen.

This is why the much-admired Robert Frost could advise, "Good fences good neighbors make." We can presume he had in mind that "good fences" are appropriate boundaries that invite honoring and respect, whereas "bad fences" are barriers to friendly and fruitful relations.

We can add furthermore that boundaries are necessary; barriers, however, are to be conquered, removed. Human life is about freedom and all barriers are its antithesis. Wherever we erect them, in our minds or environs, they impede the flow of life in both directions. To eliminate them is to open the path to new possibilities, new freedoms. Such acts inevitably require great courage and an unshakable belief in what is possible beyond the dictates of tradition or the edicts of those in control.

This explains furthermore the immense attraction human beings have to heroes. All heroes are pathfinders, barrier-breakers in whatever field they excel. We could scarcely venture far beyond the familiar and/or comfortable without their bold contributions. We would remain incarcerated by the myth of limits. And in fact, to prevent that, we must all become heroes in one way or another, must dare what author Kurt Vonnegut once suggested, namely, "to continually be jumping off cliffs and developing our wings on the way down."

Models and mentors

It has been said that seeing is believing. But an even greater truth may be that believing is seeing, such as expressed in the aphorism, "As you think, so shall it be." Bannister believed that he could explode an established assumption – and so he did! His consciousness was the first stage for that thrilling breakthrough.

Speaking in retrospect of the exhilarating experience, he emphasized that his mind felt as though disconnected from his body, as if it were out ahead of him, pulling him forward, toward victory. Which tells us that mind/consciousness, is endowed with immense powers – to be discovered and utilized.

I can testify to this mysterious power, having to deal with considerable pain since a hip replacement operation went awry. Yet, when presenting a sermon, teaching a class, counseling or writing, i.e., doing what I love, I have been able to transcend physical pain. However, when the event or activity is completed, I am once again made aware of the body and the injury it sustained.

Mind/consciousness is clearly gifted with great powers, including the capacity for transcendence, and the result of using these potentials is truly impressive. Witness, for example, the wondrous world of computers and other electronic gadgets created by human minds. Think of the world they have opened up to us! Think especially of the World Wide Web and its interconnected network of unlimited possibilities.

Yet, when comparing these advances with the rather slow progress we have made in relational and spiritual matters, one can only yearn for the day when not only the mind, but the heart as well, works at greater capacity. For unless the heart keeps pace with the mind, much can and *is* being created which serves neither humans nor life in general.

Actually, this should not really come as a surprise. After all, Hebrew Scriptures tell us at the beginning that a deep sleep fell upon Adam. Yet, despite careful further reading, you will find no reference anywhere to his waking up! We are a species asleep – asleep to ourselves, asleep to the miracle of our being, asleep to the miraculous around us. Like Adam, we need to wake up, come alive, and prepare for the race of our life, which shall take not only a sound mind, but a strong heart.

Individuals who set in motion record-breaking or life-transforming events masterfully utilize what is within: inherent powers and potentials. No longer satisfied with the way things are, they achieve what no one thought possible. Hence, when Roger Bannister electrified the sports world in 1954, he broke not only the record for running the mile, but simultaneously offered valuable insight into life, and what is untapped, yet possible, for the living.

Be it Roger Bannister, who raced the mile in 1954, or Rosa Parks, who refused to move at all in 1955, these are the heralds of a new morning. Demonstrating that barriers are first and foremost in "the head", they open pathways and possibilities for thousands of humans and ultimately all of humanity. They are beacons that draw us away from stagnation, toward breakthroughs and expansion.

Whether in the outer or inner realm, transformation can rarely be achieved without a model, a mentor. Gratitude belongs, therefore, especially to the extraordinary athletes of the spirit who symbolically have run the mile and established new records of what is possible for those who are human.

We owe much to all those who embody the splendor of the awakened self. Not surprisingly, entire cultures – the arts, philosophy, poetry, music – have flowered because of them: Abraham and Moses, Christ and Mohammed, Lao-tzu, Confucius and Buddha – visionaries of the spirit, progenitors of civilizations, living examples of the best humans can be. All of them runners, forerunners – mirrors in which we may see reflected our own humanity and yet to be discovered Self.

Thus, while athletic titans break records of speed and endurance, Olympians of the spirit plunge into new dimensions of depth and grace. They reveal the universe to us, and above all, the universe *in* us, while showing us what human beings are capable of doing when they challenge the myth of limitations.

Spiritual masters demonstrate that there is a vast source of power within, invisible, like the nucleus of the atom, and that the only limit to that power is the place where each of us draws the line.

Unfortunately, most of us draw the line far too close to home; we prefer the harbor to the sea. We feel comfortable with the familiar, the known. We mistrust and even dread the new, and especially those who are the messengers of newness, because the vast majority of us are strangers to ourselves. As such, we are naturally suspicious of what appears different, irregular, mysterious. And this is how we remain stuck in what we consider "safe". As a consequence, we soon find ourselves in a rut because we now interbreed with the same old thoughts and habits.

Yet, as noted, the only limit to the power within is the place where we construct barriers. And they often come in the shape of doubt. Doubt is the great eraser of our life's most cherished dreams. We are hypnotized into thinking that whatever we wish for can't be attained, can't be done.

Still, there is a point I would not want to miss adding. I remember years ago how a chiropractor friend, after examining an X-ray, rather somberly spoke of "the limitation of matter". He explained, "Living on Earth, our physical bodies are naturally subject to the laws of matter, regardless of how interchangeable matter and energy may be. Linear life has a beginning and an end. Certain organs when damaged cannot be regenerated; limbs when lost cannot be re-grown, at least not at this point in our evolution."

I can easily resonate with those observations. Based on them, it is not hard to concede that we don't know, for instance, whether we will ever be able to run the mile under three minutes; that may well be one of those limitations. But in between there are numerous possibilities of overcoming what have been billed as insurmountable obstacles. As a Hindu sage was fond of saying: "Be realistic, expect a miracle!"

We are made up mostly of unused, untapped potential. What, we must ask, is holding us back from actualizing those gifts? What stops us from running faster, climbing higher, diving deeper, being stronger, being kinder, being free? We may look outside and blame him, or her, blame this, or that, but ultimately we will run out of scapegoats – and must dare do what we so shrewdly try to avoid: look in the mirror. That's when authentic life finally has a chance to touch us. "If the prison is in the mind, so is the freedom." If the blockage is in us, so is the opening. On that knowing, we can build anew.

What/who holds us back? We, you and I, each in our own peculiar way. And we do it for a reason few of us would ever suspect. Author/activist Marianne Williamson has said it best. More than our inadequacies, we fear our own light, the power within. We fear being our best, our most radiant Self – afraid to display qualities that reveal our divine nature. Needless to say, that fear is an obstacle to wholeness and liberation not easily removed.

But there is a way. Learning to love ourselves, practicing self-love (and self-love is the very opposite of egotism) can emancipate us from the senseless fear of our own light and greatness. Self-love can adjust those out-of-focus lenses that prevent us from seeing that we deserve the gifts of life, deserve fulfillment, lasting happiness. And self-love can reveal to us that we are so much more than struggling egos, so much more than clever survivors; it can show us that we are made in the image of the Sacred, the Infinite – beings of worth and dignity.

Because we have unfathomable spiritual depths to draw upon, psychiatrist Victor Frankl, founder of Logotherapy, after observing himself and other prisoners under the dehumanizing conditions of concentration camps, came to a critical conclusion. Even when robbed of everything, human beings have one last freedom: their inner attitude toward any set of outer circumstances. Not what we experience, but how we respond will either set us free or enslave us. Based on that observation, he deduced that life has meaning under all circumstances, even the most dismal ones; and it is, in fact, the will to meaning that colors the whole of our existence.

That is a powerful insight and message: none of us ever needs to feel like a victim, a loser, unless we condemn ourselves to being that. We may encounter diseases and disasters, experience painful, frustrating restrictions on our outer liberty, but there is always that final freedom: to be free in the inmost part of our being. In that interior realm is where the greatest heroism can ultimately be manifested. And it is here that the most consequential of records can be broken, the most significant victories be won.

For the sake of that freedom, it behooves us to become

aware of impediments that affect how we, for instance, run the symbolic mile of our life. Roger Bannister's determination to break a world record shows that we do not have to be trapped in perceived limitations.

Moreover, his victory was not his alone, as he spurred others on to match his superb abilities. In fact, his amazing achievement directly affected, no doubt, the witnesses to his great feat, and indirectly the whole human family. Why? Because in a world of oneness, there is no self-enhancement without elevating the whole, no self-reduction without diminishing all. Who we are matters, what we do matters; for better or for worse, our influence is immense.

So what race are you running for the sake of the human race? Or, conversely, what self- and society-enhancing deeds are you postponing because you feel inadequate? There are adventures awaiting your enthusiastic Yes! There are potentials in you yearning to show themselves, to shine! There are summits to scale for your fulfillment and the benefit of humankind!

Roger Bannister demonstrated that we are faster on our feet when we believe we can be. Edmund Hillary and Charles Lindbergh erected lofty monuments to our capacity to endure and persevere. And the magnificent athletes of the spirit exemplify for us that we are greater inside, more powerful, and yes, more capable of loving than imagined. There are essentially no limits to our wholeness because, as holography has taught us, *the fragment contains the whole* – we host the universe inside of us.

The question we must finally ask ourselves is this: are we willing to be runners and climbers for a new way of life? Are we willing to break the barriers that hold us back from birthing our essence, our genuine Self? Are we willing to be friend and lover of humanity, acknowledging the Light in all we meet? Are we willing to dispense with false beliefs and eliminate the self-doubts that hold us back?

Granted, it is not going to be easy. Be it in a personal or public milieu, raising consciousness and initiating change never is. Resistance and conflict are sure to follow, and they can present a formidable wall, not easily scaled or dismantled. Yet, as repeatedly demonstrated, it is not a mission impossible.

We do thoughtless, hurtful, inane things until our eyes are opened. That is the burden we bear when unawakened. It is only in retrospect that we see how detrimental and self-defeating our behavior has been. Obviously, to wake up is the solution, how to accomplish it, the question. Will it be intentionally or must it be through some crisis, some painful, ground-shifting experience?

So many miles to run, so many mountains to climb, so many limits to overcome, so many barriers to remove, so many wounds to heal. But then again, what more can we ask for than the privilege of gaining liberation and the freedom to love?

Meditation on a New Day

Here we are
a new day, a new page
in the Book of Life,
What will you write this day
in the chapter that bears your name?
How will you use
the precious gift?
What is your vision
your commitment
your promise to
self and others?
Be
> *here*
>> *now.*
How truly present are we?
How open, how willing to be
touched, moved, changed
by life, by love
this moment, now?
> *What is it that you*
might do this day
to add depth, color
freedom to your life?

What are the barriers
the baggage that prevent you
from running the mile
with greater lightness
of foot or heart?
     Here we are:
a new morning
a kaleidoscope of possibilities.

What shall we write in the book
of our life this day?

RC

Chapter 12

DESTINATION: HOME

We come, trailing clouds of glory, from God who is our Home.
~William Wordsworth

If seeds in the black earth can turn into such beautiful roses, what might not the heart of [humans] become in its long journey toward the stars?
~G.K. Chesterton

Nothing can have as its destination anything other than its origin.
~Simone Weil

As rivers have their source in some far-off fountain, so the human spirit has its source. To find this fountain of spirit is to learn the secret of heaven and earth.
~Lao-tzu

For how long have we humans lived in ignorance, slavishly serving forces that would keep us divided, dependent and afraid? Today, a state of wholeness and genuine freedom is waiting for us on the other side of darkness, and never have circumstances been more conducive for attaining that blessed state than at this critical moment when everything stands ready to facilitate the journey through the great passage of renewal.

Indeed, after many detours, a path has opened to reconnect us with the truth of our being, to come home to who we truly are, to embrace our uniqueness, power and beauty – and in that embrace affirm our oneness with all. There is an entirely new terrain beckoning us to an exhilarating voyage of discovery.

The road shall take us from sleep to awakening, from ignorance to enlightenment, from self-abandonment to self-love, from egotism to service to others. As all the great masters have demonstrated, it is a journey worthy of our commitment and exertion.

"How do I know this is true?" China's ancient sage, Lao-tzu, asked rhetorically when speaking of the presence of the Tao, the Way of Life and Creation. "By looking inside myself," he quietly insisted. We will never find what we are seeking unless we do the same.

There are worlds within us, yearning to be known – worlds of beauty, enchantment and love.

Outer versus inner revolutions

We have ample reason to bemoan the fate that has befallen our world just when we thought we had made considerable progress. Yet, with all that has occurred, it is advisable to view the present crisis, much like the double meaning of the Chinese character, as also a tremendous opportunity. In fact, just turning our focus to a slightly different frequency, much like we tune the radio to another station, may help us to discover that humankind stands today not only at the brink of disaster, but at the threshold of a spiritual renaissance.

Several factors have led us to this point, but the overarching emphasis must be on the word *spiritual* itself. Dissatisfied with an unabashedly materialistic, purely secular way of life, and seeking to regain a deeper sense of meaning, many individuals have yearned to counterbalance the present uneasiness by refocusing on the inner dimension. As a result, a great shift toward renewal has been unfolding, possibly for several generations, that is, ever since New Thought movements made their appearance. This development has encouraged societal transformers, cultural creatives and futurists to see humanity poised at a defining moment, which, despite its perils, promises a rebirth the likes of which have not been witnessed before.

Looking back, we recognize that overthrowing tyrants and dictators of every stripe was historically achieved by mostly violent means. However, disappointment inevitably followed because so-called liberators could not resist the temptation of power and soon morphed into despots themselves. Thus, oppression was brutally repeated, even intensified, and through the generations, people remained pawns in the Machiavellian play of the ambitious and power-driven.

This remained the pattern for centuries until, in 1776, a break in the clouds of global gloominess revealed a burst of luminosity so intense that it continues to energize the longing of millions, keeping alive the vision of liberty and justice for all. Yet, not until the great convulsions of World War I and II had come to an end was humanity on the whole able to build upon that dream and its aspirations. And even then, a large portion of the world's inhabitants was compelled to exist under the harsh conditions of totalitarian regimes.

However, with the demise of communism, hope was rekindled and a new chapter seemed to have begun – until the forces and events of 9/11 shook the world to its foundations. Once the toxic dust had settled, an entirely different totalitarianism was in charge, this time on a global scale. And its nature and intentions are so cleverly disguised that it remains unrecognized as such by the vast majority of people. Therein lies the extraordinary danger of our time.

Which leads to the question: After so many centuries of tyrants and broken dreams, how was it possible that we could not see through and thus prevent the most deceitful conquest in human history? What is it that we are not getting? The answer is in many ways quite simple. We are not getting that outer changes alone, including political governance, can never be genuine or lasting unless accompanied by a change of consciousness, a change of heart, by the individual. In other words, exterior, cosmetic changes only solve problems temporarily. However, those who seek genuine progress recognize that restructuring a society must start closer to home, in fact, as close to home as possible: inside of us.

By having paid insufficient attention to that essential truth, much harm has been wrought in our world, in our name. And today some of the vanquished are resisting and revolting. We may be incensed, yet, what moral authority do we have to tell those who languish under occupation and devastation caused by military aggression and other hubristic intrusions, how to gain liberation? Yes, ideally, it should be the nonviolent

272

way, but such a criterion is not for us to place on others. While nonviolence must one day become the star that guides all our actions in support of change, it is important to remember that rare, indeed, are the incidents when freedom was gained entirely by nonviolent means. Additionally, every form of oppression is different, as are the means of the oppressed to cut the yoke that strangles them. In Tibet, for instance, a large number of Buddhist monks, and several nuns, have immolated themselves in an effort to end the Chinese occupation of their land and destruction of their culture.

At the same time, even when nonviolent resistance is exercised – demonstrations, boycotts, even negotiations – we note that the overwhelming majority of oppressors/occupiers are doggedly determined to remain in control. In fact, too often when the powerful and the powerless sit together to "resolve" their differences, it is predictable who will be the loser, who the winner. The long and fruitless "negotiations" between the "stateless" and constantly compromising Palestinians and the willful, land-seizing Israelis is a heartbreaking case in point.

While the nonviolent struggle of Gandhi and his compatriots for liberation from the British Empire – especially after the colonial master's own battle for survival during WWII – set a new criterion for similar future movements, it was, nonetheless, unique. And so was the bloodless 1989 revolution in East Germany, soon to be followed by the overthrow of unpopular governments in the rest of the Soviet satellite countries.

Such enormous changes would almost certainly have spiraled into horrendous violence had it not been for a man named Gorbachev. He knew that the controlled could no longer be kept from having a more humane governing system. And under his laudable leadership, the Soviets and their occupying armies did not to crush the people's aspirations. Thus, one after the other, chains dissolved like packs of ice in the heat of summer until the great iceberg, the Kremlin itself, which had kept multitudes in a frozen state, melted into history.

In the late autumn of 1989, copious evidence was collected in support of the argument that if we yearn for genuine change, lasting change, we must foster it from the inside out.

That was, as noted, true in the case of East Germany's principled activists, and, as results would bear out, applied no less to the last Soviet leader. For it was unmistakably Mr. Gorbachev's personal integrity and decisive authority that blocked Moscow's reactions to the uprisings from descending into a bloodbath. To watch the effects unfold and the despised Berlin Wall fall right before our disbelieving eyes became, indisputably, the spectacle of the century. (The dramatic turning point is comprehensively covered in *Envisioning a New World*.)

Ideally, real societal change must not only include, but preferably originate, with a personal awakening that leads to a more conscious, intentional, and caring way of life. When enough people reach that point, new awareness can then kindle a nonviolent grassroots movement necessary for political change. And that change also needs to focus, beyond our present "romance with rights", on a strong sense of responsibility for the interconnectedness of life, and the sacred obligations we have to the whole and one another.

Finally, I'd like to reiterate that while one would hope that all people can find liberation the nonviolent way, there are examples of injustices and crimes against humanity so egregious that they require the kind of emergency response encountered in cases of self-defense. While we are not asked to condone such acts, neither are we entitled to condemn them. Rather, seeing people despondent and desperate, e.g. the Palestinians, should galvanize us to insist that such abuses not be committed with impunity. Instead, the perpetrators must be held accountable. Only then can we break the vicious cycle of human rights violations and the exploitation of the oppressed.

Dilemmas and choices

The age in which we live is, to a large degree, the result of scientific breakthroughs and inventions brilliantly, but also selfishly and thoughtlessly, applied. As previously underscored, however, technological advances by themselves are not to blame for some of the exceedingly bitter fruits we have been reaping. Rather, our predicament is ultimately that we have not matched feats of intellectual expansion with an equivalent enlargement of the heart, and thus an increase in moral responsibility. That is why so many of our innovations bear within them the seeds of harmfulness – to ourselves and the rest of creation.

In the end, this is the cause of the dilemma we are facing: we have chosen profit over the prophetic; power over empowerment; separateness over oneness. Our loss has been in the quality of our values, in moral clarity, in human relationships. As noted, one of the disastrous results of that deficiency was the global financial catastrophe of 2008 generated by greed, deceit and utter recklessness, and given the green light by governmental deregulation in Washington.

Additionally, while there is corruption in many of our private and sociopolitical institutions, due to the unholy marriage of money and power, it is important to realize that even if citizens could overthrow all the autocrats and tycoons of this world, nothing would fundamentally change if individuals remained *inwardly* in disharmony with the laws of life. For if we cannot conquer ignorance or subdue fear, we will continue to experience an endless variety of external conditions whereby we are controlled – and sometimes even destroyed – by others.

Looking at societal conditions can easily create the impression that circumstances are beyond our influence. Yet at no time is life out to get us; rather, it (a) reflects back to us where we stand spiritually, and (b) seeks to awaken us so that we can move from believing that things are happening to us, to knowing that we significantly contribute to their occurrence.

Which is another way of saying self-reform cannot be circumvented if we hope to transform our world.

The key to creating a new world

We have for too long lived spiritually disconnected lives, despite a greatly improved physical existence and a rather comfortable living standard enjoyed by many. This makes it difficult to decipher the inner emptiness of our lives. It is, in fact, more often than not that material affluence lulls us into the illusion that we can exist disconnected from our core, can shape our lives independent of spiritual content.

But take away our toys – our flat-screen TVs, Ipods, cell phones, notebooks and dozens of other electronic gadgets – and we panic or sink into boredom. Why? Because without all that outer glitter and clutter, we sense a barrenness, and a lack of genuine connection to others and, most importantly, to our own inner being.

Kevin Reilly, Fox entertainment chairman, in a revealing response to the horrific shooting that claimed the lives of twenty first-graders and six teachers in Newtown, Connecticut, in December 2012, admitted that "Part of entertainment, part of what we do on television, is to provide escapism."

He explains, "Escapism comes in many forms. It could be laughter. It could be fantasy. It is also your worst nightmare come to life. And it makes our palms sweat and it moves us emotionally and puts us on the edge of the seat. We are engrossed in it and we forget ourselves for an hour."

Indeed, all diversions, all distractions, are a clever formula for making humans self-forgetting, for blocking remembrance of who they are. And never before has this been so all encompassing or damaging as it is today.

When we are deprived of knowing and communing with the deepest parts and truths within us, we frequently don't notice (a) how wounded we are, and (b) that healing cannot come from adding more diversions, more high decibel, high intensity 24/7 entertainment, to our life.

Instead, we must be willing to do just the opposite: turn off the distractions and focus on a source that never ceases to surprise us, never bores, never disappoints, but keeps things fresh and sparkling: the life within our mind, our heart, our soul. Incredible adventures await those who turn inward, not to escape but to come home to all that is good and true and beautiful.

As we begin the process of reconnecting with what is deepest, strongest and brightest in us, we are learning that the new life we are seeking is an idea that has been pulsating in the heart of humanity since first we gained awareness, and with it the freedom to shape or misshape our destiny.

This is why we can say that those who are presently on

this planet have definitely been born into "interesting times", thus fulfilling a wish the ancient Chinese extended to new arrivals. And indeed, is there a more propitious opportunity for self-examination, clarification and re-definition of who we are and where we are going than during a period alive with clashing values and opposing worldviews? There may be turmoil as old systems are breaking up and new ones are struggling to rise, but such moments are anything but dull.

Chinese sages focused on "interesting" times; Charles Dickens emphasized "best of times/worst of times". As previously noted, at present we certainly can echo the great 19th century novelist's sentiment, while simultaneously adding one more depiction: *maddening times*. And thus it shall remain unless we claim the power and accept the responsibility to become conscious co-creators with the fertile forces of life.

Having clarified that without a change of heart, without an inner conversion, there can be no lasting change in the external world, should we, for that reason, postpone the restructuring of society? Not at all. Inner and outer work can and, in fact, must be engaged in simultaneously. Life flows on and continually requires our attention, for all elements are entwined and affect each other – exterior and interior. However, it is only the inner realm that can give us the knowledge necessary to actualize our ideals and potentials. This makes it invaluable in helping to understand, and subsequently shape, better relations, and a brighter collective future.

Of course, subjugated people still have the traditional option of initiating change as it has been done for generations, namely, via external measures: they can forcefully overthrow dictators and dislodge unresponsive governments.

However, especially since Gandhi's victory, human beings now have the added choice of changing themselves as a prelude to, or in tandem with, changing society. This greatly increases the chances of avoiding the cyclical tragedy of overthrowing one dictatorial system only to see it replaced by another. Yet, even if inner change is not the initial step taken by the oppressed, it can still become the next and final one to guarantee that great gains are not stolen by those addicted to the arrogance of power. Either way, the key to creating a new world is, in the final analysis, always a movement from the inside out.

Purifying heart and mind

If we opt for changing the self in conjunction with reshaping society, the prospect for success in our time holds great promises. We have learned much, at least theoretically, about the inwardness of things, from the nature of atoms to our own consciousness and being. The sacred texts of the world's religions and their spiritual disciplines are available to us. There are gurus and counselors, and numerous courses and workshops in personal growth. Many seekers today have the time and the money to explore various pathways and glean valuable knowledge and skills.

Yet, while the tools at our disposal are many, I feel impelled to caution that entrenched ways are not easily dislodged. As Samuel Johnson knew, "The chains of habit are generally too small to be felt until they are too strong to be broken." Real change is demanding; it takes courage and fortitude; it is not for the faint of heart or the impatient.

Finally, if we declare ourselves committed to reach the other shore, the banks of transformed life, we must be willing to traverse the broad river of internal cleansing, of purifying heart and mind. This is where some shy away, hoping for a less demanding assignment. Unfortunately, or perhaps I should say fortunately, there is no other path but the one leading directly through our own inner being, thereby placing us fully in charge of the process, its depth and duration.

Native American wisdom proclaims, "We are the ones we have been waiting for." Fulfilling that sacred task requires comprehensive preparation. This means engaging in various phases of rigorous cleansing, whereby contaminants that have polluted the stream of our personal or public life are brought to the surface so that individuals and society can analyze them and proceed with the necessary purification. Without those steps, nothing ground-breaking can flourish for long: the old toxins will inevitably seep into the new growth and cause harm.

When we look at our world from that perspective, when we recognize the weight of the task, we no longer need to feel dejected about the sluggish progress in resolving stale and stubborn human problems. After all, be they private or public in scope, cleaning out a clogged sewer system is a messy and odorous affair. Nonetheless, it is also one that cannot be circumvented, because the health and welfare of the whole person and that of the entire community depend on it.

To soften our stance toward something that cannot really be avoided if we are to advance, I'd suggest reflecting on a pearl of wisdom extracted from Sage Bennet's inspiring *Wisdom Walk:* "If you want to do something, you'll find a way. If you don't want to do it, you'll find excuses."

I mention this to counsel being honest with ourselves.

Besides honesty, inner purification requires another important virtue and that is patience. Patience can keep discouragement at bay, and it therefore always plays a pivotal role in one's quest for self-renewal. No one can hope for success without it, especially when confronting self-defeating tendencies with the intent of extricating them. This is because, under pressure, one's resolve can easily dissipate. And when resolve is lost, anger and doubt quickly step in to thwart one's efforts.

Finally, considering how deeply most of us are asleep, it would not be realistic to expect awakening to be instantaneous. It can happen on rare occasions, but it is not something we can count on. This is where patience becomes quite indispensable.

Human consciousness is presently pregnant with new, life-transforming concepts waiting to revolutionize the world, even as spiritual pioneers already are demonstrating what is possible. Who, touched by today's winds of change, would therefore want to cling to yesterday's deficient ways?

Inner space – the final frontier

In July 1999, the Associated Press reported on a poll by the Pew Research Center for the People and the Press. The article began: "Accompanying the hum of computers and the roar of the economy at the end of the 20th century is a nagging feeling among many Americans that something has been lost."

That loss was described as "an absence of morality, a loss of innocence, a lack of trust." As one interviewee said, "There is more money, but less human caring."

Quite obviously, from an economic perspective, by the 1990s, life had significantly improved for many, but at what cost to the quality of human relationships and spiritual values?

How, one might ask, would citizens respond to such a survey today? My conjecture is, probably even more despondently in view of endless war and the shaky economic and financial status of the American Dream – not to mention the crumbling of the moral/ethical structures of shared life.

Indeed, a public opinion poll taken by *The New York Times* on April 21, 2011, showed that 70 percent of those responding were concerned that the country was heading in the wrong direction.

The American people sense that something has gone badly awry, but they do not have the tools or instructions to explore the underlying causes – or at least, so it seems. Obviously, corporate media will not reveal what is occurring behind the scenes, nor can citizens turn to their elected officials for clarification or answers because those so-called representatives work almost exclusively for special interests. In other words, they are doing anything but "the people's business". That once treasured principle is today a sham.

What can be done about it?

We must start with the recognition that the forces that usurped our country on 9/11 cannot be defeated by any of the methods of "fighting fire with fire". Ensconced in every aspect of governance and in control of every major network of communications, they cannot be disposed of by weapons, street protests, phone calls or mass mailings to Congress.

However, their influence can be diminished by a change of heart in individuals across this immense nation. It can be defused by seeing that money and possessions can never fill the emptiness we feel inside. And it can be neutralized by the realization that the numerous moral compromises and errors of judgment we make are rooted in forgetting who we are. Hence, as previously underscored, the most severe problems facing our society are related to our neglect of the interior dimension, the source of true sustenance, strength and freedom. Disconnection from that vital space makes us prone to being duped, used and abused by those who crave power and control.

We have been incredibly successful externally – doing, getting, accomplishing. But human beings live by more than bread or all the possessions and pleasures credit cards can buy. And there is no starvation worse than an undernourished spirit. Without a vision, the people perish. We have allowed our vision to become dim, and our spirit to seem superfluous.

This is how our country has been infiltrated by alien values, undermining our democratic principles and throwing us into a maelstrom of disunity, suspicion and anxiety. With temples to materialism dotting our cities and towns, it may appear that outwardly we are far from perishing, but unless we recognize the cause of our general malaise, we will feel ever more acutely that something vital has been lost – something that is inevitably leading to our decline.

What has been lost is our connection to spirit and our knowing of who we are – as individuals and a people. Additionally, our excessive focus on the outer world, and negligence of the inner, has left us without peace in both dimensions. As stated, this one-sidedness has made many Americans feel alienated, polarized and cynical. In fact, with all the greed, inequality and duplicity existing in our country today, it is sometimes hard to remember that this nation's sociopolitical system is rooted in a document declaring that all human beings are created equal and endowed with inalienable rights. Many of our treasured standards – ideals that made us a vibrant people at home and an appreciated one abroad – lie in tatters. To be reminded of that should jolt us into realizing that we need to make a far greater effort to bridge the unhealthy division between who we say we are and what we do.

It cannot be stated often enough: what matters most is inside of us. While this does not reduce the importance of our connections with others, and resultant mutual obligations, the truth is, there is no surer ticket to hardship and heartaches than living estranged from the essence of our own being.

As previously noted, especially in America, very few of us are familiar with the inner, spiritual landscape. In fact, we are quite illiterate when it comes to that realm. And such lack of self-knowing is a serious barrier to exploring what is invisible, intangible – yet no less real – and of ultimate importance. Never before has this inner knowing been more crucial to our wellbeing and the future of humanity.

Unfortunately, instead of slowing down for introspection and reflection, we are a people forever on the move. Infected with the migratory "bug", we are always looking for new geographical frontiers. We need to ask about the deeper reasons for such restlessness. Might our frequent travels and constant relocations actually be a substitute for the real journey we need to take? And is not inner space the ultimate frontier that calls us today, the part in us which psychiatrist Carl Jung so aptly named "The Undiscovered Self"?

There exists presently an epic struggle for the soul and future of humankind, requiring clarity of vision, commitment and courage. Since too many people are still largely beginners when it comes to the intricacies of the world within, those dedicated to spiritual principles are much needed to add their wisdom and guidance to the challenges we face.

As highlighted, we live in a setting of duality: inner and outer, personal and public. When these two interrelated, interdependent aspects are aligned, that is, when the hidden roots and visible branches of the tree of our life receive equal attention, then we, and humanity, can be fully nourished by a harvest of wholesome fruits brought forth by our skills and efforts.

Those alive today are here at the end of a long period of darkness and endless nightmares – and just at the cusp of dawn. This confers on us a unique privilege and a great responsibility to help restore our world to light and our life to joy.

Political versus spiritual realities

On January 8, 2011, the tranquility of a Saturday morning in Tucson and the surrounding Sonoran Desert was shattered when a mentally disturbed male attempted to assassinate Congresswoman Gabrielle Giffords. Shooting with cold precision, he gravely wounded his target and then continued to kill six constituents and bystanders, while wounding thirteen others. A stunned city and nation struggled to keep its emotional balance while seeking to comprehend a great tragedy, which, at the same time, was accentuated with acts of heroism and self-sacrifice. Across the country, life seemed to come to a momentary halt, while all eyes were on Tucson – in shock, disbelief and mourning.

Several days later, President Obama came to Tucson to offer his condolences during a memorial service at the University of Arizona. Through his poised presence, empathy, and inspiring address to the nation, he touched millions of hearts across the country, displaying an extraordinary capacity to bring a healing touch and unity to those in mourning.

Commenting on the President's remarks, McClatchy Newspapers touched upon something of great significance. "First in a moving eulogy to those who died, then in the uplifting tales of those who acted heroically, finally in his call to the nation to live up to the ideals of a slain 9-year-old girl, Obama recaptured, at least temporarily, the appeal that first thrust him onto the national stage – the sense that the country is a family that yearns to be united, not divided."

"It reminded us of how he got to be president," said Wayne Fields, an English professor at Washington University in St. Louis, and an expert on presidential rhetoric. And then he added something that should give us pause. "It wasn't because of something he was. It was something that we longed for, (and) that was to be whole."

President Obama, since his much-hailed elections of 2008 and 2012, has disappointed many of those who supported and voted for him. Now, I personally don't believe that Barack Obama made a 180-degree turn away from the promises he made during the campaigns; rather the real, albeit hidden, powers in Washington set him straight from the moment he took office as to who holds the reins, and what a president can and cannot do. They figuratively tethered him so that his uplifting rhetoric would not be able to let him and this country soar toward new horizons.

This means but one thing: Our elected officials may not be free to be themselves, may not be able to live up to their ideals, but the longing for something better, for being whole as individuals and a people, is engraved in the human heart, is within us all. And what is within will remain there for only a certain amount of time before it will burst its shell to find expression in the external realm. Actually, is this not what the voting of November 2008, and even of 2012, was all about?

Additionally, what we long for, longs no less for us. It yearns to be discovered in order that we can be healed from self-estrangement and self-wounding. That is why nobody who embarks on an inner journey will ever be disappointed. For each step of the way is an enrichment and a blessing.

Which raises the question: Have we not lived long enough in ignorance, slavishly serving the forces that would keep us divided, dependent and afraid? Today, a state of wholeness and expansive freedom is waiting for us on the other side of darkness, and never have circumstances been more favorable for attaining it than at this auspicious moment when everything stands ready to facilitate the journey through the great passage of renewal.

In light of what could be, we can see to what degree we have been lost in a wilderness of confusion and doubt, have lived estranged from the core of self, on the outskirts of our being, existing in angst and hiding.

The first part of this book was especially persistent and unrelenting along those lines, showing the degree to which we have abandoned ourselves, and how close we have come to an abyss in our blind march toward collective self-destruction. Frightened into submission by those who would lead us into temptation, we have turned a deaf ear to voices of truth and reason. We have allowed for perpetual war, torture, and the murder of countless innocents. We have not been true to ourselves. And the result has been a moral disaster.

We need openness and transparency, for in the light there are no secrets; in light, truth manifests. And there is nothing more powerful than truth (think of politics and politicians in particular!), for truth and justice are entwined; in fact, truth is the very foundation of justice, since every injustice has its genesis in hypocrisy, lies and deception.

To the degree that we learn to base our personal and collective lives on such clear principles as truth and justice, to that degree shall we be able to reduce the cycle of oppression and violence that has enslaved humanity for millennia.

Such a goal can be more easily obtained if we connect with the essence of our being and true power. This is why today we are so urgently called to come home to who we really are, to embrace our uniqueness and beauty – and yes, our divine essence, the part of us that was created "in the image of God". There are worlds within us that contain all the elements we have ever longed and languished for.

The snail, of which we were reminded in an earlier chapter, carries her home permanently on the outside of her body; we humans carry our home at all times within. Such a setup guarantees that no one can invade it, no one can steal it, no one can neglect it but us, each one of us. Our home is our castle, the royal palace of our true heritage, the seat of the Divine. We have been entitled to it from the moment of our birth, but shall never fully know that until we have claimed the "title" to it. At that moment of empowerment, that flash of clarity, our life forever changes.

Waking up is the journey

Who can count the generations that have endured the chains of falsehood and oppression, deprived of truth and freedom? We have been, spiritually speaking, on a starvation diet for centuries, and waking up from a long slumber, a nightmare, we are, in fact, disturbed to discover what an inauthentic, compromised life we have been living – how we have allowed ourselves to be used and abused by the powers of this world. Yet, despite surface appearances, much like in nature, winter and sleep have at the same time created deep underground, away from prying eyes, sprouting seeds and promises of renewal.

This is why there is today a noticeable intensification and acceleration in every aspect of common life. For the heart and mind of humanity are being dilated in order to deliver a higher degree of understanding, a fuller expression of love, a more genuine and humane way of life. If we choose, a period of rebirthing, a renaissance, can be ours.

It takes time, receptivity and a unique confluence of circumstances to reach such a point. Amazingly, however, no one can say when that exact moment of renewal will finally manifest, when we have struggled out of the egg in our push toward new freedoms and wider horizons. We may be able to speak of events or deeds that most likely contributed, but the rest we have to attribute to the proverbial straw that broke the camel's back, or in this case, the spark that ignited us into newness of being.

Birds make great sky-circles
of their freedom.
How do they learn it?
They fall, and falling
they are given wings.

Rumi

Experience has shown that renewal results most often from exposure to a period of great darkness. It is precisely the deprivation of light and disenchantment with outer conditions that compel us to look for alternatives, to go "underground", to do inner work. Significantly, it is the very oppressiveness, the weight of living a nightmare, which ultimately wakes us up, and inspires us to embrace change, bringing forth a stronger self, a clearer vision, a greater understanding, a more unshakable commitment. Our humanity, quite surprisingly, expands under inhumane circumstances because we yearn most intensely at such times for the gifts of a transformed life.

Which leads us back to one of the most encouraging spiritual messages: Within the self is the fertile ground; within the self are the seeds. And, after we have done the inner cultivation and preparation, it is all brought to life by the light, the sun, of our awakened consciousness. That is what creates the inner spring. And that's where those flowers of joy originate, those songs of exuberance: from the greening and blooming within. A flowering person is the very opposite of those living disconnected from the core, the foundation of Self.

All of this is reflective of the fisherman's wife to whom we were introduced in *Envisioning a New World* in the chapter on "Consuming Greed". Her defining characteristic was the inability to ever be satisfied. As soon as she had one desire granted by that enchanted prince turned fish, she obsessed with wanting more. And it was not only material things that she craved; she coveted power. "I want to be Empress ... Pope ... Ruler of the Universe" was her lustful cry. Wish after wish was granted, except for the last: to be the Ruler of the Universe.

That megalomanic desire was not only denied her, but at the very moment she voiced it, she was once again reduced to being a lowly fisherman's wife in a tiny cottage by the sea. Hubris and intoxication with status takes us only so far before the inevitable fall.

The story of the greedy wife ends badly; she presumably never gets the chance to discover what other option she might have had. She, like millions of others, failed to see that getting genuine riches depends on the capacity to wake up and recognize the gift of one's true self. We don't need positions of power and wealth, but we do need to be in intimate relationship with our inner being, to learn to trust ourselves and allow our intuitive voice to reveal the itinerary of our life, thus transcending the fear-based and self-limiting dictates of society to find spiritual fulfillment.

Lamentably, our society has for too long operated under the tendency to miss what matters most. This has come at a high cost, and therein lies the reason why the call for sweeping changes has become so urgent and insistent in our time. Under "normal" circumstances, we would usually have more of a choice as to how to respond, would be granted deferments and exceptions, even an outright excuse or two.

However, because we are living in an age of extremes, and in the midst of ominous threats, there is a deep sense of urgency to counterbalance with inner light, with enlightenment, the darkness and "thing-ness" of our age. And if the darkness is not as apparent to some as it ought to be, it is because our world is filled with a great deal of artificial light, with a fairyland glitter of the illusory and fake.

The challenges we are facing today are profound and manifold. Their combined pressures are thrusting the human caterpillar toward metamorphosis. Not surprising, those who have been shrewdly manipulating all the naïve caterpillars don't appreciate what is occurring. In response, they employ every method available to frighten those hapless creatures away from the process of transformation.

For several years, it was, for instance, alternating color codes that kept the petrified multitudes in line. (Presently, the only code still in use is "Code Pink", an audacious group of female activists who irreverently mock the very notion of color-coded threats.) Today it is primarily economics – volatile finances, unemployment, home foreclosures and rising costs, interspersed with a host of manufactured incidents – that keep the masses worried and in check.

All these methods still work to a large degree in America, but in other places, dissatisfaction and turmoil are growing. It must be rather frustrating for those whose greatest skill lies in controlling others to realize that despite all their tricks, something unexpected is happening.

Case in point: the Arab world, which in 2011 suddenly burst forth into a revolutionary spring that caught dictators and human rights activists alike by surprise. Here was by far the clearest indication yet of the human urge to throw off suffocating straightjackets, and be part of a whole new beginning. I would like to emphasize that there are spiritual forces at work in the Middle East, which no one needs to be apprehensive about, except those whose aim is dominance and whose tools are deception and callousness. And they, of course, will brand any who resist their sinister schemes "terrorists" and mercilessly eliminate them.

Closer to home, over the last century in particular, people ready to awaken have had many occasions, some of them harsh and brutal. For example, they have been given the opportunity to be shaken out of their slumber by wars, concentration camps, gulags, atomic bombs, AIDS, pollution, economic hardships, terror and scandals. Others might have chosen to be awakened through less cruel, but still laborious ways: the civil rights, women's rights and gay rights movements. Yet others may have had an expansion of awareness through the revelations of Quantum physics, Eastern spiritual thought, views of our precious planet from outer space, the World Wide Web, their own conscience. In other words, for all who care and are eager for change, this is, indeed, a time conducive for awakening and renewal.

Clearly, life is showing us that genuine healing of humanity's inner and outer wounds is ultimately only possible through an epiphany that shatters the illusion of separateness and leads to the realization of life's oneness and love's primacy.

Yet, as stated, despite the good news about all that lies asleep within us, it would surely not be realistic to expect waking up to be instantaneous. That's why we are talking about the opening of our eyes being a journey and a process. We may have been devoted to modifying and altering old patterns for a considerable amount of time. Yet, as noted, real change usually first happens below ground, beyond the reach of observation. Then, just as spring suddenly bursts forth to dazzle the senses, the individual is anesthetized one moment, and the next, he or she exclaims with the slave ship captain of *Amazing Grace* fame: "Was blind but now I see!"

Now, if our citizens have indeed become more aware of the schemes of those who seized power in this country, then the misbegotten deeds of the last decade are not only detrimental. For to finally see through the fog and no longer be duped is a significant gain. And without the grand masters of deceit having inflicted such stress and strain, that expansion would most likely not have taken place; rather, the sleep of the naïve and gullible would have blithely continued on the same large scale.

In slowly waking up, we are seeing to what degree we have wandered in a maze of confusion and doubt, living estranged from the core of self, existing in angst and apprehension. And while not all are participating in the great turning, enough are letting their eyes be opened by the moral clarity and courage of young individuals such as Bradley Manning and

Edward Snowden, permitting us a view of the lies and secret machinations of people in control.

Clearly, in all walks of life, waking up is the journey. With respect to this, recall the answer of the Buddha when he was asked what he was. After a litany of possibilities suggested to him by the questioner, his response was amazingly simple: "I am awake." Prince Siddhartha did not arrive at that stage without Herculean efforts, without years of intense inner struggle. The results of those efforts are confirmed by the acumen of yet another masterful explorer of depth dimensions, Carl Jung. He framed the idea persuasively: "Who looks outside dreams; who looks inside wakes."

We have all been looking outside for too long, been asleep for too long. There is nothing wrong with an outward gaze, except that it is an incomplete, partial way of seeing. The reality is, human beings develop not only thanks to sight but through insight, the gaze directed inward that perceives wisdom from the roots of being so that our becoming may be continual and strong.

Saved by love

There is no way for us to know the truth, the whole truth, and nothing but the truth. But we certainly can know love, know when we are loving, compassionate, generous. And that is what we and the whole world so desperately need: love, compassion, generosity. Without them, we are lost; with them, we have all we need to be a Mensch.

Indeed, the world will not, cannot, be saved by anything but love. We may invoke truth, we may cite the law, we may demand justice, but in the end, if we do not have love, we are all lost, or to use St. Paul's compelling phrase, we are "nothing". Love alone makes us "something", makes us "everything". When human beings experience the purest and highest expression of it, it is a love that is unconditional and healing.

There is a scene in the award-winning film *My Left Foot* that must surely rank as one of the most moving ever portrayed on the screen. The story concerns a boy afflicted with cerebral palsy born into an Irish working class family. One night while several members are occupied doing homework, the terribly handicapped child – named a "retard" by his father – is watching from a mat on the floor. Suddenly he becomes restless and his inarticulate sounds indicate that he is trying to communicate something. Finally, he laboriously pulls himself across the floor and with his left foot – the only mobile part of him – picks up a piece of chalk. With jerky movements and in the grip of great intensity he begins to scrawl, pausing again and again. Slowly, the family and we are able to see what he wanted to communicate so desperately. When he is finished there stands before us a single word: *Mother.*

Mother. Nothing in this or any other language is so powerful and emotionally charged as this single word, mother. She is the first we know and the first we love. She is the central influence of our life. This is why motherhood must surely rank as one of the great opportunities to be the giver of a love that is pure and unconditional.

What a mystery and miracle, this reality of mother and child, this conception, forming, growing, in the body of another! All the wonder of life is symbolized by this: a child in the womb of a woman. Every one of us has been in that position and condition, having been launched into life via the labor of a mother. All of us have been subject to that unique and profound connection.

In the beginning of our separateness it is total dependency. We survive only because there is mother – or others able to take her place – who can respond to our needs. And that nurturing must include a great deal more than supplying physical necessities. Otherwise, the consequences will be disastrous.

Take, for instance, an 18th century story from Germany, set into motion at the behest of Frederick the Great, King of Prussia. Having a rather inquisitive mind, he was interested in discovering what language babies would speak when they grew up if no one talked to them as children. Deciding on an orphanage as the most appropriate place for such a test, a number of children were chosen to participate.

The instructions were that the infants should be fed and otherwise be properly attended to. However, none of the caregivers was to show affection, cuddle or speak to them.

In the end, the curious king never received an answer to his inquiry. Why? Because all of the assigned orphans died. And what was the cause of their demise? An observer explained, "They could not live without the petting and joyful faces and loving words of their foster parents."

Without the human touch, without love, we cannot survive. Not as small children, at least. When we get older we learn to find substitutes for love, such as sex, food, drinks, drugs, etc. These can sometimes temporarily "help us through the night", but they can never add meaning to our life, much less true or lasting happiness.

All this underlines not only the vital and indispensable role of love, but the immense responsibility of being a parent. We are adding a new life, a new being, to the great generational chain of humankind. Beyond the individual and family, the destiny of millions may depend on it. Let us be mindful that Stalin, Hitler and Gandhi were once infants, innocent and helpless.

Parenting is serious business, and good parenting is essential not only for the health of every child, but the wellness of an entire society.

And sometimes children actually ask for it in touching ways, as the following story illustrates.

My daughter and her three-year-old son were driving home from a day in the city. Ian Christopher was sitting in his car seat in the back, entertaining himself by looking at the pages of a book.

Suddenly he inquired: "Mommy, do you have scissors?"

"Not here, honey. What do you need them for?"

"I want to make a hole in this book."

"What do you want to do that for?"

"I want to get inside the story," he replied.

Touched, Patricia replied: "What a wonderful imagination you have!"

"What is imagination?" he wanted to know.

"Oh, it is something like dreaming."

There was a pause and then a sweet little voice asked: "Mommy, will you teach me how to dream?"

Every child is part of the human family and thus related to us. And in spirit every child reaches out to each one of us and asks: Will you teach me how to dream? Will you model for me how to love? Will you help me to be the best I can be?

If, in our effort to respond, we make mistakes, let them be on the side of our humanity, for it is written: "Those who have loved much shall be forgiven much." In the end, it is far better to fail on the side of love than to fail love and one another.

Above all, let us be mindful that our journey on Earth is about more than a drive for physical survival, more than a desire for self-preservation, image or success. Our journey is about embracing and growing in love. Or, as the Nazarene advised, it is about seeking first what is of the highest spiritual value and, in response, all our other needs shall be met.

Tomorrow is now

My explorations into life and its meaning have been guided and enriched by the spiritual traditions of the world's religions. Each has something unique to say and special to teach.

A favorite source for heart expansion has been Hasidic tales. The following story, here liberally retold, underscores the power of intentionality, and the magic of believing as a potent agent of change.

Many years ago, we are told, there was a community torn apart by disagreements and discord, factions and feuds. The situation was becoming unbearable when one of the elders of the town decided to ask a rebbe (rabbi), known for his great wisdom, to pay a visit and advise the group on how to restore what seemed fatally flawed and fractured.

The venerable one arrived and spent several days in the midst of the complaining and blaming townspeople. He listened intently to various voices of discontent.

When the time had come to leave, he gathered everyone for a final meeting. "Dear friends," he solemnly intoned, "being with you these past days has led me to realize that one of you is the messiah."

Without elucidation, or entertaining a single response,

he bid the stunned audience Shalom and promised to return in a year.

In the hours, days and weeks that followed, members of the community began to ask themselves with increasing gravity: "Could it be me? Could I be the messiah?!"

As they pondered the implication, something astonishing began to happen: One by one the people started to act as though they *were* the messiah!

Upon returning the next year, the rebbe could scarcely recognize the place. Everyone appeared energized and joyful. Individuals passed by with a smile or greeted each other with a hug. Goodwill and generosity were palpable. In various settings, group members worked or played together, and they clearly loved and appreciated each other. There was a lightness of spirit and an infectious sense of confidence in the air. It was as though an inner spring had risen and enticed an entire community into blooming.

The revered visitor enjoyed his time in their midst, and before departing expressed his delight at seeing individual and communal life flourish to such a high degree. His words fell like a blessing upon their hearts and inspired even greater efforts and stronger cohesion in the years to come.

Gandhi's idea that we must be the change we want to see, that is, be a model of our ideals and live as we would like others to live, was successfully applied by the people of the village. Granted, the idea of the messiah may not work wonders for everyone, but how about the Fully Realized Person, the Enlightened or the Loving One?

So here is the challenge: one of you is a great visionary and teacher, one of you embodies the values humans strive for, one of you can make the world more vibrant, caring, just. There are too many hurdles, you say? But remember, as the good people of the Hasidic community demonstrated, it's all in the mind, *your* mind!

Having entered a new loop on the grand ascending spiral of personal and societal maturation, having broken numerous barriers on our long journey on Earth, we are getting a glimpse of once unimaginable opportunities. This is the moment not only for the exceptional but the average human being to seize the day, to become a hero within the circle of his or her own life, and in the process renew and enrich the larger life, the community of all beings.

Surprisingly, however, this is not the end, but the beginning, of our *true* journey; a voyage reflective of Kahlil Gibran's description of what occurs when we will shed this physical envelope.

He speaks eloquently of that moment in his masterwork, *The Prophet.*

> *Only when you drink from the river of*
> *silence shall you indeed sing.*
> *And when you have reached the mountain*
> *top, then shall you begin to climb.*
> *And when the earth shall claim your*
> *limbs, then shall you truly dance.*

While Gibran uses those paradoxical images to speak of the final letting go, coming home to ourselves is no less a letting go of all that would pull us away from our center. Moreover, being committed to the great quest is in many ways a form of dying, a dying to selfish, self-defeating ways, to obsolete and juvenile behavior.

Tikkun: to mend, repair and transform

The reason we do not boldly step forward and participate in the renewal of our world is that we are unaware of significant underlying truths. We are especially ill informed as to who we are, and because of that deficiency, are robbed of the ability to fully identify with others.

Not being able to do that, we remain trapped in the illusion of separateness, which is the breeding ground for distrust and fear. When adding arrogance to the mix, it is not surprising that we have ended up precisely where we are: obsessed with stockpiling weapons that can reduce everything on this planet to ruins and rust. Think of the creativity and skill, as well as the expense, that have gone into building those fiendish

295

arms of mass destruction! Yet, do they keep us safe? Has pulverizing places and people brought us peace on Earth? Hardly. We gain, at best, a ceasefire – until the next monster du jour makes its appearance, and so on ad infinitum.

Treating others with respect, seeing the worth and dignity of every person, letting our humanity touch the humanity of others – that change of heart, I would argue, can guarantee security and provide the yearned-for peace.

Yet, how best to proceed? All dedicated repairers of human relations must begin the process with an acknowledgement that those who inhabit this abode called Earth are human beings first before anything else – gender, color, ethnicity, religion, vocation or nationality. We share a common humanity, a common destiny. And yes, a common "dwelling", the foundation of which is the inherent worth and dignity of all people.

Embracing such a unifying principle, and acting accordingly, will be the surest way of walking differently in the world. And the building material needed for such an alluring enterprise is stored within each individual and ready for application this very hour.

A final reflection

The purpose of this work has been to record what is occurring in our world as clear evidence that humanity today stands indeed at a crossroads as media reports point daily to the multiple perils confronting us. Yet, despite alarming revelations, we are not without choices. And the choice of directions before us could either be immensely enriching – or rob all of humanity of a future. If it is enrichment and advancement we wish to experience, then certain prerequisites shall have to be met.

This is where the source of the idea of coming home can be located. Such a homecoming, as we learned, must be inclusive of our country, which means a return to its original purpose, its fundamental principles and values. And it must include a personal coming home to our true nature, our sacred center, our capacity for love and compassion, truth and justice.

It is in coming home to ourselves that we can finally realize that this has been the aim and purpose of our existence all along – from the moment we inhaled our first breath and proclaimed our presence with a full-throated cry.

However, over the years and generations we became orphans wandering in the wilderness of self-abandonment, living divorced from our true Self. We existed, fractured and fragmented, at the periphery of our being, in denial and fear.

This is why the journey must be about reconnecting: with our essence, our truth, our power, and our heart. We owe it to ourselves and to the generations that follow to act in ways more becoming of human beings, to shed the kind of animalistic behavior prominent in tribal and territorial thinking. Too many conflicts, wars and sorrows have resulted from such a narrow and rigid frame of mind. We deserve better – and so does this magnificent planet.

In summary, we are to recognize what it means to be human in a new way on every level of life and in all our affairs so that one day, through vision quest and concerted effort, we can reach our place in the sun to proclaim in full knowledge and complete freedom: "Here I am!" – alive, aware and fully present to love and to serve.

This is the Call

This is the fork in the road foreseen
by the sages, the parting of the ways
the severance of the old from the new –
this is the call to step out of the herd
and of hiding.

This is the opening to escape
the vicious circle, the unholy ground
of us versus them, the dungeon
of good versus evil, the slaughterhouse
of dualistic thought.

This is the call.

This is the choice set before us:
tribe and territory

or the human family and all life
as intrinsically one.

This is the moment to depart
from the cowering masses
mesmerized by the glitter of things
lulled into silence
by half-truths and fear.
This is the hour to join the child
who proclaims the emperor naked
the signal to unmask the vacuous pretender
the heartless, the false.

This is the call.

This is the time to leave the prison
of complacency, conformity, compliance –
the quagmire of compromised life.

This is the call.

This is the new rising before us –
truth breaking through walls of denial
unleashing the Power
freeing the Light within:

the human butterfly converting
death into transformation
entombment into winged life.

This is the call.

RC